MW00699740

Other Books by Richard We

LLEWELLYN'S

COMPLETE BOOK OF

DIVINATION

Photo by Jason Fell

About the Author

Richard Webster was born and raised in New Zealand. He has been interested in the psychic world since he was nine years old. As a teenager, he became involved in hypnotism and later became a professional stage hypnotist. After school, he worked in the publishing business and purchased a bookstore. The concept of reincarnation played a significant role in his decision to become a past-life specialist. Richard has also taught psychic development classes, which are based on many of his books.

Richard's first book was published in 1972, fulfilling a childhood dream of becoming an author. Richard is now the author of over a hundred books, and is still writing today. His best-selling books include *Spirit Guides & Angel Guardians* and *Creative Visualization for Beginners*.

Richard has appeared on several radio and TV programs in the United States and abroad including guest spots on Hard Copy, WMAQ-TV (Chicago), KTLA-TV (Los Angeles), KSTW-TV (Seattle), and the Mike and Matty Show (ABC). He currently resides in New Zealand with his wife and three children. He regularly travels the world to give lectures and workshops, and to continue his research.

To Write to the Author

If you wish to contact the author or would like more information about this book, please write to the author in care of Llewellyn Worldwide, and we will forward your request. Llewellyn Worldwide cannot guarantee that every letter written to the author can be answered, but all will be forwarded. Please write to:

Richard Webster
℅ Llewellyn Worldwide
2143 Wooddale Drive
Woodbury, MN 55125-2989

Please enclose a self-addressed stamped envelope for reply or $1.00 to cover costs.
If outside the USA, enclose an international postal reply coupon.

Many of Llewellyn's authors have websites with additional information and resources. For more information, please visit us at: www.llewellyn.com.

LLEWELLYN'S

COMPLETE BOOK OF

DIVINATION

**Your Definitive Source for Learning
Predictive & Prophetic Techniques**

RICHARD WEBSTER

Llewellyn Publications
Woodbury, Minnesota

FIRST EDITION
First Printing, 2017

Book design by Bob Gaul
Cover design and photo by Ellen Lawson
Cover images of cards, runes and pendulum © Lo Scarabeo
Editing by Aaron Lawrence
Bone reading on page 49, dowsing rod on page 93, diving rod on page 95, face reading on pages 104–108, rune stick on page 122, and palmistry images on pages 214–215 and 217–220 by Wen Hsu
Celtic cross spread on page 302, compass spread on page 177, geomancy on page 123 and 127–130, hexagrams on pages 139–140, 142–166, and 168, oghams on page 204, runes on page 246 and trigrams on page 136 by Llewellyn Art Deparment
Llewellyn's Classic Tarot on pages 269–293, 295–296, and 298 by Barbara Moore and Eugene Smith © 2014, Llewellyn Publications

Llewellyn Publications is a registered trademark of Llewellyn Worldwide Ltd.

Library of Congress Cataloging-in-Publication Data
Names: Webster, Richard, author.
Title: Llewellyn's complete book of divination: your definitive source for
   learning predictive & prophetic techniques / Richard Webster.
Other titles: Complete book of divination
Description: First edition. | Woodbury: Llewellyn Worldwide, Ltd., 2017. |
   Includes bibliographical references and index.
Identifiers: LCCN 2017039064 (print) | LCCN 2017034515 (ebook) | ISBN
   9780738753485 () | ISBN 9780738751757 (alk. paper)
Subjects: LCSH: Divination.
Classification: LCC BF1751 (print) | LCC BF1751 .W43 2017 (ebook) | DDC
   133.3—dc23
LC record available at https://lccn.loc.gov/2017039064

Llewellyn Publications
A Division of Llewellyn Worldwide Ltd.
2143 Wooddale Drive
Woodbury, MN 55125-2989
www.llewellyn.com

Printed in the United States of America

Contents

Acknowledgments

I'd like to thank two good friends for their help in this project: Jonathan Twidwell, aka Shiatsu Guy, in Kaneohe, Hawaii; and Danny Thorn, feng shui expert and fellow writer, in Auckland, New Zealand.

Dedication

In memory of Carl Weschcke, the true Father of the New Age, with grateful thanks for all your enthusiasm and encouragement.

Introduction

We all have questions about our lives. Everyone wants to learn more about their goals, careers, families, health, money, and travel. We all have problems and concerns and want information about matters that are going on in our lives in advance. This is why divination is just as popular today as it ever has been.

Divination is the art of predicting future events or discovering hidden knowledge using a variety of techniques, such as prophecy and intuition. There are many types of divination, and the main ones, plus some unusual ones, are covered in this book. Some are thousands of years old, while others have been developed recently.

If divination is new to you, I'm hoping this book will open your mind to a practice that has existed throughout human civilization and is still hugely popular today. I also hope you'll find some methods of divination that appeal to you, and in most cases I provide enough information to get you started. I've also included details for other books on specific subjects to enable you to learn more about the areas that interest you.

I hope this book also appeals to people who are already involved in one or more methods of divination. It's always helpful to have other methods to use in different situations. In addition, as you learn about a technique you're not already familiar with, you may find information that will prove helpful in the type of divinations you currently perform. Here's an example: I read palms, but I almost always include numerology with it, as I find it enables me to be more specific when working out the timing of future events. You might even find a method that will become as useful to you as the techniques you use now.

Even if you have no interest in performing divinations for others, I hope you'll enjoy learning about the different methods people have used when attempting to part the veil and glimpse into the future. You might try some of the techniques to help you gain access to your intuition and learn more about what's going on in your life.

Divination is a popular topic, and even though many people claim not to believe in it, you'll find they're often the first to ask if they could have their palms or cards read. Learning a form of divination guarantees your popularity at any social gathering, as you'll have a skill that's always in demand.

It takes time and practice to become good at any form of divination. Once you've gained confidence with a system, you'll be able to temporarily ignore your rational conscious mind and gain access to your intuitive side. Once you're able to do that, you'll be able to help yourself and other people in many different ways.

One

What Is Divination?

For I dipt into the future, far as human eye could see, Saw the Vision of the world, and all the wonder that would be … —Alfred, Lord Tennyson, *Locksley Hall*

Throughout history, people of every culture have used different methods to predict future events. No matter where in the world you happen to be, it's hard to find people who don't have questions about the future. Most people want to know if their personal future will include love, happiness, success, children, and good health. They also want to know about the futures of family members and other people close to them. In addition to this, they want to know how their country, and the world, will prosper in the future. It's no wonder that divination is just as popular today as it ever has been, and it plays an important role in many people's lives.

The word *divination* comes from the Latin words *divinare,* which means "to be inspired by a god," and *divinus*, which means "the divine." This shows that divination was originally concerned with determining the will of the gods (or the divine), and that information came from that particular deity.

Divination is the art of foretelling the future using a variety of natural and psychological techniques. Divination goes back to prehistoric times and has been practiced by every culture in the world. This isn't surprising, as people have always sought diviners when they felt unsure or uncertain about the future.

Divination is not the same as fortune-telling. Fortune-telling is the art of telling people about their future. Divination is the art of looking at a given situation from a different point of view. This enables the person to examine a number of potential outcomes that he or she may not have thought of before.

Divination always involves a question. Someone wants an answer to a question and is searching for information that he or she could not obtain in any other way. The questions can be general or specific. One person might ask, "Will I be happy?" Someone else might ask, "Will Molly come out with me if I ask her for a date?" or "Should I ask my boss for a pay rise on Thursday?" Before telephones were invented, people used divination techniques to ask if so-and-so was at home.

Divination is usually concerned with everyday problems and concerns and attempts to find practical solutions to these. If someone has lost a valuable object, is concerned about the future of a relationship, or has some other concern, he or she may perform a divination, or consult a diviner, to learn some possibilities about the outcome.

Some people believe that divination reveals their destiny. This isn't the case. A divination lets people see what is ahead if they carry on the way they are now. Fortunately, people possess free will, and we can all change our destinies by changing the way we think and act.

I experienced a good example of this more than thirty years ago when I used to conduct psychic parties in people's homes. I'd finished the crystal ball section and was giving brief private palm readings to everyone in a separate room. There were four young men there, one the son of the hostess. Each of them asked me something along the lines of: "Will everything work out tonight?" I had a strong feeling that they were planning something illegal, so I told them that it would be disastrous, and they shouldn't do it. The next day the hostess phoned to thank me for keeping her son honest. He, and several friends, had been planning to break into a warehouse that night. After listening to me, the four boys decided not to participate. Their friends went ahead with the robbery, and were caught.

There are many different ways to classify divination techniques. More than two thousand years ago, Cicero, the Roman politician and orator, divided divination into two groups: inductive (learned) and intuitive (natural). Astrology is an example of an inductive divination, as the basic data (day, month, year, and time of birth) is fixed and interpreted.

Intuitive divination involves the diviner receiving knowledge from the divine. Sometimes the diviner might need to enter into a trance state. The information might be seen in a crystal ball. Knowledge gained through a dream is another example of intuitive divination. An intuitive diviner must possess specific skills ("the gift"), while an inductive diviner needs to learn and practice a system.

However, divination cannot be easily divided into two groups. A tarot card reader, for instance, could be called an inductive diviner, as he or she uses a system to interpret the cards that have been dealt. However, this same reader may also be using intuition while performing the reading, and this enables him or her to provide information that was not available to another reader who had simply learned the meanings of the cards. The ability to use both together is often a sign of a great diviner, rather than a good one.

It's probably more useful to divide divination into eight main areas: omens, sortilege, the human body, astrology, numbers, augury, dreams, and intuition.

Omens involve observing what is happening in nature and making interpretations. This could be the movements of clouds, the behavior of animals, or the positions of planets in the sky. Natural disasters, such as flooding and earthquakes, were considered omens that the gods were not happy with humanity.

Sortilege is the casting of lots. Objects that have been randomly separated from a larger group are interpreted. The casting of bones, shells, sticks, dice, coins, cards, and other objects are all examples of sortilege. Rune stones and tarot cards are also good examples. Aaron used sortilege to determine which goat was for God and which was to be set free (Leviticus 16:7–10).

The human body involves observation and interpretation of parts of the human body. Palmistry is the best-known example of this. Foot reading, phrenology, knee reading, navel reading, and even nipple reading are other examples. Even bodily functions, such as sneezing and itching, have been interpreted. Two friends of mine are extremely good at interpreting the way people laugh.

Astrology has a category of its own. It involves reading the patterns made by the planets as they make their endless cycles around the Sun. Western astrology and Chinese astrology are the main examples.

Numbers interpret the mystical relationships between numbers and human activities. Numerology converts numbers, dates, and relating letters to numbers to predict future trends. There are three main forms of numerology: Kabbalistic, Chaldean, and Pythagorean.

Augury was originally divination by observing the flight of birds. Legend says that Romulus and Remus couldn't agree about the exact place to found Rome. They settled it by observing the flight of birds. Remus saw six vultures, but Romulus saw twelve, showing that the gods favored his location. Gradually, augury was extended to include the movements of other animals, as well as birds. The military used to predict success or defeat by the actions of chickens being fed. Even bird songs, as well as lightning and thunder, came to be included.

We all experience precognitive dreams from time to time. The problem for many people is remembering the dream when they wake up. One of the most famous examples of divination in a dream is related in the Bible when Joseph interpreted Pharaoh's dream that predicted the seven fat and seven lean years that were ahead for Egypt.

Intuition involves quietening the conscious mind and accessing the subconscious. It enables people to know something without using their powers of reason. Hunches and feelings are examples of this. A good example of intuition involved the film star Clark Gable. For several days before his wife, Carole Lombard, was killed in a plane crash, Gable was despondent and anxious. This was completely opposite to his usual behavior. [1]

---

1   Slate 1988, 21.

Some people are able to access their intuition whenever they wish. Some of them go into a form of trance to do this. Shamans are a good example. Most intuitive diviners, though, simply quiet their minds and pause to see what information comes to them. The pendulum also fits into this category.

How Does Divination Work?

A number of theories have been put forward about how divination works.

Carl Jung's concept of synchronicity says that two or more events may be acausally connected, outside the laws of cause and effect. These are meaningful coincidences. This means that the action of shuffling a deck of tarot cards somehow influences the particular cards that are dealt, and the person being read for receives the particular cards that are right for him or her at that particular moment.

Another theory says that everything is already known, and all you need do is access this library of knowledge and wisdom using your subconscious mind. This library is sometimes referred to as the Akashic records.

The concept of the Akashic records accepts that the future already exists. However, your life isn't all predetermined. Small changes have little impact, but any major changes you make today will have an effect on your future. Let's suppose, for example, that you've been thinking about buying a particular business. If you decide against buying it, your life will continue in much the same way it already is. If you buy the business, though, your life might change dramatically. If you make a huge success of this new venture, your standard of living will increase, and you'll be able to help all the people you care about. If the business fails, your life will change in other ways, and hopefully you'll learn some important lessons from the experience. Both success and failure will affect your future in different ways.

Many people believe that information about the future comes to them through spirits, or directly from the ultimate life force.

In his essay "Is Everything Determined?", Stephen Hawking, the English physicist and cosmologist, argued that as everything is governed by the physical rules of the universe, life is predetermined. However, we're unable to predict the future by scientific means, as the "uncertainty principle" makes it impossible for anyone to work out all the equations. The uncertainty principle says that it's impossible to work out the position and speed of a particle, as the more accurately the position is measured, the less accurate the speed would be. Dr. Hawking concludes that as everything is determined, we don't possess free will. He also writes that "it might as well not be, because we can never know what is determined."[2]

The theory I like best is that we each create our own futures by our thoughts and actions. Everything we do creates energy that not only influences the present but also extends into the future.

---

2   Hawking 1993, 115.

People who are optimistic and expect good things to happen usually enjoy happier lives than people who dwell on the negative. Both groups are creating their futures by their thoughts and actions.

Everything you think and do has the potential to change your future. This is why you can be told something during, say, a tarot card reading on one day and something completely different when you have another reading a week or two later.

All forms of divination provide ways for people to bypass their conscious minds and listen to what their subconscious minds are telling them.

One of the most fascinating things about divination is that it works. If it didn't, it would have been discarded and forgotten long ago. The mere fact of its survival shows that divination effectively guides, helps, and comforts people just as much today as it did thousands of years ago.

Is Divination Always Accurate?

Divination is accurate, but a number of factors can change the outcome. Obviously, the skill of the diviner is important. I'd much rather have my tarot cards read by someone who has studied them for twenty years than from someone who read a book on the subject last week. However, having said that, every now and again beginners produce remarkable results, and everyone has to start somewhere.

Sometimes there'll be no response at all. If you're asking a number of questions using a pendulum, you may find that sometimes the pendulum won't move, or it might indicate "I don't want to answer." This doesn't mean the answer is negative. It's more likely that the situation is in a state of flux, and you'll receive an answer if you ask the question again at a later date. I usually accept that I won't receive an answer today, but if you wish, you can ask additional questions about why the pendulum won't give a reply.

One common problem is to ask a question that is too vague or long-winded to be answered. Your questions need to be as specific as possible. It's a waste of time to ask, "Will I be happy?" as it's not specific. At the very least, this question needs a time frame, as it's unrealistic to be happy all the time.

Divinations fail at times, as readers can only see what's going to happen if you stay on the same path you're on now. Fortunately, you can change your future. The people you interact with may also change their decisions about certain matters, and this can affect your divination. However, even when a divination appears to be incorrect, it always provides information that is useful, helpful, and relevant to the situation.

Divinations sometimes include warnings. If your reading said you'll be run over by a bus on a certain day, you'd naturally change what you normally do on that particular day, which means you'd change your future. If I received such a warning, I'd avoid buses as much as possible on that day. I'd use other forms of transport and would keep as far away as possible from any bus I encountered. Because of this, the prediction probably wouldn't occur. However, this doesn't mean the prediction failed, as I'd changed my actions, which changed my destiny.

There are difficulties in reading for yourself, as your preconceived ideas will often override the true outcome. I've seen this happen many times with pregnant women. If a pregnant woman already has three boys, and is desperate for a girl, the pendulum is likely to tell her she's having a daughter, no matter what the unborn baby may be, as that's what she wants to hear. Whenever you have an emotional involvement in the outcome, you should ask someone who is totally impartial to do the reading for you.

Another difficulty with reading for yourself is that you might unintentionally misinterpret the answer. This is because you'd be looking for the answer you wanted and might overlook something negative or read it the wrong way.

Rules for Readers

When you're giving readings for others, you need to be gentle, caring, and honest. As far as your clients are concerned, you're a counsellor and advisor. This means your clients are putting a great deal of trust in you, and you have a duty to help them as much as you can.

Environment

If you're fortunate, you might have a room that you can use solely for your readings. This means you can personalize it and make it as attractive and as inviting as possible.

If you don't have the luxury of a spare room, you might be able to rent a room for your readings or choose somewhere in your home where there'll be no distractions for the length of time that's required.

Over the years, I've had a number of readings in places that I considered totally unprofessional. One of these was in someone's living room. This was fine, but the lady had a young son who kept coming in every few minutes and disturbing the reading. Another had a sleeping baby in the room. When she woke up, she put the child to her breast and carried on with reading. On several occasions I've had readings in kitchens that had piles of unwashed dishes on the bench. I've had a number of readings that were interrupted several times by the reader answering the phone. Needless to say, I never went back to any of these readers and never recommended them to others.

If there's nowhere suitable in your home, you might be able to read for your clients in a coffee shop or hotel lobby. I'd be careful about giving readings in your clients' homes, especially if you don't know them.

Wherever you choose, it should be clean, warm, and friendly.

Bad News

Even if you're convinced that something bad is going to occur to a client, you should never tell them that a specific event will occur. After all, you might be wrong, which would put your client through a great deal of stress and worry. When you're giving a reading, your words are extremely powerful, and you could create a self-fulfilling prophecy if you predict a disaster or crisis. Your job is to help, not harm.

If you foresee a potentially difficult situation, you should suggest that your client has a medical checkup, a car service, or whatever else you feel could be done to provide help without worrying your client.

You should think about what you'd say if, for instance, you were giving a tarot card reading and the Death card or the Tower came up.

You're bound to come across people who are grieving because of the loss of a loved one or some other tragedy. This is the time that many people seek someone to tell them that the future will be better than the present. You should be as caring and sympathetic as possible and willing to listen to what they have to say. As much as possible, give practical advice, and help them realize that there are many people who'd be more than willing to offer support and encouragement. Apart from professionals, most people have family and friends who'd be only too happy to help. You can also help them understand that life does go on, and no matter how bleak it may seem in the present, it will gradually get better.

Trends and Possibilities

We all have free will, which means we have the ability to change the future. Many years ago I read the palms of a young man. It looked as if he'd already served time in prison, and his hands indicated that he was going to spend much more time there in the future. My reading turned into a talk about choices. He could stay on the path he was on or make some important changes and create a wonderful future for himself. Fortunately, he did change his life, and I've seen him a few times since. His hands no longer show the possibilities indicated by the path he was on.

Because we have free will, you can't state anything with absolute certainty. You can talk about trends and possibilities, but ultimately the decision about what to do needs to be made by your client.

Naturally, your readings should be positive and encouraging. This doesn't mean you should predict glowing futures for everyone. That would be totally unrealistic, and you'd lose all credibility. You should discuss negative situations in a positive light, and try to give your clients hope and encouragement.

Look After Yourself

Being a professional reader can be exhausting, and you need to replenish yourself between readings. I used to take several slow, deep breaths and then shake my hands vigorously to eliminate negativity whenever I had one client immediately followed by another. It's a good idea to spend a few minutes on your own between readings to allow yourself enough time to restore your energy.

You should also drink plenty of water. This is good for you anyway, but is essential for anyone who's making a living using his or her voice.

You should never give a reading if you're overtired, intoxicated, unwell, or upset about something that's going on in your personal life. You have a duty to give your clients the best reading you can. If you can't do that, you shouldn't give the reading. It's dishonest and unfair. Explain what the problem is to your client, and reschedule the appointment.

Do Not Judge

Once you start giving readings to others, you'll be amazed at what people will tell you. People often open up and disclose information to strangers that they'd never consider telling anyone else.

It's not your job to judge anyone else. You shouldn't appear shocked no matter how horrifying or offensive the information may be. Simply give your advice and interpretation, and carry on with the reading.

Confidentiality

Everything a client tells you is confidential. You'd be horrified if a priest or attorney told others something you'd told him or her in confidence. The same thing applies to you. From time to time you'll hear fascinating stories that you'd love to tell others about, but you must resist that temptation.

Your Tools

You need to treat the items you use for divination with love and respect. Your clients will subconsciously realize this, and will respect them too. Would you prefer to visit a tarot card reader who handled his cards with care, and kept them wrapped in a velvet cloth, or someone who kept his cards in a beaten up old box and tossed them to one side once the reading was over?

Everything you use should be carefully looked after. This even applies to the casting cloth that you use when giving a reading. Replace decks of cards and other items that get worn or damaged on a regular basis.

As you are a professional, everything should look smart, clean, and professional. This even applies to your clothes. You don't need to wear a suit, but your clothes should be clean.

It shouldn't need saying, but personal hygiene is vitally important. As you're sitting close to your clients, your breath needs to be fresh and your body clean.

I know you'll encounter readers who break all of these rules and appear to be doing well. What they do is their business. If you have integrity and follow these guidelines, you'll experience personal satisfaction and have many satisfied clients.

Two

—··—

The History
of Divination

Divination has always played a role in humankind. No one knows when it began, but the earliest diviners were likely to have been shamans who entered into a trance state and made contact with the gods.

As well as this, people drew their omens from the world around them. They looked at the stars and planets (astrology), clouds (nephelomancy), the winds (austromancy), the flight and song of birds (ornithomancy), flowers (floromancy), the flame of a candle or lamp (lampadomancy), smoke from a fire (capnomancy), the movements of water in a stream or fountain (pegomancy), ripples caused by the wind on water (aeromancy), coming across an animal by chance (apantomancy), the crackling of laurel tossed into a fire (daphnomancy), pieces of wood (xylomancy), the howling of dogs (ololygmancy), dreams (oneiromancy), and even the ashes remaining after a sacrifice (spodomancy).

Groups of objects could be tossed on the ground to affect a divination. These include pebbles (cleromancy), knucklebones (astragalomancy), dice (cubomancy), pearls (margaritomancy), and salt (alomancy).

Parts of the body were used for divination, too. Palmistry (cheiromancy and chirognomy) is the obvious one, but faces (physiognomy), foreheads (metoposcopy), eyes (oculomancy), lips (labiomancy), teeth (odontomancy), fingernails (onychomancy), moles (moleosophy), and feet (podomancy) are other examples.

Trance states were induced by gazing into mirrors, clear pools of water, olive oil (onimancy), glasses of wine (oenomancy), glasses of water (cylicomancy), fire (pyromancy), and even finger-nails (onychomancy). These enabled the seer to receive glimpses of the future.

Throughout history, people have devised numerous methods of divination. Many are no longer practiced, but some have stood the test of time and are still being used today.

At least four thousand years ago, Babylonian and Assyrian priests were making predictions from their observations of the movements of the planets. This marked the start of astrology, which quickly spread around the known world. The oldest surviving example of a personal horoscope dates back to 410 BCE.

Early Babylonian texts discuss a variety of different forms of divination, including augury, lecanomancy and libanomancy (see appendix). The Babylonians used dice made from bone to cast lots. The Assyrians usually used dice made from clay. Dream interpretations were considered extremely important and were often used and referred to in their epic poems. The *Epic of Gilgamesh*, written in about 2,100 BCE, is considered to be the oldest surviving example of great literature. Gilgamesh, the hero of the story, has a number of precognitive dreams that are interpreted by his friend, Enkidu.

While the ancient Babylonians were gazing at the stars, half a world away, the Chinese were reading the markings created by heating tortoise shells. This ultimately developed into a variety of divination systems, including the I Ching, Chinese numerology, and geomancy.

The ancient Egyptians used divination for two main purposes: to gain information about the present situation and to plea to the gods for help in improving a particular situation. The gods who were invoked persuaded the other gods to help affect the desired change.

The ancient Greeks had oracles who spoke to the gods. There were three main oracles: Delphi, Dodona, and Trophonius. The oracle of Delphi is the most famous of these. Pythia, the priestess there, communicated with Apollo. She gave her predictions on the seventh day of the month, for nine months every year. Apollo didn't spend any time in Delphi in the colder winter months. The oracles were kept so busy that Plutarch wrote that at times there were three of them. Two worked in shifts, and the third one was available if either of them needed a rest.

The Pythia prepared herself by chewing laurel leaves and bay leaves. As laurel was associated with Apollo, she'd also wear a laurel crown while sitting on a tripod placed over a fissure in the basement of the temple. The gases that came through the fissure caused the Pythia to go into a trance. Priests led the inquirers into the room and asked the question. Once Pythia replied, the priest would interpret it.

The ancient Greeks used seers as well as oracles. They interpreted dreams and observed patterns in nature, such as the flight of birds, to help them in their divinations. The Greeks were interested in astrology, too. Plato and Hippocrates are just two of the philosophers who wrote on the subject. The ancient Mesopotamians considered the Moon to be the most important orb in the sky, but the Greeks believed the Sun was more important. It was the Greeks who named the planets, though today we know them by the Roman versions of their names: Mercury, Venus, Mars, Jupiter, and Saturn. The word *zodiac* comes from the Greeks, as well, and means "circle of animals."

Numerology was also important to the Greeks, and Pythagoras, remembered today largely because of his theorem, modernized numerology some 2,600 years ago.

Divination was just as popular in ancient Rome, and a number of authors, such as Livy and Cicero, wrote extensively about it. Divination was used to communicate with the gods and goddesses, and diviner priests were kept busy interpreting omens relating to the outcome of military expeditions and battles.

Plutarch recorded the famous warning given to Julius Caesar by a soothsayer named Spurinna: "Beware the Ides of March." Less well known are a number of other predictions that also relate to his murder. Here are two examples.

A few months earlier, a group of immigrants were clearing land for building and uncovered prehistoric graves. In one of them they found a bronze tablet that said that once the contents of the tombs were brought to light, a leading member of the Julian house would be killed by a friend.

The night before the murder, Calpurnia, Caesar's wife, had a dream in which their house crumbled and her husband, fatally stabbed, was in her arms. When Caesar woke, he wasn't feeling well and almost agreed to Calpurnia's request that he stay at home. However, his friend Decimus Brutus told him that he couldn't disappoint the crowd of people who were waiting to see him.

Various forms of augury were popular, and chickens were even taken to sea to provide advice. Ovid wrote about Admiral Pubius Claudius's experience during the First Punic War. He was about to attack the Carthaginians, and he laid out food for his chickens before the battle. The chickens refused to eat it, which meant Claudius would lose the battle. As Claudius didn't believe in divination, he ordered his men to toss the chickens overboard, saying that if they wouldn't eat, they could drink instead. Shortly afterward, Claudius lost the battle. He survived, but twenty thousand of his soldiers were captured, and almost all of his ships sank.

Divination in the Bible

The prophets of the Old Testament regularly used dreams to contact God and divine the future.

The Bible includes several different types of divination, in addition to dream interpretation (oneiromancy). Interpreting the flight of birds is one example (Ecclesiastes 10:20). The Magi knew that Jesus would be born at a certain time and place by observing the stars. Joseph practiced hydromancy (divination by water) (Genesis 44:5). The king of Babylon practiced belomancy (divination by arrows) (Ezekiel 21:21–22).

The intriguing Urim and Thummim that the high priest wore on his breastplate for divination purposes were probably two sticks or stones, one black and one white, that provided yes and no answers (Exodus 28:30).

The mysterious Witch of Endor practiced necromancy by evoking the spirit of Samuel to provide advice for Saul (1 Samuel 28:7–25).

Divination is forbidden in Deuteronomy 18:10–12 and Leviticus 19:26.

People Who Could See into the Future

Thomas the Rhymer

Thomas of Ercildoune, better known as Thomas the Rhymer, was a thirteenth century Scottish laird and poet who made his prophecies in rhyme. He is sometimes known as True Thomas, as apparently he was unable to tell a lie.

Thomas is said to have met the Queen of Elfland while sitting beside a thorn tree. She took him to the fairy "otherworld" and gave him the gift of prophecy. One of his prophecies was: "As long as the thorn tree stands, Ercildoune shall keep its lands." In 1814, more than five hundred years after his death, the tree blew down in a gale. It's said that the local people tried to revive the tree with whisky. If so, it didn't work. In the same year, the people of Ercildoune were beset with a series of financial calamities, and all the common land had to be sold to repay the debts. Thomas's prediction had come true. Today, a large plaque marks the spot where the thorn tree grew.

Thomas made many predictions, but unfortunately in the centuries after his death many people attributed their own predictions to him, and today it's impossible to know which predictions were actually made by Thomas.

Roger Bacon (c.1214–1294)

Roger Bacon was a Franciscan monk and alchemist who wrote a remarkable book called *Epistola de Secretis*. It includes detailed descriptions of cars, ships, submarines, and airplanes, all invented hundreds of years after his death. Sadly, he suffered for his work and spent fourteen years in prison.

Mother Shipton (1488–1561)

Ursula Southiel, the Yorkshire Witch better known as Mother Shipton, was born in Knaresborough. Legend says that she was born in a cave and discovered her powers while still at school. During her life she worked as a fortune-teller. Even though this was a potentially dangerous occupation at the time, she managed to live to the ripe old age of seventy-three and die in her own bed. Her first major prediction was that King Henry VIII would invade northern France in 1513. She also predicted the defeat of the Spanish Armada and the Great Fire of London. Unfortunately, after that, it's difficult to determine which of the predictions attributed to her were genuine. In his *Collections of Prophecies*, published in 1646, William Lilly wrote that sixteen out of eighteen of her prophecies had already been fulfilled.

Nostradamus (1503–1566)

Nostradamus is by far the best-known psychic of the last five hundred years. He was born in Provence, France, and his family encouraged his gift at prophecy. He became a doctor and later a professor of medicine. He married into a wealthy family and had two children. Sadly, his wife and children died of the Black Death. Nostradamus had cured many people of the plague but was unable to save his own family. His family turned against him, and with the Inquisition seeking to question him, he spent the next ten years on the road visiting most of southern Europe.

He finally returned to Provence in 1544 and remarried. He started writing an annual almanac containing his predictions. Gratified with the response he received, he started writing the quatrains that are still being read and studied today. Seven volumes of these were published between 1555 and 1557. The final three volumes were published after his death.

In 1556, Nostradamus predicted that King Henry II would be killed in a jousting accident when a splinter from a jousting staff would slip through his helmet's visor, pass behind an eye, and into the brain. Queen Catherine de Medici had him brought to Paris to question him about this, but they became good friends. Fortunately, Nostradamus was back home when every aspect of the prediction came true in 1559.

Huge numbers of people petitioned the inquisitors demanding he be burned at the stake. This would have happened if Nostradamus had not been friends with Queen Catherine.

In 1564, Catherine, and her young son, King Charles IX, visited Nostradamus and honored him by giving him the title of Counselor and Physician in Ordinary. Twenty months later he died, successfully fulfilling his final prediction that gave the date and details of his death.

One of Nostradamus's best-known minor predictions concerned the fate of two young piglets. His landlord asked him what would happen to them. Nostradamus told him that the white one would be eaten by a wolf, and he and the landlord would eat the black one.

His landlord decided to play a trick on Nostradamus and told his cook to kill and prepare the white piglet for dinner that evening. The cook did this. While the cook's back was turned, a young wolf cub that lived in the house as a pet seized the carcass and started eating it. The cook, knowing nothing of the proposed trick, killed and prepared the black piglet, and served it to the two men that evening. As they were eating the piglet, his landlord laughingly told Nostradamus that his prediction was wrong as they were eating the white piglet. Nostradamus insisted they were eating the black one. The cook was called for and told the men what had occurred. Nostradamus's landlord was forced to change his views about his famous boarder's abilities.

The Brahan Seer

The Brahan Seer's real name was Coinneach Odhar Fionsiche. He lived on the island of Brahan in Scotland in the seventeenth century and divined with a piece of a polished meteor. He also had an adder stone with a hole in it that he used.

Most of his predictions involved Scotland, but he also predicted tar-sealed roads, trains, and even pipelines carrying water. His predictions brought him fame, but also a number of powerful enemies. Shortly before he was burned at the stake, the Countess of Seaforth said that he was destined for hell. The Brahan Seer replied that he'd go to heaven, but the Countess wouldn't. He said that immediately after his death a raven and a dove would alight on his ashes. If the raven arrived first, the Countess would be right, but it would be a different story if the dove landed first. According to legend, a large crowd saw a dove and a raven appear in the sky and descend onto the Brahan Seer's ashes. The dove landed first.

Emanuel Swedenborg (1688–1772)

Emanuel Swedenborg was an eminent Swedish scientist who suddenly started seeing visions and experiencing psychic and precognitive dreams when he was fifty-three years old.

His prediction of his own death is well documented. John Wesley had been exchanging letters with Swedenborg and said he was planning to visit him shortly after he returned home from a six month journey. Swedenborg replied that Wesley's visit would be too late, as he was going into the "world of spirits" on the twenty-ninth day of the following month. Exactly as he predicted, Swedenborg died on March 29, 1772. [3]

St. John Bosco (1815–1888)

As a young priest in Turin, Italy, St. John Bosco gained fame for his work with underprivileged teenage boys. He was helped and protected by a large dog called Grigio whom he considered his guardian angel.

St. John Bosco had a gift for prophecy, and, apart from his predictions of the end times, all of his published prophecies eventuated. At the age of nine he started having prophetic dreams, and throughout his life most of his predictions came to him in his dreams.

Evangeline Adams (1865–1932)

Evangeline Adams was a celebrity astrologer in New York when she was arrested for fortune-telling. In court she asked if she could draw up a horoscope of someone totally unknown to her. She was given the birth data of this unknown person who happened to be the judge's son. The judge was so impressed with the reading she provided that he not only acquitted her, but ensured that astrology became legal in the state of New York.

She became J. P. Morgan's astrologer and gained nationwide fame with her radio program. She predicted that Warren G. Harding would become US president. She also correctly forecast the death of King Edward VII, as well as her own death in 1932.

---

3   Tafel 1847, 565.

Cheiro (1866–1936)

William John Warner, better known as Cheiro, was an Irish astrologer, palmist, and clairvoyant. He is best known for his palm readings. During his career, he read the hands of many famous people, including Mark Twain, Sarah Bernhardt, Oscar Wilde, Thomas Edison, Dame Nellie Melba, and many other prominent people. One of these was the Prince of Wales. He successfully predicted that the prince would give up everything, including the throne, for the woman he loved.

He also predicted the date that Queen Victoria would die, and the terrible fate that awaited Czar Nicholas II of Russia. Another successful prediction was that the Jews would return to Palestine, and the country would be named Israel. A number of his books, especially those on palmistry and numerology, are still in print today.

Edgar Cayce (1877–1945)

Edgar Cayce, often called the "sleeping prophet," gave more than twenty thousand readings while in a trance state. Fortunately, many of these were recorded and dated for later verification. Most of his readings involved healing and were for individuals. However, in 1931, he saw a vision of a coming war that would kill millions of people. Throughout the 1930s, he continued mentioning a war during his readings, providing accurate information about the upcoming war.

Edgar Cayce accurately predicted the stock market crash of 1929 and the start and end of the Great Depression. He predicted the rise and fall of Adolf Hitler, and the deaths of two presidents in office. A number of his predictions refer to situations that have not yet occurred.

Edgar Cayce moved to Virginia Beach, Virginia, in 1927. The Association for Research and Enlightenment that he founded still actively promotes his work.

Jeane Dixon (1904–1997)

Jeane L. Pinckert, better known to the world as Jeane Dixon, was born in Medford, Wisconsin. She first gained public attention through her syndicated astrology column, followed by a number of books.

Jeane Dixon is best known for predicting the death of President John F. Kennedy. She also predicted the assassinations of Mahatma Gandhi, Martin Luther King Jr., and Robert F. Kennedy. One month before it happened, she predicted the exact date of the partition of India on August 15, 1947. She also predicted the suicide of Marilyn Monroe.

Three

— · · —

The Main Systems of Divination

It's difficult to create a list of the main divination systems of the world, as everyone who's studied the subject will have different ideas about which systems should be included or excluded. This chapter covers the thirty-one systems that I feel should be included. Some have existed for thousands of years and are still being used today. Others are comparatively new but are widely practiced around the world. A few are seldom seen today but have been included, as they played an important role in the development of divination throughout history.

Astrology

Thousands of years ago, people gazed up at the skies and were awed by the mystery of the planets and the stars. The movements of the stars and planets must have seemed like magic to them. Not surprisingly, these movements were observed and recorded. Solon, the Greek historian, wrote that astronomical information was being recorded nine thousand years before he was born. If this is correct, people have been interested in astrology for at least eleven thousand years. It's possible that astrology is the oldest form of divination in the world.

Astrology probably originated in Mesopotamia, but almost every ancient civilization, from Babylon to Egypt, and China to Greece, studied it. Early astrologers noted that most groups of stars, known as constellations, moved around the sky together. However, five of the larger and brighter stars traveled independently. They called them "wanderers." Today we know them as planets. The astrologers thought these wanderers were gods and called them Mercury, Venus, Mars, Jupiter, and Saturn. Uranus was discovered in 1781, followed by Neptune in 1846, and Pluto in 1930. They also noted the movements of the Sun and Moon.

Astrologers gradually came to realize that people who were born at a particular time of year, when the Sun, Moon, and planets were in the same part of the sky, had a great deal in common. Even though every person is unique, these people shared many of the same interests and feelings. This enabled astrologers to construct horoscope charts for individual people. A horoscope is a picture of the heavens at the date, time, and place where the person was born. If you could lie on your back and look up at the sky at the moment you were born, you'd see all the planets in the same positions as they are in your natal chart.

Preparing your chart used to be a lengthy process, but nowadays it can be done in seconds. If you Google "free horoscope chart," you'll find many sites that'll prepare a chart for you. However, interpreting the chart is an involved process that takes years to master.

The Four Elements

The twelve signs of the zodiac are divided into four groups, each containing three of the signs. The four groups are named after the four elements that were proposed by the ancient Greek philosopher Empedocles twenty-four hundred years ago. They were believed to be the building blocks of the universe: fire, earth, air, and water. The elements express the indispensable nature of the different signs.

△ **Fire (Aries, Leo, and Sagittarius)**

Fire is positive, assertive, energetic, enthusiastic, impulsive, inspirational, courageous, powerful, passionate, and initiating.

▽ **Earth (Taurus, Virgo, and Capricorn)**

Earth is cautious, responsible, reliable, ambitious, practical, focused, disciplined, dependable, solid, and persevering.

△ **Air (Gemini, Libra, and Aquarius)**

Air is lighthearted, joyful, curious, restless, independent, communicative, impractical, entertaining, intellectual, and trusting.

▽ **Water (Cancer, Scorpio, and Pisces)**

Water is compassionate, forgiving, understanding, emotional, creative, intuitive, and spiritual.

Sun Signs

The Sun is the energy and force behind the entire solar system. Without it, life as we know it could not exist. In your horoscope the Sun represents independence, willpower, strength, energy, leadership, motivation, creativity, and even your popularity. It indicates your individuality—what you are really like inside.

Most people know what their Sun sign is, and they usually know a few of the character traits that are assigned to it. The astrological predictions that appear in many newspapers and magazines are based on the Sun signs. These are by necessity generalizations, as there are only twelve Sun signs, and this means all of humanity is divided into twelve groups. Obviously, this isn't the case, but it's a good place to start looking at your horoscope chart.

In astrology, the sky is divided into twelve sections, each representing one of the signs of the zodiac. It looks like a circular cake cut into twelve equal slices. At the moment you were born, the Sun was in one of those twelve sections, and that determines what sign of the zodiac you belong to. The Sun spends thirty days in each section, which means it takes a whole year to visit each section and circle the zodiac. The dates change by a day or two from year to year. Consequently, if you were born near the beginning or end of a sign, it would pay to check the year you were born in to find what sign you were born in. Incidentally, when I was young, someone told me that people who were born "on the cusp," which means at the start or end of a sign, pick up the positive aspects of each sign and miss out on the negatives. This isn't totally true, but it's amazing how many people who are born on the cusp have a positive outlook on life.

Each section provides its own particular energy to the people who are born in it. Thousands of years ago, astrologers used the names of animals, people, and objects to describe this energy. This is why we have: Aries the Ram, Taurus the Bull, Gemini the Twins, Cancer the Crab, Leo the Lion, Virgo the Virgin, Libra the Scales, Scorpio the Scorpion, Sagittarius the Centaur, Capricorn the Goat, Aquarius the Water Carrier, and Pisces the Fish.

♈ Aries March 21–April 20

Element: Fire

Ruling Planet: Mars

People born under the sign of Aries are leaders and pioneers. They enjoy responsibility and are happiest when managing and organizing others. They are magnetic and outgoing and can inspire others to action with their dynamic leadership. They are courageous and prepared to take calculated risks, and they fight for what they believe in. They need to be busy to be happy.

Arians are often happiest when working for themselves, but also rise to positions of leadership and responsibility when working for others. They are curious and have a keen interest in everything that's going on.

Because they're quick-witted and like to get to the heart of any problem, they can get impatient with people who take time to come to a decision. They enjoy talking and look forward to social activities. They make warm and lively friends.

♉ Taurus April 21–May 21

Element: Earth

Ruling Planet: Venus

People born under the sign of Taurus are practical, patient, and determined. They're naturally cautious and think matters through before acting. Because of this, they can appear stubborn and obstinate to others. They like to do things their own way. Taureans can be extremely generous, but they always keep something in reserve, as security is important to them. They are generally good at managing their financial affairs. They are persistent and possess enormous drive and determination.

Taureans love beauty and work best in harmonious surroundings. Their homes invariably display good quality and tasteful objects, and whenever they buy something, it has to be of good quality.

The main lesson Taureans need to learn is how to control obstinacy. Once they've made up their minds on something, it's almost impossible to change it. This can make them inflexible and unforgiving, which is out of tune with the calm, harmonious approach they usually have.

♊ Gemini May 22–June 21

Element: Air

Ruling Planet: Mercury

People born under the sign of Gemini are ingenious, versatile, restless, and quick-thinking. They love meeting new people, and have an unquenchable thirst for knowledge. They are good with words, and can talk at great length on almost anything. They enjoy occupations that use their voices in some way. They enjoy mental stimulation, but often waste time on idle chatter. They are easygoing and get on well with almost everyone. They're versatile, highly creative, and often artistic. They need a great deal of variety in their lives. This endless search for variety often means they leave a trail of half-finished projects behind them. They possess a great deal of nervous energy and always seek quick results. They have the ability to see both sides of a problem.

♋ Cancer June 22–July 22

Element: Water

Ruling Planet: Moon

People born under the sign of Cancer are romantic, emotional, and imaginative. They are ruled largely by their feelings. They are highly sensitive and easily hurt, but are able to fight back when pushed into a corner. They have the ability to charm and captivate others and use this to devastating effect when they know what they want. Because they're incredibly tenacious, they ultimately achieve their goals.

Cancerians are ruled by the Moon, which emphasizes the sensitive, emotional side of their natures. Consequently, they may sometimes appear unwilling to commit in case they get hurt.

Cancerians love the security of home and family, and they make extremely good parents. They can be self-indulgent and spend money freely, yet they're also extremely good at getting a bargain. They are usually highly intuitive, and have the potential to develop considerable psychic ability.

♌ Leo July 23–August 22

Element: Fire

Ruling Planet: Sun

People born under the sign of Leo are ambitious, determined people with open, friendly natures. They are born leaders and instinctively gravitate to positions where their leadership potential can be utilized. They're open, honest, and enthusiastic about every aspect of their lives. Because they're generally happy, they want everyone close to them to be happy too. They are confident and determined and always make their presence felt in everything they do. They invariably get where they want to go, though overconfidence can cause delays and problems along the way.

Pride is very important to Leos, and they hate being ridiculed or demeaned. They are susceptible to flattery and need to learn how to control this. They are generous and enjoy making magnanimous gestures. They spread their warmth and enthusiasm everywhere they go. They can exaggerate or distort the truth at times, as they like to weave a good story.

♍ Virgo August 23–September 23

Element: Earth

Ruling Planet: Mercury

People born under the sign of Virgo are modest, down-to-earth, and matter of fact. They have a shrewd outlook on life. They are intelligent, cautious, conforming people who invariably look respectable and tidy. They enjoy doing detailed and precise work, and this, coupled with good memories, makes them highly capable administrators. They can assess people quickly, though they usually keep their thoughts to themselves. They are naturally reserved, and this makes it hard to get close to them until they're ready to let you in. They make good friends once this happens.

They are their own worst critics, as they constantly aim for perfection and set high standards for themselves. They enjoy analyzing things and can sometimes pay excessive attention to tiny details. They are self-motivated but find it impossible to complete anything to the high standards they require. This can cause significant worry. They generally prefer working behind the scenes but enjoy the inner satisfaction of a job well done. They can be outspoken and critical, and this often comes into play when they feel that justice and fair play are absent.

♎ Libra September 24–October 22

Element: Air

Ruling Planet: Venus

People born under the sign of Libra are harmonious, well-balanced, and friendly. They have a tendency to be indecisive. They are good talkers but prefer to avoid arguments and confrontations. They're honest and sincere and expect others to be the same. They feel their emotions deeply and are very involved in the lives of the people they care for. They love beauty and have good taste.

Librans find it hard to make decisions. They like to think about the matter, agonize over it, and weigh it up carefully before making a decision. This can cause impatience in other people, especially when the indecision is over something that is unimportant. However, once the decision has been made, they'll follow it through with great determination.

Librans have a strong sense of justice and fair play. They often side with the underdog.

♏ Scorpio October 23–November 21

Element: Water

Ruling Planet: Mars

People born under the sign of Scorpio are forceful and determined. They have enormous powers of concentration, but don't always reveal this side of themselves as they're also secretive and never reveal their true nature to anyone. They're intuitive, and this gives them great insight into how other people work and react.

Scorpios are individualistic. They're prepared to take risks, but they're always carefully calculated first. They watch and wait for opportunities, using the element of surprise to their advantage. Scorpios usually know what it is that they want, and they possess incredible determination and tenacity, which helps them reach their goals.

♐ Sagittarius November 22–December 22

Element: Fire

Ruling Planet: Jupiter

People born under the sign of Sagittarius are friendly, open, and optimistic. They are naturally enthusiastic and have a great zest for life. They're honest and loyal, but can be outspoken and tactless at times. Independence is important to them, and they need space and room around them in order to thrive. Because of this, they're often interested in sports and other outdoor activities. Sagittarians need to learn to channel their energies, as they often try to do too many different things at the same time. This is especially the case when they're young, and it can be frustrating to others who can see their potential.

Sagittarians enjoy learning, and often do this on their own, as they feel hemmed in and restricted in classrooms. They possess considerable foresight and vision, and over a lifetime develop a strong philosophy of life.

♑ Capricorn December 23–January 20

Element: Earth

Ruling Planet: Saturn

People born under the sign of Capricorn are solid, practical, and hardworking. They have a serious approach to life and slowly but steadily reach their goals. They are cautious, logical, careful, and fair. They're ambitious and set their sights on far off distant goals that they invariably achieve. They are practical, conservative people who like to work everything out carefully before acting. They are thrifty and careful with money. They enjoy saving money but are happy to use it for specific purposes.

They find it hard to express their emotions but can be extremely romantic with the right partner. They enjoy family life and are good, responsible, and loving parents.

♒ Aquarius January 21–February 19

Element: Air

Ruling Planet: Uranus

People born under the sign of Aquarius are sympathetic, broad-minded, tolerant, unconventional, and completely lacking in prejudice. They're inclined to be independent, intellectual, inventive, and altruistic. They possess strong humanitarian ideals and are happiest when they're involved in helping others. Their humanitarianism extends to all humanity.

Aquarians have a scientific frame of mind and are always progressive and frequently radical in their ideas. They're constantly looking ahead, trying to turn their dreams into reality. They accept people for who they are and accept their needs and idiosyncrasies. They make excellent, long-lasting friendships.

Aquarians seek the truth of life in everything they do. They learn using both logic and intuition. They live largely on a mental plane and enjoy coming up with original ideas.

♓ Pisces February 20–March 20

Element: Water

Ruling Planet: Neptune

People born under the sign of Pisces are gentle, imaginative, thoughtful, philanthropic, and creative. Although they can be vague and indecisive at times, they are generally popular and make successes of their lives. They're sensitive and easily hurt, and this can lead to disappointments and emotional crises. They need encouragement to perform well.

Pisceans are intuitive, receptive, and sympathetic. This makes them good judges of character. However, it also means they get easily hurt, and they suffer in silence when rebuffed or dismissed. They are extremely compassionate and are always available with a shoulder to lean on. They are happiest in any occupation that involves helping others.

The Ascendant

The second most important part of a horoscope chart is called the ascendant, or rising sign. Because of the Earth's rotation on its axis, the zodiac appears to revolve once every twenty-four hours. This means that one of the twelve signs was on the eastern horizon at the time you were born. This sign is called the ascendant. If you were born between 4:00 a.m. and 6:00 a.m., for instance, the sign coming over the horizon would be the same as your Sun sign. If you were born between 6:00 a.m. and 8:00 a.m., your ascendant would be the sign that immediately follows your Sun sign.

Your Sun sign describes your individuality, and your ascendant reveals your personality. It also has an effect on your physical appearance and how you present your individuality in everyday life.

If your ascendant is a *fire* sign (Aries, Leo, and Sagittarius), you'll appear enthusiastic, optimistic, and full of energy.

If your ascendant is an *earth* sign (Taurus, Virgo, and Capricorn), you'll appear cautious, reserved, practical, and serious.

If your ascendant is an *air* sign (Gemini, Libra, and Aquarius), you'll appear sociable, friendly, and communicative.

If your ascendant is a *water* sign (Cancer, Scorpio, and Pisces), you'll appear emotional, intuitive, and sensitive.

If you don't know your time of birth, astrologers normally use 6:00 a.m. This places your Sun Sign in the first house. However, you should use your time of birth if you know what it is. Sometimes your friends might be able to help you decide on a possible ascendant by comparing you to the qualities provided by the four elements.

Your horoscope sign and ascendant provide valuable insights into you and your nature. They also explain why two people of the same sign can be completely different to each other. Someone born under the sign of Aries, with a Leo ascendant, will be outspoken and enjoy being the center of attention. Another Arian, with a Pisces ascendant, will be quieter and more sensitive.

The Ten Planets

Astrologers refer to the Sun and the Moon as planets when doing their calculations. Of course they know this isn't actually the case, but because they have a strong influence on our lives, it's convenient to consider them as planets when looking at a horoscope chart. Accordingly, the ten planets are: the Sun, the Moon, Mercury, Venus, Mars, Jupiter, Saturn, Uranus, Neptune, and Pluto. Each of these relates to a different side of our personality.

☉ The Sun

The Sun passes through every sign of the zodiac for approximately one month every year. It reveals what we want out of life. The Sun is the giver of life, radiating energy, inspiration, self-awareness, enthusiasm, and wisdom. However, the warm rays of the Sun can be used for both good and ill. When adversely affected, this creates pride, anger, conceit, and egotism. The Sun relates to the conscious mind.

☽ The Moon

The Moon symbolizes fertility and relates to sensitivity, imagination, feelings, emotions, the subconscious, and intuition. It also relates to nurturing, domesticity, and home and family life. People who are ruled by the Moon are essentially emotional, sensitive, and changeable. The Moon relates to the subconscious mind.

☿ Mercury

Mercury governs the nervous system and intellect. It relates to self-expression and getting on with others. The keyword for Mercury is communication, which is why it's related to rapid thought, adaptability, eloquence, quick perceptions, and the intellect. It's also related to travel.

♀ Venus

Venus is the goddess of love and sexuality. It represents gentility, sociability, beauty, and the arts. It controls the deeper and finer human emotions, such as appreciation, love, and devotion. Venus reveals what you enjoy and how you handle close relationships.

♂ Mars

Mars, the god of war, symbolizes courage, force, bravery, assertiveness, and physical drive. It gives the qualities of boldness, frankness, endurance, and initiative. Mars reveals your energy and sexuality. People influenced by Mars are better at doing things, rather than planning them. When Mars is well situated in a chart it gives strength of character, leadership ability, and a strong desire to succeed. It also provides moral courage and the ability to carry ideas through to completion.

♃ Jupiter

Ancient astrologers considered Jupiter as being second only to the Sun. It symbolizes wisdom, moderation, and generosity. Jupiter reveals how we enjoy ourselves. Good fortune and luck have always been associated with this planet. Jupiter is also related to wisdom, knowledge, higher learning, philosophy, ethics, understanding, and the intellect. Because it's always looking ahead, Jupiter is also associated with ambition and career.

♄ Saturn

Saturn is the planet of restriction and restraint, and gives its name to the word *saturnine*. It reveals our sense of discipline, responsibility, focus, and strength of character. It gives tenacity, prudence, self-control, and concentration. When harnessed and directed, Saturn can be a positive energy that helps people achieve their aims.

♅ Uranus

Uranus is the planet of transformation and regeneration. It pioneers new ideas and concepts and brings out people's highest potential. It reveals originality, individuality, and creativity. It also provides a humanitarian outlook and an interest in metaphysical pursuits.

♆ Neptune

Neptune rules our innermost feelings, psychic abilities, sensitivity, and imagination. Its positive traits are receptiveness, intuition, spiritual development, psychic perception, and compassion. It reveals spirituality and humanitarian ideals.

♇ Pluto

Pluto, ruler of the underworld, represents the subconscious. It reveals your capacity for change, regeneration, growth, healing, and knowledge. As it takes Pluto two hundred and fifty years to circle the zodiac, Pluto's influence has an effect on generations of people, and can influence world conditions.

Like the Sun, the planets visit all of the signs in turn, and the planet and sign combination can be interpreted. Here are some examples:

If Mercury was in Cancer, you could say, "thinking would be influenced by emotions."

If Mars was in Capricorn, you might say, "plenty of ambition, with a strong desire to succeed."

If Jupiter was in Taurus, you might say, "luck in moneymaking ventures. Materialistic approach."

If Saturn was in Gemini, you might say, "security gained through some form of communication."

Aspects

The angles between the different planets in a horoscope are called aspects. They can strengthen, weaken, and affect the readings for each planet. There are both favorable and unfavorable aspects. Often a planet can be in a favorable aspect to one or more planets and at the same time be in an unfavorable aspect to others. Interestingly, people use their aspects differently. One person might suffer greatly under the effects of a discordant aspect, while someone else with the exact same aspect will look for the positive energies inside the aspect and work with them.

Favorable Aspects

The favorable aspects emphasize the positive, beneficial energies of the planets. They indicate the areas of life where you can accomplish what you set out to do with little effort. Because of this, many people take them for granted and become lazy. It's important to work just as hard in these areas as anywhere else to make the most of the blessings you've been given. The favorable aspects are:

- ☌ *Conjunction:* This occurs when two planets are within 8 degrees of each other. The conjunctions usually indicate areas that will show good results.

- △ *Trine:* This occurs when the planets are approximately 120 degrees apart, with a leeway of 8 degrees on either side. The trine is the most fortunate aspect, as the energies of the two planets harmonize easily. This aspect often shows you where your greatest strengths are.

- ✳ *Sextile:* This occurs when the planets are approximately 60 degrees apart, with a leeway of 8 degrees on either side. This is an "easy" aspect that generally works in your favor without much input from you.

- ⊻ *Semi-sextile:* This occurs when the planets are approximately 30 degrees apart, again with a leeway of 8 degrees on either side. This is also an "easy" aspect. Despite this, you shouldn't take it for granted, as it indicates areas where you can shine.

Unfavorable Aspects

The unfavorable aspects emphasize the negative characteristics of the planets involved. The unfavorable aspects often motivate people to action, as they want to overcome the challenges and difficulties the particular aspect produces.

- ☍ *Opposition:* This occurs when the two planets are approximately 180 degrees apart with a leeway of 8 degrees on either side. This is a difficult aspect, and it takes a great deal of effort to overcome any problems it creates.

- □ *Square:* This occurs when the two planets are approximately 90 degrees apart, with a leeway of 8 degrees on either side. This aspect works against your best interests, and it takes a great deal of hard work to eliminate the negativity it creates.

The Houses

There are twelve houses in astrology. They represent the areas of life in which the planets and signs operate. As there are also twelve signs in astrology, it's easy to think the twelve houses are part of the same wheel or chart. However, this isn't the case. The signs are dictated by the apparent annual rotation of the Sun, while the houses represent the Earth's twenty-four hour rotation around its axis.

The planets and signs exhibit their characteristics best in the areas of life dictated by the house they happen to be in. It's common for a chart to have a number of houses with no planets in them. These houses are still interpreted, but are not as important in the person's life as houses that contain one or more planets.

First House

This is the house of the self. It's responsible for the person's appearance, physical body, vitality, and temperament. It includes likes, dislikes, thoughts, personal activities and interests, and anything else that appeals to the person. The ruler of the first house is Aries.

Second House

This is the house of money, possessions, resources, and feelings. It reveals the person's ability to earn and to spend. This house is ruled by Taurus.

Third House

This is the house of communications, mental stimulation, short journeys, and relationships, especially brothers and sisters. The third house is ruled by Gemini, the Twins, which relates to the family relationships.

Fourth House

This house represents the home and early childhood. Consequently, it's usually related to the person's mother. It is also related to anything that's private or concealed. This house is ruled by Cancer.

Fifth House

This house governs pleasure, love, creativity, and the element of chance. The fifth house is ruled by Leo.

Sixth House

This is the house of system and order, practical work, and service to others. It is also related to matters concerning health and hygiene. It's ruled by Virgo.

Seventh House

The seventh house governs partnerships, such as marriage, close friendships, and business partnerships. As this house is involved in bringing people together, it's also related to enemies, as not every contact can be a happy one. It's ruled by Libra.

Eighth House

This is the house of death, legacies, possessions that are gained from someone else, strong feelings, and anything that's hidden. It's ruled by Scorpio.

Ninth House

The ninth house governs long journeys, higher education, prophecy, and philosophy. It's ruled by Sagittarius.

Tenth House

The tenth house governs the person's status, importance, and aspirations. It's involved with practical matters, security, and the drive to succeed. It's often related to the father. It is ruled by Capricorn.

Eleventh House

This is the house of humanitarianism, ideals, connections, and casual friendships with people who support a common cause or interest. Traditionally, this is the house of "hopes and wishes." It's ruled by Aquarius.

Twelfth House

The twelfth house relates to the occult, the psychic, and the person's unconscious. It also relates to health problems, and the fact that not everything should be taken at face value. The twelfth house is ruled by Pisces.

Putting It Together

With this information, it's possible to provide a detailed description of the person's personality, including his or her strengths and weaknesses, emotions, parental influences, ability to find happiness and fulfilment, lifestyle and career, love and sex. In fact, it's possible to look at a chart and receive information on any aspect of the person's personality and makeup.

Here's an example. Let's assume the chart is for a young man who is thinking of starting his own business. His Sun sign is Taurus, so we know he's prepared to work hard and expects to receive the rewards of his labor. His Sun is in the second house, a particularly harmonious combination, and one that would certainly help him in business. His Sun is conjunct Venus. This means he'll be charming and able to get along with others. He'll be positive and optimistic. Although he'll be ambitious, this side of his character will be softened, making him less competitive and more relaxed.

His Sun is also trine Saturn in the ninth house. This means he'll be responsible and ethical. He'll overcome the difficulties in his life relatively easily and will always try to do what is right. He's likely to travel extensively.

His Sun is in opposition to Uranus in the seventh house. This means he'll look at everything from his own personal point of view. He'll have original ideas, but is likely to need others to help him as he's impractical. He'll have a strong desire for independence, which encourages self-employment. Uranus in the seventh house could well indicate a business partnership.

In this example we've looked briefly at the Sun and three planets. Imagine the detail an astrologer would find if he or she examined all the planets, all the aspects, and all the houses.

Into the Future

Astrology doesn't claim to accurately predict the future. However, using a variety of methods, it reveals the influences and tendencies that will appear in the future.

A natal horoscope chart is constructed for someone at the moment of their birth. This chart can be progressed to any time in the future of that person. There are a variety of ways to do this.

Transits

Probably the easiest and most popular way of doing this is to examine the planetary transits. Transits describe the movements of the different planets as they move around the horoscope. You'll need the person's natal horoscope (the chart drawn up from their birth data) and a book called an ephemeris. This is a listing of the positions of all the planets on any given date. Ephemerides are also available online. You look at the ephemeris for the particular date you're interested in and see what planets listed there are in aspect to any of the planets in the birth chart. Most astrologers work with a 1 or 2 degree leeway when doing this, rather than the 8 degrees often used for a natal chart.

Speaking generally, the aspects between the slower moving planets (Jupiter, Saturn, Uranus, Neptune, and Pluto) are more powerful than the faster moving planets. This is because the aspects created by faster moving planets exist for only a short period of time. No astrologer would look at the transits created by the Sun or Moon, for instance. The transit created by the Sun lasts for about two and a half days, and the Moon a mere four hours. The transits of the outer planets reveal the trends of a person's life, while the transits of the inner planets usually indicate an event.

Planetary Returns

A planetary return occurs when a planet returns to the position it was in at the time of the person's birth. They signify a new cycle of experience is about to start. The planets take varying degrees of time to return to where they were when someone was born:

Jupiter takes approximately twelve years. It's a time to move forward as there's considerable potential for achievement and success.

Saturn takes approximately twenty-nine years. It's a time to reassess one's life and to change direction, if need be.

Uranus takes eighty-four years. Many people never experience this. Consequently, the half-return at the age of forty-two is examined. It's a stressful time, but it opens doors for new interests.

Solar Return

In this method a chart is erected when the Sun has returned to the same position it was in the natal chart. This chart provides insights into the next twelve months. The ascendant of this progressed chart gives a strong clue as to how the person will handle him or herself in the next twelve months. The house the progressed Sun is in indicates the person's focus for the next year.

A Day for a Year

People often ask astrologers about the trends of their lives. "I seem to be going through a rough patch." "Back then everything seemed to just fall into place." "How come I made money so easily last year, but this year it's a struggle?" We all have ups and downs in our lives.

In astrology there's the concept of "one day for one year" when progressing an astrology chart. In other words, if you turned thirty-five today, your current astrology chart would show every planet moved forward thirty-five days from the position they were in when you were born. This is an ancient technique that is still used by many astrologers. There are other methods for determining future trends with astrology, but the "one day for one year" method is perfect for most needs. It's a quick and easy way to forecast future trends, and it's not surprising that many professional astrologers use it.

Horary Astrology

Horary astrology is a method to answer specific questions. A chart is erected for the date, time, and place where the question was asked. The chart is then interpreted to help answer the question.

William Lilly, the seventeenth century English astrologer, used horary astrology most of the time, as many of his clients were not sure when they were born. He wrote a detailed explanation of the technique in his book *Christian Astrology*.

Mundane Astrology

Mundane astrology isn't interested in the future of a single person. It focuses on the future of nations, political parties, and world events. A chart is erected for the capital city of a country, or the date of birth of the people most involved, such as a president or prime minister.

Newspaper Astrology

Everyone is familiar with the Sun sign forecasts printed in newspapers and magazines around the world. For some years, I prepared daily horoscopes for a national radio station and was amazed at the amount of positive feedback I received, as I was using nothing but the ten planets and the twelve houses.

If you're preparing a Sun sign forecast for an Arian, you'd place Aries in the first house, Taurus in the second, and so on. If the person happened to be a Virgo, you'd place Virgo in the first house, Libra in the second, and so on. As the planets travel through the twelve houses, they stimulate the houses they pass through, and this provides the Sun sign astrologers with the information they need to prepare their forecasts.

Consequently, if Venus happened to be in the third house, it would enhance all forms of communication and fill it with love and affection. When Uranus is in the third house, it would behave completely differently. You could expect disruptions and other problems in your communications and dealings with others.

The signs the planets are in at any given moment are available online, enabling you to create your own Sun sign readings in much greater detail than you'd find in your daily paper.

Suggested Reading

Clement, Stephanie Jean. *Mapping Your Birthchart*. St. Paul, MN: Llewellyn Publications, 2003.

Mann, A. T. *The Round Art: The Astrology of Time and Space*. Cheltenham, UK: Dragon's World Ltd., 1979.

Oken, Alan. *Alan Oken's Complete Astrology*. New York: Bantam Books, Inc., 1980.

Parker, Karren Curry. Understanding Human Design. San Antonio, TX: Hierophant Publishing, 2013.

Riske, Kris Brandt. *Mapping Your Future*. St. Paul, MN: Llewellyn Publications, 2004.

Webster, Richard. *The Stars and Your Destiny*. Auckland, NZ: Brookfield Press, 1982.

Woolfolk, Joanna Martine. *The Only Astrology Book You'll Ever Need*. Boulder, CO: Taylor Trade Publishing, 1982. Updated edition 2012.

Augury

When I was a child, I'd get annoyed when I asked my grandmother a question and her reply was, "A little bird told me." This phrase is very old and can be found in the Koran and in Shakespeare's *Henry IV*. It meant my grandmother wasn't prepared to answer my question. Augury is the art of divining from the actions and sounds of birds and other animals.

Divination by observing the signs of nature to determine the desires of the gods probably dates back to Chaldean times. As it originally referred to the movements and sounds of birds, augury possibly began because the ability of birds to fly enabled them to get closer to the gods. There's even a reference to it in the Old Testament when King Solomon says: "for a bird of the air shall carry the voice, and that which hath wings shall tell the matter" (Ecclesiastes 10:20).

Augury was practiced by both the ancient Greeks and Romans. At the time of Julius Caesar in the first century BCE, the Romans employed sixteen priests as full-time augurs, and they had developed an extensive system to interpret a wide range of possible actions. There were four colleges of priests, one of which was the college of augurs. Augury was used to determine the will of the gods. This enabled them to take a certain course of action, if the gods approved, or to make new plans if they didn't.

Types of Augury
Ex caelo

The most important auguries to the Romans were those that the augurs specifically looked for, such as thunder, lightning, and the appearance of comets or meteors. Lightning and thunder were signs from Jupiter and could be both favorable and unfavorable according to which side of the augur they came from and whether the number of claps of thunder were odd or even.

Ex avibus

This category observes the flight patterns and sounds made by different birds. The name given to birds whose flight patterns were observed was *Alites*. The most important birds in this group were eagles, hawks, vultures, and starlings. Birds who gave omens through their singing belonged to the *Oscines*. Examples of these included crows, owls, ravens, and woodpeckers. Their singing was interpreted as being a positive or negative sign depending on which side of the augur's special area they appeared on.

Ex tripudiis

Tripudium means "sacred dance." This category interpreted the eating patterns of sacred chickens. The chickens were kept in cages. These coops were opened when an augury was needed, and the chickens were enticed with bread crumbs or corn. It was a negative sign if the chickens refused to come out of their cages, wouldn't eat, cried, or flapped their wings. It was a positive sign if a chicken left its cage and ate greedily. It was even more auspicious if a few morsels of food fell from its beak onto the ground.

The Greeks also had sacred fowls, but they used them in a different manner. Letters of the alphabet were placed on the ground and grains were scattered over them. The order in which the grains were picked up were interpreted to provide the answer.

Ex quadrupedibus

This category was a late addition to augury and was never used for affairs of state. It describes the movements of four-legged animals, such as wolves, foxes, horses, dogs, and goats. These were interpreted if one of these was found in an unusual location, crossed someone's path, or ran in a particular direction.

Ex diris

This category included unusual incidents that weren't covered in the other four categories. These included unexpected noises, as well as people sneezing, hiccupping, stumbling, or even seeing an apparition. The list of possible auguries in this category increased so much that the college of augurs was forced to limit the number of unexpected activities that could be considered an augury.

Attus Navius

Cicero recorded the story of a humble man called Attus Navius. When one of his pigs escaped, he told the gods that if it was found, he'd give them the biggest grapes he could find from his vineyard. Once the pig had been found, Attus, holding his augur's wand, stood in the middle of his vineyard facing south. He mentally divided his vineyard into four quarters. He noticed that the birds appeared to favor a certain quarter. He went to the center of this quarter and again divided it into four parts. Again, the birds favored a certain quarter. He walked in that direction and found a bunch of incredibly large grapes, which he offered to the gods. The story became well known, and it was eventually heard by King Tarquinius Priscus, who ordered him to come to Rome.

The king was planning to enlarge his army, and asked Attus Navius to do an augury for him. He was furious when he was told that the omens were unfavorable. He asked Attus Navius to perform an augury to see if he could do what the king was thinking. He did this, and he told the king that whatever it was he was thinking about would occur. The king laughed and said that he was wondering if Attus Navius could cut a whetstone in half with a razor. The implements were gathered, and Navius successfully cut the whetstone in half. Navius was immediately made one of the king's augurs. [4]

How to Perform an Augury

1. Select a suitable area of high ground.

2. Draw a *templum* on the ground. You do this by drawing a line from east to west. This is called a *cardo*. A second line, called a *decumanus*, is drawn from north to south. As the cardo is drawn from where the Sun rises and sets on the day of the divination, it may not be exactly east and west. The *decumanus* is gauged from the position of Polaris, rather than a compass. Two parallel lines are drawn to create a rectangle, with the longer sides running from north to south.

3. A square tent, called a *tabernaculum*, which only opens on one side, is erected in the center of the rectangle with the open side facing south. This tent is often erected the night before the augury takes place, and the augur sleeps in it.

4. The person who is doing the augury sits inside the tent on a firm chair facing south. (The chair needs to be firm to avoid any possibly of it squeaking. Any extraneous sounds, such as something being dropped on the ground, are considered unfavorable.) Because the other sides are closed, he or she cannot be distracted by anything that happens outside the field of vision so focus is solely on the sky in front of him or her. This person holds a wand (called a *lituus*) made from an unblemished tree branch with a naturally curved end.

---

4   Cicero, *De Divinatione 1*, 31.

5. The flute players start playing and continue throughout the entire ritual. This is done to please the gods. Incense may be burned as well.

6. The person conducting the augury drinks a libation to Jupiter from an earthenware cup. He or she explains why the augury is being performed, and asks for his approval.

7. The augur draws another templum in the air with his or her wand. This templum is mentally divided into four quarters that are each divided into four, creating sixteen sections. (Our word *temple* is derived from the Latin *templum*. It's interesting to think that *templum* originally indicate a space marked out in the air, rather than a sacred building.)

8. The augur prays to Jupiter, asking him to provide the required signs within the *templum*.

9. The augur sits quietly and gazes steadily at the sky in front of him or her and starts looking for signs.

10. The augur remains sitting until the augury is over. This can be any length of time that is decided beforehand. It might be as short as sixty minutes or as long as a day. During this time, all the omens, both good and bad, are observed, and interpreted later.

The Signs

The Roman name for the omens that are observed is *auspices*. The English word *auspicious* is derived from this. The questions that are asked can always be answered with a yes or a no. Consequently, the different omens that have appeared during the augury need to be evaluated to determine the correct answer. A rare or unusual bird would, for instance, be considered more important than a common one.

It's a sign that the gods are not interested in the matter if no omens appear during the augury. This means the person can safely proceed, though it is usually considered better to confirm this by performing the augury again on another day.

Interpreting the Augury

The signs that augurs look for are interpreted in different ways depending on the augur's background and culture. One of the ways the ancient Romans interpreted their auguries was by waiting for a single bird to appear in the four quarters the augur had mentally constructed in the sky. Where the bird came from, as well as the direction it took, and where it vanished from sight was observed. All of these factors were interpreted.

Birds flying to the right indicated a positive outcome, while birds flying to the left were a sign of problems and delays. Birds flying directly at the augur were a sign of good times ahead. Conversely, birds flying away indicated a lack of opportunities in the near future. It was a good sign if the birds flew high in the air, as this indicated a positive outcome. A bird that sang as it flew was a good omen, and showed that it was the right time to proceed. A flock of birds was always a good omen.

The Romans thought that every bird had a particular quality that indicated good or bad fortune. Eagles were extremely propitious and were a sign of prosperity. Vultures were considered auspicious by some augurs and a sign of bad luck by others. Herons and doves were considered lucky. Falcon hawks were considered especially lucky for anything relating to relationships and money. Buzzards, magpies, swallows, and owls were a sign of bad luck. However, owls were considered extremely lucky in Greece, and were sacred to the goddess Minerva. In ancient Greece, ravens were sacred to Apollo, who was considered the patron of augurs.

Is Augury Practiced Today?

I've seen people practicing augury in Thailand and India. In both cases, a parrot selected a reading for someone from a selection of cards containing different readings.

The Groundhog Day tradition could be considered a form of augury. Folklore says that if a groundhog emerges from its burrow and sees its own shadow, it will return underground and winter will last another six weeks.

Popular folklore endows certain birds with a variety of meanings, both good and bad. In North America, the robin is considered a sign of good luck. It's a sign of good luck if the robin flies upward, but bad luck if it flies down. You're supposed to make a wish whenever you see a robin.

One of the reasons canaries are kept in homes is because they encourage faithfulness and a happy home and family life.

The cuckoo has always been considered a strange bird that has the gift of "double sight," which enables it to see into the future. This superstition is derived from the two syllables of its call. It's a bad sign to hear a cuckoo's call coming from the north. However, it's highly positive if it comes from the south. It's a sign of good luck if you hear it from the west, and a good omen of success in love if you hear it from the east. To complicate matters, it's considered bad luck to hear a cuckoo's call if you're standing on firm ground, good luck if you're standing on soft ground, and bad luck whenever you're sitting on the ground.

Crows have always been considered birds that bring bad luck with them. Even today, some people bow to a single crow to avert the bad luck that a crow on its own signifies. Two crows flying together are a sign of good luck. If the first crow you see in the spring is flying, it's a sign that you'll soon be taking a journey. It's a sign of bad luck if a crow flies to your left, and a warning to be careful that day if it flies to your right.

However, it's not all bad. If you see a crow gliding through the air, you can make a wish. If it doesn't flap its wings before it disappears from view, your wish will come true. If it does happen to flap its wings, you must turn away. If the crow has disappeared from view when you look back, your wish may still come true.

It's a sign of a loss of some sort if you see a hawk catching its prey. An old belief of the ancient Greeks and Romans is that if you see a hawk flying overhead while you're making a decision, it will prove successful. Similarly, if you're involved in a contest of some sort, or even a battle, and happen to see a hawk overhead, the outcome will be positive. It's a good omen to see a hawk on your right-hand side.

Blackbirds, doves, ducks, hummingbirds, kingfishers, martins, robins, storks, swallows, woodpeckers, and wrens are all said to bring good luck. Blue and red birds do the same. Even the humble sparrow is considered lucky in some parts of the world. However, all around the world people believe that it's bad luck to kill one.

Even though augury, as practiced by the Greeks and the Romans, died out long ago, people still consider birds to be lucky or unlucky. Because of this, augury still survives today.

Suggested Reading

Brown, W. J. *The Gods had Wings*. London, UK: Constable and Company Ltd., 1936.

Encyclopaedia Britannica. Micropaedia1. 647–648. Chicago: Encycloæpdia Britannica, Inc. 15th Edition, 1983.

Loewe, Michael, and Carmen Blacker. *Oracles and Divination*. Boulder, CO: Shambhala Publications, Inc., 1981.

Spafte, Dianne. *When Oracles Speak*. London: Thorsons, 1997.

Automatic Writing

Automatic writing is the ability to write or draw in a state of altered consciousness—without using the conscious mind. Rudyard Kipling explained it well when he wrote: "the pen took charge, and I watched it write." [5] Alfred Lord Tennyson, William Butler Yeats, and Gertrude Stein are three other examples of authors who have used automatic writing to enhance their creativity. There are also many examples of people with no noticeable creative talents who were able to produce remarkable work through automatic writing.

Most people produce automatic writing while holding a pen or pencil, while others use a planchette. This is a triangular or heart-shaped device with legs on two of its corners. These two legs have small wheels or ball bearings to facilitate movement. A pencil fulfils the role of the third leg. A planchette is usually made of wood and is approximately six inches in length. The planchette is placed on a sheet of paper that is taped to a table, and the operator rests his or her hands lightly on it. The operator usually closes his or her eyes and enters into a relaxed, meditative state. Some people enter into a trance, while others remain totally alert. Some people distract their conscious mind by reciting poetry, reading a book, or talking with a friend. After a period of time, which varies from person to person, the person's subconscious mind causes the planchette to move and produce shapes and words on the paper.

---

5   Inglis 1987, 40.

The most common example of this is the doodles that people create while conversing on the telephone. These drawings are produced effortlessly, with virtually no conscious input, and the results often surprise the creator.

A few people achieve good results immediately. However, most people need to be patient and practice regularly until the planchette starts to move. Even then, the writing that's initially produced is likely to be illegible scribbles and random shapes. With practice, though, words and sentences appear. One complication is that all the words are joined together as, most of the time, the pencil lead never leaves the paper. Some people even produce automatic writing in reverse, and a mirror is needed to read it. Other people produce writing that's so small a magnifying glass is needed to read it. I've even seen someone producing automatic writing backward and upside down, which meant the sheet of paper had to be turned around to read it.

Once the person has developed skill at automatic writing, he or she can carry on a conversation with someone while the hand on the planchette continues to write. People who are skilled at automatic writing can produce up to two thousand words an hour. The Reverend George Vale Owen was said to receive an average of twenty-four words a minute, and he continued doing this four nights a week for months on end. One of the fascinating things about automatic writing is that you can do it for long periods of time without becoming physically tired.

Automatic writers experience what they are doing in two completely different ways. The first group remains unaware of what their hand is writing until they read the information afterward. These people are often surprised at what they've written. The second group receives ideas that relate to what their hand is writing as they write.

Automatic writing is normally associated with writing books and poetry. However, it can be a highly effective way of gaining answers to questions. A woman I know asked, "Why does no one like me?" She received a detailed reply that explained why she had become so reclusive and timid, and it gave her detailed suggestions on various things she could do to gain friends. She now has a number of friends and makes her living answering questions for people with her automatic writing skills.

Because it's such an effective way of answering questions, automatic writing can be a useful divination tool. Simply ask a question pertaining to the future, and see what responses you get. Some answers will be detailed and specific. At other times, the answers appear in the form of symbols that need to be interpreted. Naturally, you should evaluate the answers carefully before acting on the information.

Automatic Writing in the Far East

Automatic writing is called *Fu Kay* in China and Hong Kong. It's thought that it began as a game in which children received answers to their questions from the Purple Goddess. Adults began playing it during periods of repression, which is why Fu Kay became a private activity performed in people's homes. This applies even today. However, despite this, Fu Kay is also practiced in Taoist temples.

Some years ago I was fortunate enough to see Fu Kay in action at the Ching Chung Koon Temple in the New Territories of Hong Kong. This is the largest Taoist temple in Hong Kong, and it has a special shrine room that is used solely for Fu Kay. Most Fu Kay rooms are richly decorated with lanterns, plaques, and red and gold satin wall coverings, as well as an altar and Fu Kay table. The Fu Kay room in the Ching Chung Koon Temple is almost austere in comparison. In front of the altar are offerings of fruit and flowers, and burning joss sticks. Above the altar is the God of Mediums. The Fu Kay table is a simple shallow box containing sand or sawdust.

The medium uses a special stick, usually made from willow, to answer the questions. One end is T-shaped and the other end tapers to a point. The medium rests the T end of the stick on both hands. When a question is asked, the pointed end moves rapidly over the sand creating a series of Chinese characters that answer the question. The answers are in the form of ancient Chinese classical verse, which needs to be interpreted.

Many Taoists believe that the medium's answer comes from Lao Tzu, the legendary sixth century BCE philosopher who is credited with founding philosophical Taoism. He is considered a deity in religious Taoism.

Where Does the Writing Come From?

Spiritualists claim that automatic writing involves communication with spirits from the "other side." However, it's more likely to be an example of the ideomotor response, which also activates the pendulum and Ouija board. This enables the person to retrieve messages from his or her subconscious mind. However, apart from accessing the universal life force, this doesn't explain how valuable information that no one knows is able to come through with automatic writing.

A 2012 university study discovered that when a person is writing normally, the cerebral cortex is highly active. This is not the case with automatic writing, and this planning section of the brain slows down when someone starts automatic writing. The researchers were unable to discover what parts of the brain were active when someone is automatic writing. This indicates that simple relaxation is not an explanation for automatic writing. [6]

Another intriguing factor is that many automatic writers produce work that is well beyond their normal intellectual capabilities.

How to Do It

1. Gather the items you'll need. At the very least you'll need pen and paper. I use a ballpoint pen, but many people I know prefer to use a pencil. When you start, you should use a large sheet of paper, as you don't know where your pen will take you. A certain amount of tiredness in the writing arm is helpful. Consequently, no part of this arm should contact the table. If this proves too difficult, you might be able to construct a sling that you can rest

---

6   Peres 2012.

your wrist on to prevent your arm from getting overly tired. Your writing arm should create a 90-degree angle at the elbow.

2. Find a space where you won't be interrupted for at least thirty minutes. It should be comfortable, and contain a table and chair.

3. Fasten a large sheet of paper to the table with tape. Alternatively, you might like to use a large-sized artist's drawing pad.

4. Sit down at the table and hold your pen or pencil normally with the lead touching the paper. If you're using a planchette, gently rest your middle three fingers on it. Take five slow deep breaths, inhaling to the count of three, holding it for three, and exhaling to the count of five. If it makes it easier to relax, close your eyes and allow all your muscles to become slack and loose.

5. Forget about what you're doing and focus solely on relaxing your body as much as you can. I usually start with the toes of one foot, and then allow the relaxation to drift into my foot. I repeat this with the other foot and then gradually allow the relaxation to drift all the way up my body to the top of my head.

6. This step can be ignored if you're not requesting specific information. If you're asking a question, silently ask it now. Repeat it several times before moving on to the next step.

7. When you feel completely relaxed, focus on your breathing for a few seconds, and then visualize a beautiful scene in your mind. This might be a place you've been to, or it could be something you've imagined. Animate this scene in various ways. You might "see" birds flying, people walking or playing, or anything else that seems right for the scene. Add sounds and smells. Continue doing this for as long as you can. If you have someone with you, you can describe the scene to them, and allow them to suggest suitable additions. The important thing is to pay no attention whatsoever to your writing hand.

8. Stay as long as you can in this detached state. Enjoy the pleasant relaxation and the beautiful scene in your mind. Pay no attention whatsoever to what your writing hand is doing. Automatic writing is unconscious writing, and you'll lose contact as soon as you start paying conscious attention to it.

9. When you feel ready, dismiss the scene from your mind and become familiar again with the room that you're in. Take a few slow, deep breaths and open your eyes.

10. If this is the first time you've practiced automatic writing, you might feel disappointed with the results. Your pencil may not have moved at all, and if it has moved, you might see nothing more than a few shapes, squiggles, or letters. This doesn't matter. The more you practice, the better you'll become. However, you need patience. Repeat the experiment again on another day, and continue doing this until you can enter the desired state quickly and easily.

Evaluate the results carefully. Even after you've gained experience at automatic writing, you'll occasionally receive messages that are silly, dishonest, or mischievous. A good example is if you ask if a certain person will give birth to a boy or a girl. Your pen might write *girl*, but the baby turns out to be a boy. The rule is not to ask any questions that you have a close personal involvement in, as you're likely to get the answer you want rather than the correct answer. Consequently, you need to use your own common sense when thinking about what you've produced.

Another reason to evaluate your results is that you might be writing your messages backward or upside down. It's rare, but you may even write messages in a foreign language.

Notes

It's natural to feel skeptical when you first start experimenting with automatic writing. You must be willing to suspend disbelief and allow the process to work through you.

It's better to practice at approximately the same time every day. Don't practice for more than twenty minutes at a time. It's better to have a number of short sessions, rather than an hour or more once a week.

If you're using a planchette, you might like to try contacting it with more or fewer fingers. You might even find you get better results using both hands, rather than one.

Instead of consciously relaxing your body, you could experiment with reading a book while holding a pencil or resting your fingers on a planchette. You could also try reciting favorite poems or chatting with a like-minded friend. Another method is to silently count a number with each exhalation. Anything that helps you to quieten your mind will work.

It can be helpful to consciously write a few words with your pen or planchette before starting the experiment.

If the pen fails to move after several minutes, ask a friend to create a few shapes using the hand that you're holding the pencil with. When this person lets go of your hand, it will often continue moving and start producing automatic writing.

You might like to try holding the pen in your nondominant hand. I haven't had any success with this, but I know people who have better results when they use their other hand.

No matter how skilled you become at automatic writing, you'll have days when nothing comes through. There is no need to worry about this. It simply means nothing is available for you at that time.

Automatic Drawing and Painting

My first experience of automatic drawing was at a spiritualist church more than forty years ago. While the medium was giving messages, a woman in the front row made sketches of the spirit guides of the people he was speaking to. I was impressed with the quality of her drawings, but what amazed me the most was the speed at which she produced them. When I spoke to her afterward, she told me that she amazed herself with her speed and quality. Apparently, the drawings she created when she drew consciously were of a much lower standard than the works she produced when in a light trance.

Automatic paintings are usually produced at great speed, too. There have even been reported cases where automatic painting was performed in the dark.

Suggested Reading

Koutstaal, Wilma. "Skirting the Abyss: A History of Experimental Explorations of Automatic Writing in Psychology." *Journal of the History of the Behavioral Sciences*, Volume 28, January 1992. http://www.tc.umn.edu/~kouts003/Koutstaal_Journal_HistBehScience_1992.pdf.

Lodge, Sir Oliver. *Raymond, or Life and Death*. New York: George H. Doran Company, 1916.

Pole, Wellesley Tudor. *Private Dowding*. London: John M. Watkins, 1917.

Bibliomancy

Bibliomancy is divination using a book. Traditionally, the book was the Bible or some other sacred book, but any book can be used. Naturally, different cultures used different sacred books. The Koran, for instance, is used in Islamic cultures. The book is opened to a random page, and the person either closes his or her eyes or turns away before touching somewhere on the page. The sentence or paragraph his or her finger indicates is interpreted to answer a question or to divine the future.

Using information chosen from books dates back to the ancient Greeks. They used verses from the *Iliad* and the *Odyssey*. The Romans preferred Virgil's *Aeneid*. The verses were written on a series of discs that were attached to a length of string. A question was asked, and one of the discs was selected randomly to provide the answer.

The Bible and a Key

A Bible and a key were used by young women to see if the person they were attracted to would make a good husband. The girl who was wanting to know the answer to this question would place her door key between the pages of the Song of Solomon, with the handle protruding. The key would be firmly bound into the Bible with her garter belt. Two friends balanced the Bible by placing their middle fingers on the protruding part of the key. Once this had been done, all three of them would recite verse seven of chapter eight: "Many waters cannot quench love, neither can the floods drown it: if a man would give all the substance of his house for love, it would utterly be contemned."

It's a sign of a happy marriage if the Bible moves or falls to the ground while these words are being said. If it fails to move, the girl is destined to remain a spinster and will never marry.

The same ritual can be performed to see if one's lover is faithful. If the Bible turns slightly toward the right, he or she is true, and there's no need for any concern.

Young women can also perform this ritual to find out the initials of their future partner's names. The letters of the alphabet are recited until the Bible moves.

Young men and woman were able to have dreams about their future partners by inserting six-pence into the Book of Ruth and placing it under their pillows.

A Bible and key were also used to assess the guilt or innocence of possible thieves. The names of the suspects were read out while other people recited passages from the Bible. The guilty party would be revealed when the Bible turned at the same time as his name was spoken.

Another version of this involved writing each suspect's name on a small piece of paper that was pushed into the central part of the key. Psalm 50, verse 8 ("When thou sawest a thief") was recited while the Bible was suspended by two people using the key. If the Bible moved while these words were being said, the suspect whose name was on the slip of paper inside the key was guilty. The first written record of this was in 1303, and Reginald Scot wrote about it in his book *The Discoverie of Witchcraft*.

Another method for determining guilt or innocence was to seat the suspects around a table. A Bible was placed in the center of the table and a key was spun on it. When the key stopped moving, it would be pointing at the guilty person.

Yet another method involved used the key as a pendulum. It was suspended on a ribbon or thread above a Bible and would move when the guilty person's name was mentioned. Thomas Hardy mentions this form of bibliomancy in his book, *Far from the Madding Crowd*.

How to Do It

The first thing you need to do is to formulate a question. It can be as general or as specific as you wish. You might ask, "Am I going in the right direction?" "Will I be happy?" or "What will the next twelve months be like?" It might be: "Will Sarah agree to have dinner with me on Saturday night?" or "Is it a good time to ask my boss for a pay rise?" Your question needs to be serious in nature. You shouldn't, for instance, ask: "What color dress will I wear next Wednesday?" Bibliomancy isn't a game, and frivolous questions get the answers they deserve.

You also need to choose a book—or the book needs to choose you. If a book falls off a book-shelf while you're searching for a different book, it may be asking you to practice bibliomancy with it. If you're thinking of travel, you might choose an atlas. If you're religious, you might choose the Bible, the Torah, the Koran, or some other spiritual book. You might choose the I Ching, a favorite novel, a book of quotations, an encyclopedia, or a nonfiction book on any topic. On one occasion I received an extremely useful answer from a book on wine. I have a large library, and I sometimes choose a book entirely by chance. However, I also have particular books that I use more frequently than others. One is a book containing the thoughts and advice of Marcus Aurelius.

If you decide not to use a spiritual book, ideally choose a book that you love, or a book that is important to you for some reason. If you have problems choosing a book, close your eyes and run your hand over the spines of the books in your bookcase. The book you stop on will be the ideal book for this particular divination.

1. Sit down comfortably holding the book you're going to use. Quieten your mind and think about your question. A minute or two of relaxation will help the entire divination process.

2. When you feel ready, you'll need to choose a random page. There are a number of ways to do this. You might close your eyes or turn your head and open the book somewhere. You might rest the book on its spine, and allow it to open itself at a page. You might place the closed book on a table with the spine facing you, and without looking, insert a playing card or piece of card between two pages. You might riffle through the pages and stop when you feel like it.

   One problem with doing any of these with a favorite book is that the book is likely to open at frequently read pages. One way to eliminate that is to use dice. Before starting, determine how many throws you'll make to pick a page. Let's assume you've decided to make five throws, and have thrown 3, 2, 5, 5, and 6. This totals 21. However, this isn't satisfactory, as the highest possible page you could reach with this method is 30. The solution is to use two dice. Each time you roll the dice, record both numbers to create a two digit number. The lower number is written down first. Consequently, if you roll a 5 and a 3, you'd write down 35. Let's assume you've decided to roll the dice five times, as before. You roll 2 and 6, 5 and 4, 6 and 2, 5 and 5, and 4 and 6. This totals 198, and you'd open the book to that page. A friend of mine has written the numbers 1 to 300 on blank business cards. He keeps these in a shoe box. When he needs a number, he shakes the box vigorously and selects a card with his eyes closed. If he chooses 296 when the book has 280 pages, he'll simply go through the process again.

3. The book is now open to the page you selected by chance. You now need to choose a line or paragraph. Close your eyes or turn away, think of your question, and then touch somewhere on the page with a finger or pin. You might like to create circles or random designs with your forefinger before allowing it to stop.

4. Your reading starts from where your finger indicated. Read the selected passage without relating it to your question. Make sure you understand exactly what it means. You might read a few words, a line, a paragraph, or the whole page. In fact, if you happen to pick a spot at the bottom of a page, your reading might be on the next page.

5. Go through the reading again with your question in mind. Sometimes, as happened with Robert Browning, the answer will be obvious. At other times the passage you selected may not seem to have anything to do with your question. On these occasions, you'll have to think about both your question and the answer you received. Rest assured, it will come. On one occasion, when the answer wasn't clear, I wrote it on a sheet of paper and looked at it whenever I had a spare moment. It took three days, but eventually the answer made perfect sense.

You can evaluate the reading in a variety of ways. You might receive the answer directly. The answer might come in the form of a symbol that you can relate to your question. Is the reading positive or negative? This is useful with yes or no questions. It can be helpful to read the passage out loud and see what emotions it creates in your body. There's no point in trying to force an answer. Give it time, and it will come to you.

If all else fails, you can count the number of letters in the sentence your finger indicated. An even number of letters indicates a positive outcome, while an odd number indicates the opposite.

Bibliomancy with the Bible

You shouldn't use a Bible for bibliomantic purposes unless you're a Christian. Non-Jews shouldn't use the Torah. You can use any spiritual book you wish, as long as it relates to your own beliefs. Many people use the Book of Psalms. It's a slim book compared to the complete Bible, but it covers virtually every aspect of human life.

The procedure begins with a short prayer, which can be read silently or spoken out loud. After this, a question is asked, again silently or out loud.

The holy book is then opened somewhere at random, and a passage chosen by allowing a finger to move around the page until it feels the right time to stop.

The selected passage is read. Sometimes its meaning will be clear, but at other times it will not seem relevant to the question that was asked. When this occurs, a positive message indicates a positive answer, and the opposite applies if the message is negative. Here's an example.

Let's assume a young woman is asking if her current relationship will continue to grow and develop. If her finger happened to land on the sixth verse of Psalm 35 ("Let their way be dark and slippery: and let the angel of the Lord persecute them."), the answer would be negative. If her finger stopped on John 6, verse 35 ("And Jesus said unto them, I am the bread of life: he that cometh to me shall never hunger; and he that believeth on me shall never thirst."), the answer would be positive.

Bibliomancy with the I Ching

Bibliomancy with the I Ching does not require coins or yarrow stalks. A question is asked, and the book is opened randomly anywhere. The hexagram on that page is interpreted to answer the question. There are several translations of the I Ching, and you should find one that you personally like. I like the Richard Wilhelm translation. However, when I'm helping someone else perform bibliomancy with the I Ching, I use the illustrated version by Koh Kok Kiang. This is because every hexagram is explained and illustrated in the form of a cartoon strip. It's a good way to introduce the I Ching to people who don't know much about it.

If you wish, you don't need to ask a specific question. Go through the process of selecting a page and a hexagram. With the cartoon version you may land on one of the six lines that make up the hexagram. The interpretation of this, and that of the hexagram, will help you to understand what is going on in your life. You shouldn't consult the I Ching more than three times a day.

Bibliomancy in Fiction

The popularity of bibliomancy is confirmed by the number of times it has appeared in fiction. Thousands of years ago, the ancient Greeks used the works of Homer for bibliomantic purposes. The Romans did the same thing with the works of Virgil. In more modern times, the narrator in Wilkie Collins's book *The Moonstone* (1868) regularly used bibliomancy with Daniel Defoe's *Robinson Crusoe*. A friend found a copy of *The Book of Webster's* by J. N. Williamson in a bookstore and bought it for me purely because of its name. I was pleasantly surprised to find one of the characters regularly performed bibliomancy with a dictionary as he thought it revealed the secrets of life and death.[7] Other examples are *Michael Strogoff* by Jules Verne, *The Man in the High Castle* by Philip K. Dick, and *Running with Scissors* by Augusten Burroughs.

What Would Shakespeare Say?

Some years ago, I became friendly with someone on a Shakespeare forum. In an e-mail, he told me that his sister used quotes from William Shakespeare to help her make decisions. She had a small box full of folded slips of paper. Each one contained a quote from the works of Shakespeare. Whenever she had a question, she'd mix the pieces of paper inside the box and pull one out. My friend told me that the message was always helpful.

I was intrigued with this and began experimenting. Instead of using slips of paper, I wrote the quotes on blank business card stock. This meant that I could mix the cards with the messages facing downward and choose one at random. Initially I used fifty cards, but I reduced this to thirty-six when I started using this system to answer other people's questions.

I start by showing my client the cards, and read one or two of them out loud. I then ask the person to mix the cards while thinking about his or her question. Obviously, he or she could simply take any card from the mixed deck to answer his or her question. That is how I originally did it.

However, one night I had a dream where I was using the cards, along with two dice. This was so startling that I woke up and immediately tried the method I'd seen in my dream. It quickly became a ritual. In fact, it worked so well that I've used it ever since.

Once the cards have been mixed, I ask the person to deal the top six cards face down in a horizontal row. He or she then deals the rest of the cards in rows underneath this, creating a six by six grid of cards. The person having the reading then rolls one of the dice. Let's assume he or she rolls a four. This indicates the fourth vertical column. This dice is placed above this column with the four on top. The second die is rolled, and this indicates the specific card in the column. Let's assume he or she rolls a five. This die is placed alongside the other one with the five on top.

I then recap, explaining that the person mixed the cards, laid them out, and rolled the two dice to arrive at a column and a number in that column. The person then turns over the selected card and reads what William Shakespeare has to say.

---

7   Williamson 1993.

If I don't have at least one die with me, I ask the person to roll two imaginary dice and tell me what numbers show up.

I use quotes from Shakespeare as I love his plays and poetry. His writing is full of potential answers to questions. It would be a simple matter to find thirty-six suitable quotes from *Hamlet*, let alone the rest of his work. However, you don't need to use Shakespeare. Choose an author who appeals to you. A couple of years ago I helped someone find thirty-six suitable quotes from Agatha Christie novels.

Suggested Reading

van der Horst, Pieter W. "Ancient Jewish Bibliomancy." *Journal of Greco-Roman Christianity and Judaism, Volume 1*. Sheffield, UK: Sheffield Phoenix Press, 2000.

Bone Reading

Bones are the longest surviving part of the human body, and can be considered symbols of both life and death. Even today in some parts of the world, pointing a bone at someone can cause death. Some people believe that the spirit of a dead person can be summoned by an individual possessing one of his or her bones. Crushed bones are still used as medicines and aphrodisiacs.

Bones are frequently marked to identify them. The markings are sometimes carved into the bone, but it's more common for them to be marked with paint or dye.

The ancient Romans used bones as a form of dice. Interestingly, they were marked on four, rather than all six, sides.

Bone reading began in ancient Egypt and has been practiced for well over 3,500 years. Astragalomancy, a form of divination using knucklebones, is possibly the oldest form of bone reading. Bone reading is still practiced today.

The Zulu sangoma healer diviners of South Africa use bones, along with a variety of other items, such as pebbles, shells, teeth, and nut kernels, that the diviner has collected.

The Venda diviners from the Transvaal in South Africa use a specially made bowl for their bone divinations. The rim of the bowl contains pictures of different qualities and situations, such as god, goddess, home, caution, danger, and travel. In the center of the bowl is a picture of a cowry shell. Five knucklebones are tossed into the bowl, and the results interpreted. Each of the knucklebones has a meaning, and its position in the bowl relating to the pictures around the rim and the cowry shell, as well as its relationship to the other bones, helps build up a complete reading.

African-American hoodoo diviners use chicken bones, along with other items they've collected. No matter how many other items are used, the reading is still called tossing or throwing the bones. In Mongolia, four knucklebones are used in a technique known as *shagai*.

Divination bones are usually stored in a bag or basket that is kept close to the practitioner's altar or work space. Traditionally, bone reading was performed by throwing the bones onto an animal hide, mat, or inscribed circle on the ground. However, all the bone readers I've seen toss the bones onto a tabletop. This often has a casting cloth on it. Most readers use bones from several different animals, but some use several bones from the same animal. Each bone has a meaning. The wishbone from a chicken, for instance, is a sign of good luck.

Bones are frequently marked to identify them. The markings are sometimes carved into the bone, but it's more common for them to be marked with paint or dye. Other forms of reading, such as dice and domino readings, developed from marked bones.

Some bone readers, especially in Africa, do not consciously interpret the spreads. The information comes from the ancestors, and the diviner picks this up clairvoyantly and passes it on to the client. However, other bone readers work with a system that provides them with everything they need to know to give satisfactory readings to their clients.

How to Do It

There are many ways of reading bones, and some are extremely complicated. Here's an example of a relatively easy bone reading that uses numerology.

Required

Ten chicken leg bones, each about four inches in length. You can use bones from any animal, and some readers like to have eight bones, each from a different animal.

A casting cloth, with a circle of at least twelve inches in diameter marked on it. Alternatively, you can create a circle using chalk, small stones, or a piece of chain or rope. You can also draw a circle on the ground with your wand.

The Bones

Chicken bones are easy to obtain. Choose ten leg bones that are as similar as possible. There are two main ways to prepare them for use.

1. This method is the one you should use if you want beautifully white bones. Clean the bones as much as possible, and place them in a container of dishwashing liquid and water for several days. This degreases them. Dry the bones, and place them in a container of hydrogen peroxide and water for another week. The liquid should be 50 percent hydrogen peroxide and 50 percent water. Cover, but don't seal the container. Check the bones every few days, and keep them in the liquid until they've achieved the degree of whiteness you prefer.

2. Clean the bones, and bury them in salt for a few weeks to dry them out. Mark the bones and spray them with a light coat of clear varnish.

Marking the Bones

The bones need to be marked to identify them. You'll notice that the bones have two distinct ends. One end is slightly concave, and the other end is flatter and wider. The bones are numbered from one to nine on the wider flattened ends. The bones need to be marked on both sides. The markings can be anything you wish. You might choose to number them from one to nine, use astrological glyphs, or any other system you wish to let you know what each bone represents. The tenth bone is broken in half. The half that includes the concave end will be your wand.

The Circle

The circle the bones are tossed into is sometimes divided into four quarters to represent different areas of the person's life. Many readers use the four quarters, but prefer to imagine the two lines that create them, rather than including them on the chart.

The four quarters can be used for a variety of purposes, depending on the question that's being asked. For a general question, the quarters relate to love, health, money, and other concerns. If the person is asking a question about his or her finances, the four quadrants could be work, money, problems, and investments.

The Reading

The person having the reading thinks of a question while the diviner holds the nine bones in his or her fist with the concave ends protruding. The person asking the question takes three of the bones, and tosses them, either one at a time, or all together, into the circle. The diviner then interprets them using numerology, or whatever system he or she is using, and the topic covered by the particular quarter of the circle the particular bone is in.

It's a sign that the client's goals will be realized if the marked end of the bone points toward the diviner. Similarly, if the marked end points away from the diviner, whatever it is the client seeks is flowing away. If the bone lands with each end pointing sideways to the reader, the concern needs more time before it can be answered. It also indicates the status quo.

Timing is done by the position of the bone in the quadrant it happens to be in. The closer it is to the reader, the sooner the event will occur.

The wand, the broken half leg bone, is used to indicate the various matters the diviner talks about during the reading. It can also be used to clarify a situation. If the three bones fail to answer the question, the wand can be tossed into the circle. Where it lands, and the direction its broken end indicates, help clarify the reading.

Some readers toss the bones again to determine the timing of different events. The immediate future is directly in front of the diviner, and the four quadrants indicate up to three, six, nine, or twelve months into the future. These are read counterclockwise, starting with the "up to three months" in the quadrant immediately to the right of the diviner, and the "up to twelve months" in the quadrant to his or her immediate left.

Mo Ku

Mo Ku is Chinese for "touch bones," which is a highly unusual form of bone reading. In the eighth century CE, Tao-Shi, a blind Taoist priest, achieved fame by predicting people's futures by feeling their bones, usually bones in their arms.

In the 1980s and '90s, Gwan Hsi, a blind Taiwanese bone reader, became extremely popular at predicting people's futures by touching the hands of his clients. [8]

Suggested Reading

Temple, Robert K. G. *Conversations with Eternity*. London: Rider & Company, 1984.

Candle Reading

Candles have been important throughout history, as they relate to the element of fire and create light where there is dark. Candles can be related to humanity. The wax symbolizes the physical body, the wick relates to the mind, and the flame represents the spirit, soul, or life force. It's no wonder that throughout history candles have been used for divination purposes.

Sometimes candles are used to create the right atmosphere or mood for other forms of divination, while at other times they're used as the medium to gain access to future trends.

Many people have experienced the trance-like state that occurs when they gaze at a fire or the flame of a candle. This is how people perform candle-scrying.

---

8   Bloomfield 1983, 145.

The ancient Greeks had an interesting method of divination using four candles. Three of them formed a triangle, and the fourth was placed in the center. All four candles were lit, but the center candle was the only one that was interpreted. A question was asked and the flame of the center candle provided the answer. It was a sign of success if the flame burned brightly. A dim flame was a sign of disappointment, a flickering flame indicated wavering fortunes, and a flame that went out indicated a death.[9]

Lychnomancy

This is derived from the ancient Greek method mentioned above. Three candles are placed to mark the three corners of a triangle. The candles are lit, and, unlike the ancient Greek version, the flames from all three candles are interpreted. Wavering flames indicate a change, rising and falling flames are a sign of danger, and flames creating a spiral are warnings. It's a sign of loss if a flame goes out. One flame burning more brightly than the others is a sign of good luck.

The sounds that candles make as they're burning can be interpreted, too. It's a good sign if the sounds are so quiet you have to strain to hear them. This means that everything is going the way it should be, whether you're aware of it or not. The louder the candles "talk," the more problems there are that need to be attended to.

How to Do It

It takes time and practice to develop skills as a candlescryer. The best way to practice is to set aside twenty or thirty minutes when you won't be disturbed. Sit in a dark room with a lit candle in front of you. Your eyes should be six or seven feet away from the flame, which should be at the same level as your eyes.

1. Take several slow, deep breaths. This relaxes you and enables you to symbolically release all the cares and stresses of everyday life. Relax your body and mind as much as you can.

2. Gaze at the candle, but focus on an imaginary spot about three feet beyond the flame.

3. Allow your eyes to feel heavy as you relax, and feel a sense of being "drawn into" the candle flame. You'll gradually enter into a hypnotic, daydreamlike state.

4. You may notice flashes of light or movement in your peripheral vision. Don't change your focus to look at them. Keep gazing at the same spot.

5. You'll gradually start seeing more and more in and around the candle flame. At first they'll be formless shapes, but with practice you'll be able to see images, scenes, symbols, pictures, figures, and even words.

---

9   Maven 1992, 175.

6. Try not to evaluate anything that comes to you until the divination is over. When you first start experimenting with this, you'll find it hard to stay in the necessary dreamlike state for more than a few minutes. However, with practice, you'll be able to enter the desired state freely whenever you wish and remain in it for as long as you wish.

Candle Magistellus

Magistellus means "little master." It's a familiar spirit that can foretell the future. You can use a candle as your magistellus, and you will find it effective at answering yes or no questions.

Required: One white candle that has never been lit, and olive oil (If you prefer, you can buy special oils for anointing candles online or at some New Age stores.)

Method

1. Choose an odd number from one to thirteen.

2. Dress or anoint the candle with olive oil. There's a special way to do this. Pour a small amount of oil on your fingers and rub your hands together.

3. Pick up the candle and rub the oil on it from the center of the candle to the wick. You do this as many times as the number you chose.

4. Repeat this rubbing from the center of the candle to the bottom.

5. Hold the candle in both hands, and say to it firmly, and in a strong, clear voice: "Candle, my candle, I command thee to be my magistellus. I need you to be both my guide and servant. Candle, my candle, you are now my magistellus."

6. Light the candle and place it on a table in front of you.

7. Sit down and gaze intently at the candle. Blink when necessary, as you don't want to fall into a trance.

8. Will the flame to rise. Once it has, will it to fall. You'll find after some experimentation that you can make the flame rise or fall whenever you wish using nothing but the power of your mind. If you prefer, you can credit the flame's rise and fall to the magistellus.

9. Once you're satisfied that the flame will rise or fall according to your will, you can ask it any questions you like that can be answered with a yes or no response. If the answer's yes, the flame will rise. If the answer's no, the flame will fall. It's important that you keep your mind focused solely on the question and allow the magistellus to provide the answer. As you know, you can use the power of your mind to influence the rise and fall of the candle flame. You don't want to overrule the correct answer by influencing the candle with your mind.

Yes–No Candle Divination

This is another method that can provide a positive or negative answer.

Required: Two identical candles

Method

1. Place both candles side by side on a table.

2. Think about your question.

3. Light the candles.

4. Decide which candle will indicate yes, and which one will indicate no.

5. The first candle to burn down and go out provides the answer.

Ceromancy

Ceromancy is the art of interpreting melted wax. In many ways, it's similar to tea leaf reading, as the shapes that are created by the wax can be interpreted.

Traditionally, wax was melted in a brass bowl and then carefully poured into a bowl full of water. The shapes that the wax produces are incredibly varied. With a reasonable amount of imagination, a fascinating story can be told about the images that have been created.

If you wish to try this, be aware that candles and fire can be dangerous. Heat the wax in a double boiler, as it's too dangerous to melt it over an open flame. Once it's melted, pour a small amount into a large container of cold water. The container should be glass or ceramic. The wax will instantly solidify, and the shape or shapes that have been created can be interpreted. Take the wax out of the water so you can examine it from every angle. Your first impressions are usually the best ones. Continue pouring small amounts of wax into the water until you've created a satisfying reading for yourself or for someone else.

Another version of this involves a candle and a bowl of water. Think of your question as you light the candle. Allow the candle to burn for a few minutes, and then hold it about an inch from the surface of the water. Tip the candle slightly to allow some molten wax to fall into the container of water. The first drops will be attracted to the side of the bowl to create a border. This border provides clues as to the outcome of the divination. A clear, unbroken border is an excellent sign that indicates a positive answer to the question. A wavy border indicates a change of plans, and a broken border indicates a negative outcome.

Continue pouring drops of wax into the water. These will form a variety of shapes that can be interpreted. Some will be obvious, but you may have to use your imagination to work out what the other ones represent. Bear in mind that the droplets of wax may form a complete picture that can be interpreted. Numbers usually relate to time, and could indicate any period from days to years, depending on the question. Some people are naturally good at reading the shapes created by wax, but it's a skill anyone can develop with practice.

When you first experiment with this, you'll find dark colored candles produce wax shapes that are easier to interpret than lighter colors. Naturally, you should use a color that contrasts with the color of the container you're using. Once you've gained experience, the colors won't make any difference.

Wax is not the only substance that can be dropped into a bowl of water for divination purposes. Oil was used in ancient Babylon. Molten lead, and the white of an egg, can also be used. Please don't try divining with molten lead. It's too dangerous, and the vapors of molten lead are toxic.

Capnomancy

Capnomancy is the art of interpreting the patterns of smoke created by a fire or flame. It was originally practiced by the ancient Babylonians, who studied the smoke created when cedar branches were burned.

If the candle smoke wafts toward you, the answer to your question is positive. If it wafts away from you, you might need to reconsider the situation. Success is still possible, but it will take a huge amount of persistence, determination, and hard work to achieve your goal. If the smoke drifts to your left, it's a sign that you're letting your emotions overrule your question, and you should either perform the ritual again at a later date, or ask someone who has no emotional interest in the outcome to ask the question for you. If the smoke drifts to your right, you'll need to use cold, hard logic to resolve the situation.

Shadow Divination

I've always enjoyed a form of scrying known as shadow divination. This is partly because it's best done in the evening, and the only light is a candle flame. Instead of gazing into the flame, you look at the shadows cast by the flickering candle on a light background, such as a wall or sheet of cardboard. There's no right or wrong way of doing this. I usually start by staring into the candle flame until my eyes feel tired, and then gaze at the shadows.

It's important to have no expectations about what you'll see. Simply look at the flickering shadows and see what comes into your mind. You might "see" moving figures inside the shadows. You might see nothing, but receive information in your mind. Stop once you receive the information you need, or you cease receiving anything from the shadows. When you start experimenting with this, you'll receive visions for a mere second or two, but this will increase with practice.

The important thing is to remain calm and relaxed. If you're stressed or try to force a picture to appear, you're unlikely to receive anything.

You don't need to restrict yourself to one candle either. Three, four, or even more candles produce fascinating shadows. Shadow divination can also be performed with any other type of flame, such as a fire, as long as you're able to gaze at the shadows rather than the flame.

Disposal of the Candle Wax

Any wax you've used for divination purposes should be thanked before you dispose of it. Some people make a small ritual out of this. After all, the wax has guided and helped you and needs to be treated with respect. A good method is to wrap it in a white paper napkin and thank it. Only after this should it be put out with the trash. If the results of your divination were negative, you should wrap the wax and paper napkin in aluminum foil to contain the negativity.

Suggested Reading

Buckland, Raymond. *Practical Candleburning Rituals*. St. Paul, MN: Llewellyn Publications, 1970.

Malbrough, Reverend Ray T. *The Magical Power of the Saints: Evocation and Candle Rituals*. St. Paul, MN: Llewellyn Publications, 1998.

Pajeon, Kala and Ketz. *The Candle Magick Workbook*. Secaucus, NJ: Citadel Press, 1991.

Webster, Richard. *Candle Magic for Beginners*. Woodbury, MN: Llewellyn Publications, 2004.

Chinese Astrology

Like many other divination systems, Chinese astrology began in prehistoric times, and there are many myths and stories about its origins. One story I've always liked involves the naming of the twelve animal signs.

Apparently, the Jade Emperor decided to assign a different animal to each year to enable people to remember the signs of the zodiac, which up until then had been identified with ideograms. He called all the animals to a meeting so he could choose twelve of them. Back then, the cat and the rat were good friends. They discussed the meeting and decided to go together. As the cat usually slept in until about noon, he asked the rat to wake him up early on the morning of the meeting. The rat said he would, and the cat slept soundly, knowing the rat would wake him. The rat woke up early and went to the meeting on his own. He was the first to arrive, and the Jade Emperor made him the first of the twelve animal signs. When the cat finally woke up, he raced to the meeting, but was too late. All the twelve positions had been taken. Ever since then, the cat and the rat have been sworn enemies, which is why cats chase rats.

This is an amusing story, but obviously that's all it is. The real reason why the cat is not one of the twelve animals is that the system was created well before cats were introduced into China. Interestingly, the cat replaces the rabbit in Vietnamese astrology.

The twelve animal signs are just a small part of Chinese astrology, but, like the twelve zodiac signs in Western astrology, they're the only part of the art that most people know about. This is probably because people hear about them at the time of the Chinese New Year, and discover that the following twelve months will be the Year of the Rat, the Ox, and so on. In addition to the element and animal provided by your year of birth, you also have elements and animals for your month, day, and hour of birth. These are called the Four Pillars.

The Twelve Animal Signs
The Rat
1900, 1912, 1924, 1936, 1948, 1960, 1972, 1984, 1996, 2008, 2020

People born in the Year of the Rat are charming, inquisitive, gregarious, sociable, and curious. They're ambitious, entrepreneurial, and opportunistic. They seek to do well financially and enjoy making and spending money. They enjoy helping and advising others.

The Rat is most compatible with the Ox, and least compatible with the Horse.

The year of the rat is a year of prosperity and abundance. It's a good year for investment, as long as you act cautiously.

The Ox
1901, 1913, 1935, 1937, 1949, 1961, 1973, 1985, 1997, 2009, 2021

People born in the year of the Ox are determined, reliable, down-to-earth, patient, and persistent. They are loyal, possessive, and affectionate with their friends. They often do well financially, using caution, tenacity, patience, and a methodical approach.

The Ox is most compatible with the Rat and least compatible with the Sheep.

The year of the ox is a year of hard work. It can be a good year as long as you're patient and prepared to wait for the results to appear.

The Tiger
1902, 1914, 1926, 1938, 1950, 1962, 1974, 1986, 1998, 2010, 2022

People born in the year of the Tiger are creative, independent, active, and courageous. They make natural leaders, as they can stimulate and inspire others. They're unconventional and can be rash, impetuous, and outspoken.

The Tiger is most compatible with the Pig and least compatible with the Monkey.

The year of the tiger is a turbulent year full of surprises and unexpected developments. You need to be cautious in everything you do.

The Rabbit
1903, 1915, 1927, 1939, 1951, 1963, 1975, 1987, 1999, 2011, 2023

People born in the year of the Rabbit are talented, affectionate, sociable, and compassionate. Good luck seems to follow them, and they get along well with others. They are good judges of character and can assess other people's motives at a glance.

The Rabbit is most compatible with the Dog and least compatible with the Rooster.

The year of the rabbit is a pleasant, relaxing year. You'll probably need to push yourself to make the progress, and achieve the results, you desire.

The Dragon

1904, 1916, 1928, 1940, 1952, 1964, 1976, 1988, 2000, 2012, 2024

People born in the year of the Dragon are passionate, imaginative, and extroverted. They like to feel appreciated and seek positions in the spotlight. They're full of ideas and are better at starting projects than they are at finishing them.

The Dragon is most compatible with the Rooster and least compatible with the Dog.

The year of the dragon is a busy, active year. It's a good year for all new beginnings, such as marriage, childbirth, and new ventures.

The Snake

1905, 1917, 1929, 1941, 1953, 1965, 1977, 1989, 2001, 2013, 2025

People born in the year of the Snake are subtle, refined, and ingenious. They're willing to take calculated chances and know how to be in the right place at the right time. They possess good taste in their attire and home surroundings. They are sometimes known as little dragons.

The Snake is most compatible with the Monkey and least compatible with the Pig.

The year of the snake is a calm and peaceful year, as long as you don't cause or spread gossip or any other negative energy. It's a good time to evaluate your progress.

The Horse

1906, 1918, 1930, 1942, 1954, 1966, 1978, 1990, 2002, 2014, 2026

People born in the year of the Horse are adventurous, sociable, and conversational. They make good friends and enjoy careers that involve a great deal of people contact. They're hardworking, competitive, positive, and realistic about their chances of success.

The Horse is most compatible with the Sheep and least compatible with the Rat.

The year of the horse is an exciting and busy year. It's a good time to bring matters to a conclusion, and to start planning for new adventures.

The Sheep

1907, 1919, 1931, 1943, 1955, 1967, 1979, 1991, 2003, 2015, 2027

People born in the year of the Sheep are well-behaved, obedient, cheerful, and diplomatic. They're affectionate, caring, and loyal. Generally, they avoid leadership roles, but are happy to express their views in any situation. They often do well in business.

The Sheep is most compatible with the Horse and least compatible with the Ox.

The year of the sheep is a relaxing year and a good time to act on your feelings, rather than logic. It's a good year for any form of creativity.

The Monkey

1908, 1920, 1932, 1944, 1956, 1968, 1980, 1992, 2004, 2016, 2028

People born in the year of the Monkey are mischievous, curious, versatile, active, and light-hearted. People enjoy their company, but their sense of humor and an apparent flippant attitude means their good ideas are not always recognized or appreciated.

The Monkey is most compatible with the Snake and least compatible with the Tiger.

The year of the monkey is a good time to seize new opportunities. Expect surprises, and be bold enough to take advantage of them.

The Rooster

1909, 1921, 1933, 1945, 1957, 1969, 1981, 1993, 2005, 2017, 2029

People born in the year of the Rooster are well organized, ambitious, determined, courageous, and confident. They're forthright and say what they think. This frequently causes problems with others. They have high ideals and expect the best from everyone.

The Rooster is most compatible with the Dragon and least compatible with the Rabbit.

The year of the rooster is a busy, but fun-filled, time, and you'll be tempted to scatter your energies. You'll achieve better results if you focus on what needs to be done.

The Dog

1910, 1922, 1934, 1946, 1958, 1970, 1982, 1994, 2006, 2018, 2030

People born in the year of the Dog are dependable, honest, and likable. They make friends easily. Their conservative outlook holds them back, and they find it hard to make major decisions or changes. They're always busy, but they are willing to make time for family and friends.

The Dog is most compatible with the Rabbit and least compatible with the Dragon.

The year of the dog is an idealistic and generous time. As long as your intentions are honorable, you'll achieve good results.

The Pig

1911, 1923, 1935, 1947, 1959, 1971, 1983, 1995, 2007, 2019, 2031

People born in the year of the Pig are conscientious, hardworking, and good with details. They enjoy responsibility and often find themselves in a leadership role. They frequently do well financially.

The Pig is most compatible with the Tiger and least compatible with the Snake.

The year of the pig is a prosperous year. There'll be a tendency to overindulge and waste time and energy on frivolous activities.

Your animal sign is the most important sign in your chart. It's also the first sign in your own twelve-year cycle of the different signs. Each time it reoccurs, you have an opportunity to start something new, or to move an existing project forward.

The Five Elements

The ancient Chinese believed that everything in the world could be classified into the five elements of fire, earth, metal, water, and wood. A Chinese horoscope contains all, or most, of these elements. They play an important role, as they determine your personality and the degree of success you'll have in life.

Wood

Wood is creative and innovative. If you have a large amount of wood in your chart, you'll want to express yourself creatively. Wood is sociable, generous, considerate, and community minded. Wood can be flexible and bending (willow), or strong and unyielding (oak).

Fire

Fire provides enthusiasm and energy but can also be destructive. Fire warms and cheers but can also burn and destroy. Fire provides strong principles but also has a tendency to be rigid and stubborn. Natural leaders have plenty of fire in their charts.

Earth

Earth is stable, patient, honest, and methodical. It also relates to real estate and legacies. However, earth can be stubborn and smothering. It sometimes expects and demands too much.

Metal

Metal relates to business and financial success. Not surprisingly, it's often referred to as gold. However, as it also relates to swords and knives, metal can be rigid, violent, and destructive. Metal likes to be in a leadership position, controlling and influencing others.

Water

Water relates to learning, travel, and communication. It also relates to literature, the arts, and the media. Water can be both gentle (gentle rain) and violent (a hurricane). Water nourishes all living things, but over time it can also wear away the hardest rock.

The five elements can be arranged into three cycles. The Cycle of Production is fire, earth, metal, water, and wood. This is because fire produces earth (ash). Earth is strengthened as fire is weakened. Earth creates metal (minerals), strengthening metal and weakening earth. Metal can be liquefied and evolve into water. Consequently, water is strengthened as metal is weakened. Water nurtures wood (plants and trees). Wood is strengthened, and water is weakened. Wood can be burned to create fire. This strengthens fire and weakens wood.

There is also a Cycle of Destruction, which shows which elements overpower others. Fire dominates metal because the heat of the fire can melt it. Metal destroys wood. Wood destroys earth, and earth dams and overpowers water. Finally, water can put out fire.

Finally, there is the Cycle of Reduction. This can correct any imbalances in the chart caused by the Cycle of Destruction. In the Cycle of Reduction, water is placed between metal and wood to neutralize any potential negative effects. In the Cycle of Destruction, fire overpowers metal. Consequently, earth can be placed between them, as earth puts out fire and neutralizes the negativity. Consequently, the Cycle of Reduction is: fire, earth, metal, water, and wood.

Your personal element is determined by your year of birth. There are many sites on the Internet where this information can be obtained, and you should do this if you were born in January or February, as the starting and ending dates vary from year to year. If you were born at any other time of year, you can use the following list:

- If the last number in your year of birth is 0 or 1, your element is *metal.*

- If the last number in your year of birth is 2 or 3, your element is *water.*

- If the last number in your year of birth is 4 or 5, your element is *wood.*

- If the last number in your year of birth is 6 or 7, your element is *fire.*

- If the last number in your year of birth is 8 or 9, your element is *earth.*

Element at the Time of Birth

The second most important element in your chart is the element from your time of birth. These are called the Twelve Earthly Branches:

Time	Element	Animal
11:00 p.m. to 1:00 a.m.	Wood	Rat
1:00 a.m. to 3:00 a.m.	Wood	Ox
3:00 a.m. to 5:00 a.m.	Fire	Tiger
5:00 a.m. to 7:00 a.m.	Fire	Rabbit
7:00 a.m. to 9:00 a.m.	Earth	Dragon
9:00 a.m. to 11:00 a.m.	Earth	Snake
11:00 a.m. to 1:00 p.m.	Metal	Horse
1:00 p.m. to 3:00 p.m.	Metal	Sheep
3:00 p.m. to 5:00 p.m.	Water	Monkey

Time	Element	Animal
5:00 p.m. to 7:00 p.m.	Water	Rooster
7:00 p.m. to 9:00 p.m.	Water	Dog
9:00 p.m. to 11:00 p.m.	Water	Pig

These times are GMT (Greenwich Mean Time) and will need to be adjusted for the local time where you were born.

Once you know the element of your year of birth, and the element of your time of birth, you can see if they harmonize with each other, are neutral, or try to destroy each other. Someone born in London, England, at 4:50 p.m. would have a time element of water, and the monkey as his or her day animal. If this person was born in 1946, he or she would be a fire dog. As fire and water are destructive, you can neutralize this by using wood, which is the element between fire and water in the cycle of reduction.

The animal associated with your time of birth has the same characteristics as the animal of your year of birth. However, the animal of your year of birth indicates your natural, innate characteristics, while the characteristics of the animal of your hour of birth will be apparent only in what you do.

The Mansions of the Moon

In addition to the twelve animals of the zodiac, there are also twenty-eight animals that symbolize the twenty-eight days of the lunar month. These day animals are important as their relationship with the animal sign of your year of birth indicates the best times for you to move forward. They also have an influence on your day to day activities.

It's a simple process to work out your day animal. For the sake of example, let's assume we're looking at the chart of someone born on January 11, 1996.

In the chart below, January is at the bottom of the first column. On the far right in the same row as January is number 27. As this person was born in 1996, the second step is to find the number related to that year. 1996 is on the twelfth row down, and on the far right of this row is number 12. These two numbers are then added to the person's day of birth, which happens to be the 11th: 27 + 12 + 11 = 50.

The next stage is to find out if this person was born in a leap year. In the chart below, all the leap years are indicated by a *. If this person was born in a leap year and his or her birthday was after March 1, you need to add 1 to your total. In the example above, the person was born in a leap year, but as it occurred before March 1, the 1 is not added to the total.

If the total of the day, month, and year of birth is greater than 56, you need to subtract 56 from the total. If your number is greater than 28, you need to subtract 28 from your total. In our example, the total is 50. Consequently, you need to subtract 28. 50 − 28 = 22.

This total indicates the person's day animal. If you check the list below the chart, you'll find that 22 is Anteater, and incidentally, this person was born on a Thursday.

Here's another example, this time someone who was born on August 15, 1985. In the chart below, August is 15, the year is 27, and the day of birth is 15. 15 + 27 + 15 = 57. As this is more than 56, that has to be removed, leaving 1. 1 relates to the salamander, and this person was born on a Thursday.

Month	Years	Number
January	1920*, 1942, 1987	1
February/March	1943, 1965, 1988*, 2010	2
	1921, 1944, 1966, 2011	3
	1922, 1967, 1989, 2012*	4
April	1923, 1945, 1968*, 2010	5
	1924*, 1946, 1991, 2013	6
May	1947, 1969, 1992, 2014	7
	1925, 1948*, 1970, 2015	8
	1926, 1971, 1993, 2016*	9
June	1927, 1949, 1972*, 1994	10
	1928*, 1950, 1995, 2017	11
July	1951, 1973, 1996*, 2018	12
	1929, 1952, 1974, 2019	13
	1930, 1975, 1997, 2020*	14
August	1931, 1953, 1976*, 1998	15
	1932*, 1954, 1999, 2021	16
	1955, 1977, 2000*, 2022	17
September	1933, 1956*, 1978, 2023	18
	1934, 1979, 2001, 2024*	19
October	1935, 1957, 1980*, 2002	20
	1936, 1958, 2003, 2025	21
	1959, 1981, 2004*, 2026	22

Month	Years	Number
November	1937, 1960*, 1982, 2027	23
	1938, 1983, 2005, 2028*	24
December	1939, 1961, 1984*, 2006	25
	1940*, 1962, 2007, 2029	26
January	1963, 1985, 2008*, 2030	27
	1941, 1964*, 1986, 2031	28

The Day Animals

There are twenty-eight day animals, divided into four families.

Family of the Azure Dragon——Season: Spring

1. *Salamander: Thursday*

   The salamander is the first of the twenty-eight animals and relates to generation and growth. It encourages creativity and imagination. People born under it are inventive and original.

2. *Sky Dragon: Friday*

   This is a good animal for people who are prepared to be patient and work hard. Dragon people are usually charming, and get on well with others.

3. *Badger: Saturday*

   Badger people need to pay particular care in dealing with people in positions of power and authority. These people can help them progress, but can also cause major problems when they don't feel respected.

4. *Hare: Sunday*

   People born under the sign of the hare lead happy, and usually long, lives surrounded by good friends and some of the luxuries life has to offer.

5. *Fox: Monday*

   People born under the sign of the fox are intelligent, charming, and shrewd. They enjoy working in artistic, creative fields.

6. *Tiger: Tuesday*

   This is a fortunate sign, financially. It often means a worthwhile inheritance and the ability to earn an excellent income.

7. *Leopard: Wednesday*

If people under the sign of the leopard keep focused on their own careers and work hard, they'll do well for themselves.

Family of the Black Tortoise—Season: Winter

8. *Unicorn: Thursday*

People born under the sign of the unicorn have the gift of foresight. They can also detect falsehood and deceit in others.

9. *Ox: Friday*

People born under the sign of the ox are hardworking, conscientious, and honest. They work steadily toward their goals.

10. *Bat: Saturday*

People born under the sign of the bat are naturally lucky, though they often fail to realize it as they can be plagued with doubt and indecision.

11. *Rat: Sunday*

The rat marks the middle of winter. People born under this sign are audacious, determined, motivated, and ambitious to achieve their goals.

12. *Swallow: Monday*

People born under the sign of the swallow like adventure, excitement, and challenges. They need to be careful not to take too many risks, as their luck sometimes runs out.

13. *Pig: Tuesday*

People born under the sign of the pig enjoy happy and fulfilled lives. They're successful, especially when working toward worthwhile goals.

14. *Porcupine: Wednesday*

People born under the sign of the porcupine are usually financially successful, as they're shrewd and prepared to work hard to achieve their goals.

Family of the White Tiger—Season: Autumn

15. *Wolf: Thursday*

People born under the sign of the wolf travel extensively. They're highly protective and enjoy looking after their family and family interests.

16. *Dog: Friday*

People born under this sign do well in all areas of life if they choose loyal friends who share similar goals, values, and attitudes.

17. *Pheasant: Saturday*

People born under the sign of the pheasant are fortunate, as they normally get what they desire. They enjoy beautiful surroundings and attractive possessions.

18. *Rooster: Sunday*

People born under the rooster are outgoing, popular, and usually successful. They're motivated by a strong desire for the best of everything.

19. *Raven: Monday*

People born under the sign of the raven are invariably successful when they know what they want. They plan ahead and go directly toward whatever it is they desire.

20. *Sky Monkey: Tuesday*

People born under this sign are happiest when living and working in pleasant surroundings, and they enjoy their family time.

21. *Gibbon: Wednesday*

People born under the sign of the gibbon are responsible from an early age. They get on well with others, and people often seek them out for advice, which is always freely given.

Family of the Vermillion Phoenix—Season: Summer

22. *Anteater: Thursday*

People born under the sign of the anteater do well in any field involving communication and self-expression, such as radio, television, and theater.

23. *Sheep: Friday*

People born under the sign of the sheep are charming, attractive, and highly intuitive. They waste a great deal of time before finding what they want to do in life.

24. *Buck: Saturday*

People born under the sign of the buck are friendly and get along well with others. They possess clairvoyant abilities and develop these skills over a lifetime.

25. *Horse: Sunday*

People born under the sign of the horse are warm-hearted, generous, independent, and persistent. They enjoy challenges and stick at anything they start until it's completed.

26. *Deer: Monday*

People born under the sign of the deer are impulsive, generous, and kind. They're the first to offer help when it's needed.

27. *Snake: Tuesday*

People born under the sign of the snake know how to present themselves for their best advantage. They enjoy the best of everything, and this motivates them to achieve success.

28. *Earthworm: Wednesday*

People born under the sign of the earthworm are quiet achievers who seek their own goals with little fuss or input from others.

The Rhythm of Life

This is an ancient way of determining fortunate and inopportune years for different activities. It assumes that human lives, just like every other form of life, are governed by rhythms. There's a time for planting, a time for sprouting, a time for flowering, and so on. Each cycle lasts for six years. The numbers in the chart below relate to your age. If you're currently thirty-one, for instance, you'd be in a sowing year, as thiry-one is six down in the sowing column.

Sowing	Taking Root	Sprouting	Flowering	Maturing	Vegetating
1	2	3	4	5	6
7	8	9	10	11	12
13	14	15	16	17	18
19	20	21	22	23	24
25	26	27	28	29	30
31	32	33	34	35	36
37	38	39	40	41	42
43	44	45	46	47	48
49	50	51	52	53	54
55	56	57	58	59	60
61	62	63	64	65	66
67	68	69	70	71	72
73	74	75	76	77	78
79	80	81	82	83	84
85	86	87	88	89	90
91	92	93	94	95	96
97	98	99	100	101	102

The first year of the cycle (sowing) is a good time to plant the seeds of future action. However, it's only the beginning, and nothing further can be done during this year.

The second and third years of the cycle (taking root and sprouting) are the best years to start working on any important projects.

By the fourth year (flowering), whatever it is should be well underway and moving forward in the direction you want.

Year five (maturing) is when the enterprise or undertaking reaches its peak.

In year six (vegetating) the project has reached its natural conclusion, and should be allowed to vegetate.

Consequently, if you're currently thirty-seven, thirty-eight, or thirty-nine years old, it's a good time to start anything, as it will build and grow during those years. However, if you're forty, forty-one, or forty-two, you shouldn't start anything new, but instead concentrate on what you've already started.

If a project is not completed by the end of the sixth year, you should consider the first year of the new cycle as a time of consolidation and start progressing again in years two and three.

Suggested Reading

de Kermadec, Jean-Michel Huon. *The Way to Chinese Astrology: The Four Pillars of Destiny.* London: Unwin Paperbacks, 1983.

Kwok, Man-Ho. *Chinese Astrology: Learn Your Future from Your Chinese Horoscope.* Boston: Charles E. Tuttle Co., Inc., 1997.

Walters, Derek. *Chinese Astrology.* Wellingborough, UK: The Aquarian Press, 1987.

Coin Divination

There are many ways in which coins can be used to give a reading. The simplest method uses just one coin and provides yes and no answers. Before tossing the coin you need to decide if heads or tails indicates yes. (Traditionally, heads means yes.) The coin is tossed and either heads or tails will be on top, providing an answer to the question.

A slightly more advanced form of this uses three coins of different denominations. These indicate the past, present, and future. Traditionally, the person being read had to hold the three coins for a few minutes to warm them, and to enable his or her energies to enter into the coins. Once this has been done, the coins are cast, either by the reader or the person being read.

Here's a system I devised many years ago when I needed a different form of reading for corporate events. The system gradually developed over time, and has been extremely useful, both for me and the people I taught it to.

Required: You'll need about thirty coins. The denominations can vary, but half of them should be copper and the rest silver. You'll also need one coin that is noticeably different to the others. In the United States, a half-dollar would be perfect. This is called the *success* coin. I keep my coins in a velvet bag. You'll also need a small cloth with a twelve-inch circle marked on it.

How to Do It

Ask the person having the reading to think of a question while putting his or her left hand into the bag and grabbing as few or as many coins as desired. This person holds his or her fist about six inches above the cloth, and opens it, allowing the coins to drop onto the cloth. Some will land inside the circle, and these are the ones that are read. If all the coins land outside the circle, the person has to go through the process again.

Interpretation

1. Count the number of coins inside the circle. If there are more than nine, bring the total down to a single digit by adding the two numbers together. (13, for instance, reduces to 4, as $1 + 3 = 4$.) This number represents the future, or the outcome of the question. It, and the other numbers, is interpreted using numerology.

2. Silver coins are considered more powerful than copper coins. Consequently, it's a good sign if there are more silver than copper coins in the circle. Count the silver coins, again reducing the total to a single digit if necessary. Silver coins represent the present situation.

3. Repeat this with the copper coins. They represent the past.

4. Count the number of coins that have landed head-side up. They indicate circumstances that the person can control.

5. Count the number of coins that are tail-side up. They indicate circumstances that are out of the person's control.

6. If the success coin is one of the coins inside the circle, the future is positive, no matter what negative indications are shown elsewhere. If the success coin ends up outside the circle, the outcome could still be positive, but it will be achieved only with a great deal of work and effort.

This coin reading can be made more exotic by using a selection of coins from different countries. You might find an eight-sided coin or a coin with a hole in it to act as the success coin.

Four Coin Divination

Required: Four coins of the same denomination. It doesn't matter what they are as long as you can hold them all comfortably in one hand. I prefer small coins, such as pennies, as they're easier to mix in your closed hand.

How to Do It

Think of a question while mixing the coins in your hand. When you feel ready, toss the coins onto a table or divination mat.

Interpretation

The number of coins that are heads up provides the answer. If all four coins land heads up, the answer is extremely positive. Three heads and one tail is also a good sign. Two heads and two tails shows the result can go either way. It's usually interpreted as a possible "yes." When this occurs, you can ask a different, but related, question and toss the coins again. One head and three tails is a mild "no." This means you can still turn the question into a positive with a great deal of effort. You need to decide if all that hard work will be worth it. Four tails is a definite "no."

Suggested Reading

Buckland, Ray. *Coin Divination: Pocket Fortuneteller*. St. Paul, MN: Llewellyn Publications, 2000.

Da, Liu. *I Ching Coin Prediction*. New York: Harper & Row, Inc., 1975.

Crystals and Gemstones

Crystals are natural geometric formations. Throughout history, people have always considered them beautiful, powerful, and mystical. In fact, they were the first precious objects owned by people. They've been considered to have magical powers for almost the same length of time.

In the legends about Atlantis, crystals were used to generate power for their cities. Ancient people loved all crystals, but some were considered more precious than others. The diamond has always been considered valuable, as its name shows. The word *diamond* comes from the Latin word *adamas*. According to the Bible, Adam was the first man. The word *adamant* comes from the same root and describes someone who is unshakable in resolve or intention. Diamonds are considered hard and unyielding, too.

A gold and turquoise bracelet, dating back 7,500 years, was found on the mummy of an ancient Egyptian queen. [10]

In the Bible, precious stones were worn on the breastplate of Joseph. In Ephesians 2:20, Jesus was called "the chief corner stone." Jesus also gave the name Peter to Simon Bar-Jonah. Peter comes from the Latin *petra*, which means a rock or a stone (Matthew 16:18).

As people instinctively felt that precious stones contained special power, they've been used as protective amulets throughout history.

Gemstones are ornamental stones. Most of them are minerals, and they're frequently tumbled in a rotating drum with an abrasive grit to make them smooth for decorative, protective, and divinatory purposes.

---

10   Knuth 1999, 1.

How to Divine with Crystals and Gemstones

There are many different ways to divine using crystals and gemstones. Arguably the easiest method is to use nine gemstones of different colors. These should be the seven colors of the rainbow, plus rose or pink, and gold. Here are some of the gemstones you might use:

- *Red*: Coral, garnet, red jasper, and ruby

- *Orange*: Carnelian and fire opal

- *Yellow*: Moonstone, amber, and topaz

- *Green*: Chrysoprase, emerald, green jasper, green tourmaline, jade, moss agate, and peridot

- *Blue*: Aquamarine, blue topaz, chrysocolla, howlite, lapis lazuli, sapphire, sodalite, and turquoise

- *Indigo*: Azurite, indigo sapphire, sodalite, and blue tiger's eye

- *Violet*: Amethyst and fluorite

- *Rose/Pink*: Kunzite, rhodochrosite, rhodonite, and rose quartz

- *Gold*: Citrine, goldstone, and gold tiger's eye

These colors all have a meaning:

- *Red*: Strength, love, sexuality, creativity, courage, independence, pioneer, active

- *Orange*: Adaptable, tactful, cooperative, kind, gentle, diplomatic, nurturing, encouraging

- *Yellow*: Happy, joyful, pleasure seeking, entertaining, optimistic, charming, communicative

- *Green*: Organized, disciplined, reliable, energetic, loyal, solid, stable, hardworking

- *Blue*: Adventurous, seeks change and variety, understanding, sincere, sensual, travel, truth

- *Indigo*: Home, family, conscientious, sympathetic, protective, responsible

- *Violet*: Intellectual, spiritual, analytical, philosophical, intuitive, wise, solitude

- *Rose/Pink*: Ambitious, practical, generous, honest, seeks financial success

- *Gold*:Humanitarian, benevolent, compassionate, understanding, capable, philanthropic

Each of these colors relates to letters of the alphabet:

Red	A	J	S
Orange	B	K	T
Yellow	C	L	U
Green	D	M	V
Blue	E	N	W
Indigo	F	O	X
Violet	G	P	Y
Rose/Pink	H	Q	Z
Gold	I	R	

With this information, you can give someone a brief reading. Use the name the person normally uses. Someone called Margaret might be known as Maggie, Margie, Mags, or Peggy, for instance. Here's a sample reading for Judy Garland:

- *J:* Red
- *U:* Yellow
- *D:* Green
- *Y:* Violet
- *G:* Violet
- *A:* Red
- *R:* Gold
- *L:* Yellow
- *A:* Red
- *N:* Blue
- *D:* Green

Judy Garland's name has 3 red, 2 yellow, 2 green, 1 blue, 2 violet, and 1 gold. The three reds show that she was strong, creative, courageous, and independent. Two each of yellow, green, and violet reveal different sides of her nature. Yellow gave her entertainment skills and showed she could be charming, happy, and joyful at times. The violet reveals a more serious side, as well as a need for time on her own. The two greens show she was hardworking, disciplined, and reliable. With one gold she was also compassionate, understanding, and benevolent.

Just as important are the colors that are missing in her name. She has no orange, indigo, or rose/pink. Wearing clothes, jewelry, or gemstones of these colors would have helped fill up these gaps, and it may have made her life easier.

A reading of this sort provides clues about her character, but it doesn't provide any information about the future. Fortunately, you can use these nine stones to learn about someone's past, present, and future.

Required: Nine gemstones, an attractive drawstring bag to carry the gemstones in, and a small mat, about the size of a mouse pad, to display the selected gemstones on.

How to Do It

1. If you're giving a reading to someone, start by pouring the gemstones out of the bag onto the mat, and ask the person to pick up the gemstone that she finds most appealing.

2. Return the other stones to the bag, ask the person to hold the stone she chose in her left hand, and tell her what the stone means. If she, for instance, chose red Jasper, tell her something along the lines of: "At this time you have more strength and courage than you probably realize. You might need to demonstrate your independence in some sort of way. Do something creative, and enjoy fun times with people you're close to."

3. Replace the gemstone in the bag. Mix the gemstones, and ask the person you're reading for to put their hand in and grab any gemstone. This represents the past. Place this on the mat to the person's left. If she's sitting opposite you, this will be to your right.

4. Ask her to do this twice more, choosing a stone for the present and a final stone for the future. The stone representing the present is placed in the middle of the mat, and the final stone is placed to your client's right.

5. You can now interpret the stones and give a reading for the person's past, present, and future. Let's assume she chose green for the past, indigo for the present, and red for the future. Pick up the stone that represents the past and hold it in your left hand. You might say: "In the past you probably had to work hard. This means you were well organized and reliable. If a job had to be done, you'd get busy and make it happen. Does that sound right to you?" Discuss this stone for a minute or two and then place it back on the table. Pick up the stone indicating the present (indigo in this example). Say something along the lines of: "At this stage in your life you might not be able to do the things you want to do because of the needs of others. Right now it's good that you're conscientious and responsible, and your home and family are the prime focus in your life. Would you say that described your life at present?" After discussing it, replace it on the table, and pick up the stone relating to the future. "You've picked red Jasper again! This is excellent, as it shows you'll soon be entering a new phase of your life, and you will be able to focus more on your own needs and desires.

This new independence will express itself in different ways. It could mean you'll have time for creative activities and fun times with friends. Be assertive when necessary. You might start something new and enjoy taking it as far as you can. You'll be able to express yourself emotionally as well, and any special relationships will become closer than ever before. You are on the right track. Do you have any questions about the future?"

6. You want your client to be actively involved in the reading. Asking her questions encourages this, and you may spend a few minutes answering any queries she may have.

7. At the end of the reading, replace all the gemstones in the bag, close it with the drawstring, and place it on top of the mat. This signifies that the reading is over.

A reading of this sort can be made more accurate by having at least three of each gemstone in the bag. This makes it possible for the same gemstone to appear more than once, as the person's fortune may not necessarily change.

Brian Howard, a friend of mine in the United Kingdom who sadly died some years ago, specialized in gemstone readings. He used ten of each gemstone and had them laid out in rows on a tray when his clients came into his reading room. They made an extremely attractive display.

Brian asked his clients to choose ten stones, one at a time, in response to questions he asked them. They were placed on his mat in the shape of a pyramid. Each stone covered a certain part of the client's life:

1. The character of the client.

2. The present time.

3. Health and future prospects.

4. Working life, career, and future prospects.

5. Financial prospects.

6. Marriage and relationships.

7. Possible changes, such as work, change of house, divorce, and new relationships.

8. Vacations and travel.

9. Enemies, or people to watch out for.

10. Parents, family illnesses, accidents, etc.

It took several minutes for my friend's clients to choose ten stones, and they provided all the information he needed to give a helpful, incisive reading.

Useful Stones for Divination

You can use any stones that appeal to you for divination purposes. However, there are some stones that have been traditionally used for this purpose and have long-established divinatory meanings.

- *Agate*: Acceptance, cooperation, understanding, and creativity.

- *Amber*: Provides balance, absorbs negative energy, and helps reduce pain.

- *Amethyst*: Spirituality, intuition, purity, peace, and tranquility. Focus on realistic goals.

- *Aquamarine*: Logic, common sense, and clear thinking. Releases anxiety and gives peace of mind. Avoid gossip and people who talk but have nothing to say.

- *Beryl*: Promotes harmony in all close relationships. Stimulates the brain. Provides courage.

- *Bloodstone*: Courage, friendship, and loyalty. Aids concentration, and provides money-making ideas.

- *Blue topaz*: Calmness and tranquility.

- *Carnelian*: Provides energy and overcomes procrastination. Grounding.

- *Chrysoprase*: Useful for overcoming addictions and greed. Heals broken hearts.

- *Citrine*: Attracts prosperity, warmth, and good friends.

- *Coral*: Self-sacrifice. Desire to help others.

- *Diamond*: Prosperity, abundance, innocence, and purity.

- *Emerald*: Openness, love, and integrity.

- *Fire opal*: Passion, physicality, and strength. Aids clairvoyance.

- *Garnet*: Commitment. Strengthens loving relationships. Passion and sensuality.

- *Iron pyrite* (commonly known as fool's gold): Deception, dishonesty, and acting before thinking.

- *Jade*: Resolving problems and concerns. Aids constructive dreaming.

- *Labradorite*: The wish stone. Think carefully, set a goal, and follow it through.

- *Lapis lazuli*: Courage, protection, and ability to stand up for oneself. Aids psychic development.

- *Malachite*: Patience, endurance, and restraint. Let go of the past and start making future plans.

- *Moonstone*: Aids telepathy, clairvoyance, and precognition. Go with the flow.

- *Moss agate*: Peace of mind, end of a stressful situation.

- *Pearl*: Forgiveness, loyalty, sincerity, and resolving problems or difficulties.

- *Peridot*: Change, growth, and spiritual awareness.

- *Quartz*: Awareness and perception. Aids communication.

- *Red jasper*: Strong emotions that are never far from the surface. Keep focused on practical, realistic goals.

- *Rose quartz*: Healing of mind, body, and spirit. Tenderness, love, and good friends. Stimulates the heart.

- *Ruby*: Attention to detail, and a desire to learn. Potential for wealth.

- *Rutilated quartz*: Creativity, new ideas.

- *Sapphire*: Prosperity, and happiness after experiencing melancholy and sadness.

- *Tiger's eye*: Independence, concentration, positivity, and change. A good luck stone.

- *Topaz*: Optimism, happiness, and success. Lead by example.

- *Tourmaline*: Calmness, and balance of mind, body, and spirit.

- *Turquoise*: Peace, tranquility, creativity, honesty, and protection.

Pick a Number

Required: At least three each of nine or ten gemstones, a velvet cloth approximately 8.5" × 11" to lay the chosen gemstones on, and a tray to hold the gemstones.

How to Do It

1. Ask the querent to think of a question that relates to his or her future.

2. After this, ask the querent to choose, one at a time, a number of stones. I suggest that he or she take more than six, and most people take seven or nine.

3. Tell the person to place each gemstone wherever they wish on the velvet cloth.

4. Once all the gemstones have been placed in position, you can interpret them in two ways: the meanings of the individual gemstones they chose, and where they placed them on the cloth.

5. You do this by mentally dividing the velvet mat into four. The area of the mat to the left of the imaginary center line (from your client's point of view) represents the past. The area to the right of the imaginary center line represents the future. The area an inch or so to the left and right of the center line indicates the present.

   The horizontal line dividing the cloth in half is also important. The top left quarter of the cloth indicates positive influences from the past, and the bottom left quarter indicates negative influences from the past. The top right quarter indicates positive influences yet to come, and the bottom right quarter signifies negative influences that will appear in the future.

   The center vertical line indicates the present. The further left you go, the more you travel into the past. Similarly, the far right of the cloth indicates well into the future, and close to the center line indicates the near future.

6. The gemstones are interpreted using the meanings of each one, and the timing is done using the four quadrants. In addition to this, any gemstones that are placed close together gain strength from each other, making the combination more powerful than would have been the case if they'd been placed well apart.

If you wish, you can also interpret the number of gemstones the querent chose. I find it helpful to see which stones the querent picked up and then replaced, as they can sometimes relate to his or her concern

Sortilege with Crystals and Gemstones

There are many forms of sortilege, the area of divination that involves objects that are either cast or drawn. At least five thousand years ago, people were tossing pebbles onto the ground and making predictions from how they fell. Rune stones and dice are two popular forms of sortilege that developed from this.

The simplest example of this is to mix a bag holding a variety of gemstones before asking a question. Place your hand into the bag and remove one gemstone. This is interpreted to answer the question. That's useful for quick answers, but you'll need some sort of chart or grid to answer more complex or detailed questions.

Today many people toss gemstones onto a chart or grid for divination purposes. One example of this is to draw a circle on a large sheet of paper and then surround it with two more circles, creating what looks like a bull's-eye. The area between the circumference of the second and third circles indicates the past, the area between the circumference of the first and second circles indicates the present, and the area inside the circumference of the innermost circle symbolizes the future.

You'll need a bag holding a selection of different gemstones, ideally three each of the nine traditional colors. Mix the stones inside the bag, and then grasp a handful of them in your fist. Hold these about six inches above the center of the innermost circle. Think of your question, and then open your fist, allowing the gemstones to fall onto your three circles.

Remove any gemstones that have rolled outside all three circles and place them back in the bag. Look at the gemstones that are between the circumferences of the second and third circles. These represent the past. Interpret them, and see how they relate to your question. Interpret the gemstones that have fallen into the "present" part of your drawing (between the first and second circles), and interpret these. Finally, look at the stones that are inside the innermost circle. These indicate the future.

Determine which stone is closest to the center. This stone is the most important one in the reading, and determines the outcome. The other stones inside this circle modify the interpretation.

Let's assume your question was, "Will I receive a pay rise this year?" and the four stones that landed in this circle are ruby (closest to center), carnelian, sodalite, and turquoise.

You can tell right away that the answer is affirmative, as ruby (red) is enthusiastic, independent, progressive, and determined. The stone closest to it is carnelian (orange). This shows that it might take longer than you'd like, and you'll need to be patient, cooperative, and kind. The other two stones are sodalite and turquoise (blue). This shows that there's likely to be a change of some sort, which could mean increased responsibility or even the offer of a new position. There'll be more variety in your life, as well.

Clock Reading

This reading also uses a circle. You might like to draw it with twelve equal divisions. Some people prefer to use a simple circle and imagine a clock face superimposed onto it. I create a circle using a gold chain that someone gave me to wear many years ago. I never used it around my neck, but it plays a useful role in many of my stone divinations.

A handful of crystals or gemstones are dropped onto the circle while the question is asked. The answer is given using a combination of numerology and crystallomancy. Any stones that land in the first division (12:00 to 1:00 a.m. or p.m.) are interpreted using number one, as well as the meaning for the particular gemstone. The reading continues in a clockwise direction until all twelve segments have contributed to the reading. The numbers 10, 11, and 12 are interpreted as higher vibrations of 1, 2, and 3.

Twelve Houses

The chart you toss your gemstones onto can be as simple or as complex as you wish. A popular and useful chart, as it covers twelve areas of life, is a circle containing the twelve houses of astrology.

Again, stones are tossed onto the chart and interpreted using a combination of numerology, the meaning of each gemstone, and the area of life indicated by the houses the stones happen to be in.

A simplified chart, still using the astrological theme, is to divide the circle into four quarters. Each of these represents one of the elements used in astrology: fire, earth, air, and water. Fire relates to enthusiasm, energy, and zest for life. Earth relates to the physical body and the practical areas of life. Air relates to thought, ideas, and intellectual matters. Water relates to the emotions, as well as the spiritual and intuitive areas of life.

Yes or No

This is a simple and quick way to answer questions. You'll need several gemstones to indicate yes, and an equal number to indicate no. Mix these in your velvet bag, ask the question, and quickly grab one gemstone from the bag. It will tell you yes or no.

You can use stones of any color for this experiment. I like to use green stones for yes and red stones for no, purely because they relate to the colors used on traffic lights to indicate go (yes) and stop (no).

Another method involves stones of many colors. Ask your question while gently mixing the stones in their bag. When you feel ready, grab a handful of stones from the bag. Count the number of stones you've removed. An odd number means no and an even number means yes. However, I know several crystal diviners who read the stones the other way round, with an odd number meaning yes and an even number indicating no. This is because odd numbers have traditionally been considered luckier than even numbers. You'll need to decide for yourself which system to use before using this method.

Three Stone Reading

Mix the stones in their bag while thinking of a question. Close your eyes and remove three stones, one at a time. Place these in a row in front of you. The first stone drawn indicates the past, the second the present, and the third the future. These are interpreted using the meanings of the stones.

Cleansing Your Crystals and Gemstones

It's important to cleanse your gemstones between readings when you're reading for others. This is because they pick up negativity that needs to be released before you use them again.

If time allows, you might lay them out outdoors and allow the rays of the Moon to cleanse them overnight. You could expose them to sunlight for ten minutes. You can also wash them in salty water, rinse them in fresh running water, and allow them to dry naturally. Unfortunately, you won't have time to use these methods when you have a number of people, all wanting a reading, one after the other.

In this case, you can quickly cleanse your gemstones by gathering them together in the center of a table and holding your hands on either side of them, with your palms facing and encircling the gemstones. Visualize the stones being cleansed and revitalized. You might feel a slight tingling in the palms of your hands as you do this. When you sense that the stones have been cleansed, silently thank them for working with you, and replace them in their bag or in position on your tray, ready for your next client.

Suggested Reading

Butler, Gail. *Crystal & Gemstone Divination*. Baldwin Park, CA: Gem Guides Book Company, 2008.

Hobrin (Brian Howard). *Gemstone Reading for Profit*. Auckland: Brookfield Press, 1988.

Knuth, Bruce G. *Gems in Myth, Legend and Lore*. Thornton, CO: Jewelers Press, 1999.

Dice Divination

The technical name for dice divination is cleromancy. It's also known as cubomancy. It began some five thousand years ago with the casting of bones. The earliest dice were made from the anklebones or knucklebones of sheep and other animals. It didn't take long for people to learn they could make dice out of clay. Cube-shaped dice dating back some four thousand years have been found in Egyptian tombs. The Greeks used them about three thousand years ago, and the same dice were being used in China 2,600 years ago. These early dice were probably made for divination purposes, rather than for games. Some biblical scholars believe that the oracular devices called Urim and Thummim that were kept in the high priest's breastplate were a form of dice.

Divination with dice has always been popular in Tibet, where it's called *Mo*. It's performed by Lamas to help people make decisions about matters that are occurring in their lives. According to an article in the *New Yorker*, the Dalai Lama uses Mo divination when he needs an answer to an important question. [11]

How to Do It

Dice make a convenient form of divination, as all you need are a few dice. If you're going to take it seriously, you should invest in a dice cup as well. You can use this to throw the dice, and can also store them in it. You might wrap the dice and cup in your casting cloth to ensure that you have everything you need when you want to perform a dice divination.

Three Dice Reading

Required: Three dice. A casting cloth and dice cup are useful additions, but are not essential.

How to Do It

1. Place the casting cloth in front of the querent. If you don't have one, draw a circle eight to twelve inches in diameter on a sheet of paper and use that.

2. Ask your client to think of a question while you shake the dice inside the cup using both hands. You can shake them in your cupped hands if you don't have a dice cup.

---

11   Osnos 2010, 63.

3. Call out "dice three!" in a loud voice and roll the dice into the middle of your circle. You can, if you wish, ask the querent to roll his or her own dice.

4. It's important that all three dice land inside the circle. If one ends up outside the circle, it's a sign that the querent will have obstacles and delays before achieving his or her goal. The dice need to be tossed again, and again if necessary, until all three dice are inside the circle. If at least one die has remained outside the circle after three attempts, the person is not able to have a reading that day. It's an indication of a disagreement if two dice end up outside the circle. However, if all three dice end up outside the circle, it's a sign of good luck. It's also a lucky sign if one die lands on top of another.

5. The dice are interpreted to provide the querent with a reading. If two of the dice have the same number of spots on top after they've been cast, it's a sign that the querent is about to start a fortunate stage of his or her life. This is even better if all three dice have the same number on top.

There are sixteen traditional interpretations:

- *Three*: This is the least number of spots that can appear when using three dice. It's extremely fortunate if all three numbers are the same. It's a sign that your social life will improve and everything will go your way for the next three days. There could be a pleasant surprise.

- *Four*: This is a sign to move ahead cautiously. There are likely to be delays and frustrations. After four days, something you've been waiting for will happen.

- *Five*: You should do something different, simply for the fun of it. It could provide opportunities for friendships and interesting experiences. Expect a pleasant surprise.

- *Six*: Expect a minor setback. Be careful with money, as there's a potential for loss.

- *Seven*: Be discreet and cautious. Avoid passing on gossip as it will rebound. Be careful with money matters. Gypsy fortune-tellers say that number seven is a sign of a possible scandal.

- *Eight*: You might be blamed for something you didn't do. Avoid anything underhanded or unethical. Work hard and keep focused on the future.

- *Nine*: This is a lucky number in dice divination. You're likely to receive an invitation to an important event and enjoy fun times with friends. There's also the possibility of romance for you, or someone close to you.

- *Ten*: Traditionally, this means the birth of a baby. This is because one means a new start in numerology, and ten is a higher form of one ($1 + 0 = 1$). Start something new.

- *Eleven*: This indicates the temporary parting of two friends. It can also mean an inheritance, in which case the parting would be permanent. There's a possibility of minor health problems.

- *Twelve*: You'll receive a long-awaited message. In the past, this would come by mail, but nowadays it could come in any form. Seek legal advice if it involves money.

- *Thirteen*: This is an unlucky throw. Something is causing you to worry, and you need to do something about it.

- *Fourteen*: There's a possibility of love and romance. A new friendship will blossom. You're likely to receive help from an unexpected source.

- *Fifteen*: Someone is trying to include you in something that will cause problems. Avoid becoming involved. Be cautious and trust your intuition.

- *Sixteen*: Possibility of travel in the near future. It will prove worthwhile on a number of levels.

- *Seventeen*: This indicates the start of a happy and productive stage of your life. You'll progress quickly.

- *Eighteen*: This is the luckiest number you can throw. It's a sign of great success and happiness.

Numerological Dice

Required: Two dice.

How to Do It

1. The querent asks his or her question while shaking the two dice in one hand.

2. The dice are tossed onto a table.

3. The numbers on top of each die are noted, and then added together.

4. All three numbers are interpreted using numerology to answer the question.

Let's assume the querent asks: "Will I make new friends while on vacation?" Let's assume she rolls a 2 and a 3. As 2 + 3 = 5, there are three numbers that will answer this question: 2, 3, and 5. The meanings of these numbers can be found in the section on Numerology. Two relates to getting on with people, 3 is a sign of social activities and communication, and 5 relates to variety and change. It sounds as if the querent will make new friends and have a wonderful time on vacation.

Three Phrase Dice Reading

Required: Three dice.

How to Do It

The dice are thrown three times, and the numbers on top are added together after each throw and then reduced to a single digit. These numbers are recorded. The three numbers that are generated can be used for any three aspects of life. It could, for instance, be used for a past, present, and future reading. It could also be used to provide three answers to a particular question. If the concern was love, for instance, the person might ask: When will I find love? Will we be happy? and will we have children? Most of the time this reading covers three different areas of someone's life. The person might start by asking about the general influences that are surrounding him or her, followed by a question on money, love, health, or anything else that is concerning him or her at the time of the reading.

Obviously, this process can be used to ask just one question, but it can be helpful to have three questions answered at the same time. Every now and again, the outcome of one question will affect the others. If, for instance, you're searching for love, but discover that you're going to have money problems, you might decide to forget about love for a while and focus on your finances. Likewise, you might be wanting to expand your business, but discover you're likely to have a few health concerns. In this case, it would be better to delay your plans for business growth and concentrate on improving your health.

Advice from the Kings

Required: Two dice and one deck of playing cards.

The kings are happy to give advice to ladies. The playing cards are thoroughly mixed and then dealt into a pile on the table. When the first king appears, it is removed and placed separately on the table. The dealing starts again until the second king appears. It is placed to the right of the first king. The third king is placed below the first king, and the fourth king is placed to the third king's right. This creates a square of four kings. The other cards are put away, as they aren't needed.

Mix the two dice and toss them onto the table. The die with the higher number on top is the one that will be used for the rest of the procedure. If both have the same number on top, they're tossed again. If the second toss also provides a pair of numbers, it's an indication that the cards don't want to answer today, and the cards and dice will need to be put away until the following day.

Usually one die will have a higher number on top than the other one. The die with the lower number is discarded. Kiss the other die and hold it about a foot above the four kings. Drop it onto the table—the king that it lands on provides the answer. If the die doesn't come to rest on a king, continue dropping it until it does.

It's also essential that it comes to rest with an even number on top. This number, and the king it is resting on, are interpreted. Here are the traditional interpretations:

King of spades

Two spots: ignore the flattery of a tall, fair-haired man.

Four spots: expect an interesting suggestion from a good friend.

Six spots: you'll be tempted to enter into a relationship that will cause grief.

King of diamonds

Two spots: be extremely cautious with all relationships for at least four weeks.

Four spots: expect a kind, caring, gentle suitor who finds it hard to express his feelings.

Six spots: you'll have to choose between two men.

King of hearts

Two spots: expect a short-lived romance with a dark-complexioned man.

Four spots: enjoy happy times with a fun-loving man, until you discover his dark side.

Six spots: you'll shortly meet a charming, affectionate, fun-loving young man.

King of clubs

Two spots: you'll be tempted to marry a young man who seems to have good prospects. Be careful, as this is likely to be a bad move.

Four spots: you'll put your faith and trust in a young man who doesn't deserve it.

Six spots: You'll shortly meet a young man who has more potential than you think he has.

Advice from the Queens

It's hardly fair for men to be excluded from this form of divination. Fortunately, they can follow almost the same procedure as advice from the kngs, and seek advice from the queens. The only difference is that a man interprets the odd rather than the even numbers on top of the die.

Queen of spades

One spot: you'll meet a fair-haired woman who'll bring you joy and happiness.

Three spots: you'll experience disappointment with a dark-haired woman.

Five spots: you'll find it hard to remove yourself from an unsuitable relationship.

Queen of diamonds

One spot: someone who doesn't appeal to you will express her love and affection for you.

Three spots: you'll become involved with an intriguing, but potentially dangerous, woman.

Five spots: you're about to meet someone who'll bring you great happiness.

Queen of hearts

One spot: you need to be careful with an older woman who is conspiring against you.

Three spots: a girl you are keen on will turn you down.

Five spots: you'll become involved in a short-term relationship with a jealous woman.

Queen of clubs

One spot: you'll meet a dark-haired woman who appears too good to be true. Be careful.

Three spots: an older woman will provide hospitality, help, and good advice.

Five spots: you'll meet a woman who immediately falls in love with you.

Astrological Dice

Required: Three dice and a casting cloth with a circle divided into twelve sections on it. The sections should be numbered from one to twelve.

The twelve sections represent the twelve houses of astrology:

1. The present. Personal interests.

2. Money matters.

3. Communications and travel.

4. Home and family matters.

5. Entertainments, creativity, and loved ones.

6. Physical fitness and health matters.

7. Relationships and legal matters.

8. Values and other people's money.

9. Learning, education, and spirituality.

10. Reputation and career.

11. Friends, community activities, and luck.

12. Matters that are hidden, or beyond your control.

The question is asked, and the three dice are tossed into the circle. Only the dice that land inside the circle are read, and this is done using both the numerological value of the number on top of the dice, and the particular house it is sitting in.

Let's assume you asked, "Will I progress in my career this year?" You roll the dice and cast: number three in house three, number one in house ten, and number one in house nine.

Number three (pleasure and fun) in house three (communications and travel) might not seem to relate to the question unless your career involves travel or communication. However, you might win a trip or have a pleasant vacation away from home.

Number one (independence and attainment) in house ten (reputation and career) is a highly positive sign, and this shows that you'll make a big step forward in your career this year. You'll have more status and your contributions will be recognized.

The third dice also indicates number one and lands in house nine (learning and spirituality). You'll be growing in knowledge and wisdom during the year, and presumably at least some of that will relate to your work.

I've seen dice readers use a variety of casting cloths with different patterns and words on them. A common form is to have the wheel divided into eight segments, each containing a word or two about good and bad luck. Here are some possible words that could be used: good luck, happiness, success, money, travel, love, loss, bad luck, misfortune, failure, sadness, and ill health. Some of these casting cloths have a blank section or a large question mark. If a die lands here, the person can make a wish.

Suggested Reading

Line, David and Julia. *Fortune Telling by Dice*. Wellingborough, UK: Aquarian Press, 1984.

Zed, Sarah. *Predicting the Future with Dice*. Hod Hosharon, Israel: Astrolog Publishing Company, 2002.

Domino Divination

Many people believe that dominoes were invented in China in about the twelfth century BCE by Keung T'ai Kung. However, this is unlikely. They were invented in China, but the earliest written records date back only as far as the twelfth century CE. Surviving examples show that they contained pictures as well as spots. They reached Europe in the eighteenth century and may have been introduced to England by French prisoners of war at the end of the century. The derivation of the name *domino* isn't known. However, in eighteenth century Europe, a loose cloak with a half mask was called a domino mask. It was used to conceal people's identities at balls and masquerades. It was black with two holes for the eyes. As dominoes are black with white spots (eyes), it's possible that the name may have come from that.

Modern-day dominoes come in sets of twenty-eight. They depict all the possible combinations of rolling two six-sided dice, as well as all six possibilities of a single die and a double-blank domino.

How to Do It

Dominoes should be read no more than once a week. This is because it can take that long for the message of the reading to be fully understood. I've met a number of people who say dominoes should never be read on a Monday or a Friday, as they are inauspicious days. Dominoes that are used for playing games should never be used for divination purposes. All divination tools need to be treated with respect. Consequently, if domino reading appeals to you, it's better to buy a set that you use purely for divination purposes.

Three Dominos

This is how dominoes are usually read. It provides a quick look at the person's past, present, and future. The three selected dominoes can also be used to answer specific questions.

Required: A set of twenty-eight dominoes.

How to Do It

1. The dominoes are thoroughly mixed facedown on a table while the querent thinks of his or her question.

2. The querent removes one domino and writes down what it is. This represents the person's past.

3. The domino is replaced with the others, and all the dominoes are thoroughly mixed again.

4. A second domino is removed and recorded. This indicates the querent's present situation. It's a good sign if the same domino is picked again, as it means the interpretation will happen quickly.

5. The domino is returned and all the dominoes are mixed again.

6. A third domino is removed, and its identity is written down. This reveals the person's future.

7. The three dominoes are interpreted.

8. The dominoes are thanked and replaced in their box or bag.

Note: It's possible to add to the reading by using numerology to interpret the number of spots on each domino, as well as the total number of spots reduced to a single digit.

If you have a simple question, or are in a hurry, you can select a single domino and interpret it. However, whenever possible use three dominoes as they provide a more detailed reading.

The Dominos

- *6:6* This is the luckiest domino of all. It promises prosperity, success, and a good relationship. The question that was asked will work out in the querent's favor.

- *6:5* Persistence pays off, and any good deeds you perform will be recognized and appreciated. You may need patience, but the outcome is positive.

- *6:4* A time of problems, frustrations, and difficulties. Seek legal advice if necessary. Don't try to progress until this time is over.

- *6:3* Potential for travel to a place you haven't visited before. You'll return with many happy memories.

- *6:2* Honesty pays off. The future looks promising with plenty of opportunities for progress and financial reward.

- *6:1* A good time spent with friends and loved ones. Potential for a celebration.

- *6:0* Be careful of false friends, people who gossip, and people who say one thing but mean another. Think before speaking.

- *5:5* This is a sign of a potential move that will provide great benefit to everyone involved. It could indicate a change of location, a change at work, or a new relationship. The answer to the querent's question is a definite yes.

- *5:4* You'll be offered an opportunity to progress financially.

- *5:3* A visitor will provide you with important news. Evaluate the information carefully.

- *5:2* Family discussions enable you to resolve an old problem. A happy social event will change your outlook.

- *5:1* Possibility of love and romance. If you're already in a relationship, you'll enjoy a happy time in each other's company.

- *5:0* Someone close to you will be going through a difficult time and you'll need to provide help and advice.

- *4:4* Your hard work has paid off and celebrations are in order. Make the most of this happy time. The answer to the querent's question is positive.

- *4:3* A misunderstanding may cause stress at home. You'll need to choose your words carefully to resolve it.

- *4:2* Possibility of deception. Someone will try to cheat you out of something. Be on your guard.

- *4:1* Be careful how much you spend, as there's the potential for overreaching yourself. Be cautious in all financial dealings.

- *4:0* You'll receive news that will annoy and aggravate you. Take as much time as necessary to formulate a response.

- *3:3* Potential for financial reward and recognition. Make the most of this happy time.

- *3:2* Unexpected activities provide great joy and happiness.

- *3:1* Take nothing on trust, and be careful with money matters. The answer to the querent's question is negative.

- *3:0* There'll be disagreements over small matters. Resolve them as quickly as you can to avoid stress and difficulties with others.

- *2:2* Your achievements will be recognized by others. Realize that not everyone will be happy with your success.

- *2:1* A minor frustration turns into a major problem. Fortunately, a new opportunity is presented to you once it's been resolved.

- *2:0* A good time for travel and new experiences. Luck is on your side.

- *1:1* Happiness in your home and working life. Take time out to relax and enjoy the present.

- *1:0* Unexpected news will be a mixed blessing. You'll appreciate it more later rather than in the present.

- *0:0* Obstacles, hindrances, and delays hold you back. There's no point in striving for success at this time. Wait until the road ahead is clear.

Astro-Numerological Dominoes

Required: A set of twenty-eight dominoes and a circular grid showing the twelve houses of astrology.

How to Do It

1. The dominoes are mixed facedown on a table.

2. Twelve dominoes are chosen one at a time and placed into each of the twelve houses.

3. The number of spots on the domino in house one are counted. If the answer is a two-digit number, the two digits are reduced to a single digit.

4. This number is interpreted by relating it to the qualities of the first house. (1 relates to the self, 2 relates to money and possessions, etc. See Astrology for further information.)

5. Steps three and four are repeated with each house in turn until all twelve houses have played their part in the reading.

Note: A more accurate reading can be obtained by making a note of each domino and replacing it with the others. All the dominoes are mixed again before another domino is chosen.

The Next Twelve Months

A good time to perform this divination is at the start of the year. It can also be used to see what the month ahead is going to be like.

Required: A set of twenty-eight dominoes.

How to Do It

1. The dominoes are thoroughly mixed and one is chosen.

2. This domino is placed horizontally in front of the querent and the number of spots it contains are added together.

The total number of spots is then interpreted.

- *Twelve*: A happy, fun-filled year. Enjoy new friends and activities.

- *Eleven*: Enjoy coming up with new ideas and making plans. Remember that it's nothing more than daydreaming unless you start acting on them.

- *Ten*: An active, energetic year. This is a good time for starting anything new.

- *Nine*: A time to let go of anything that has outlived its use. You'll feel a sense of completion and will start making plans for the future.

- *Eight*: This is the perfect time to move ahead and to receive the rewards of your hard work.

- *Seven*: A quiet, introspective year. A good time to learn, think, meditate, and grow inwardly.

- *Six*: Home and family responsibilities. This is a rewarding year, but you may not be able to do everything you want because of the needs of others.

- *Five*: This is an exciting year full of opportunities. It's a good time to start anything new or different.

- *Four*: A busy year. All the hard work pays off, but you may feel that you're making slow progress until you look back at the end of the year and realize just how much you've accomplished.

- *Three*: A happy, social year with plenty of fun activities. A good time for any form of creativity.

- *Two*: Slow progress. You'll be cooperating with others and waiting for the right opportunity. This is a good year for relationships that are going well and for making new friends.

- *One*: New beginnings. You'll be feeling independent, enthusiastic, and ready for new opportunities.

Suggested Reading

Buckland, Ray. *Buckland's Domino Divination*. Sunland, CA: Pendraig Publishing, 2010.

Dowsing

Dowsing is the popular name for rhabdomancy, which means divination using a rod, wand, or stick. Other common names are water witching and water divining. It usually refers to divining for water, oil, gold, or other minerals hidden below the earth's surface. As it can be used to locate almost anything, I call dowsing "divining for something that's desired." The world's greatest living dowser is the Israeli psychic Uri Geller, who specializes in dowsing for oil.

Dowsing is extremely old. Pictographs in the Tassili n'Ajjer caves in southeast Libya show a group of people watching a diviner with a forked stick. These famous drawings could be eight thousand years old.

Throughout history, many eminent men and women have dowsed successfully. These include Leonardo da Vinci, Robert Boyle, Sir Isaac Newton, Lloyd George, Thomas A. Edison, and Dr. Albert Einstein.

How to Do It

The most popular tools for dowsing are angle rods, a forked stick, and the pendulum. Some people prefer to use a wand made from a three-foot length of springy wood or plastic. Other people use nothing but their hands. They're often called "hand tremblers," as their hands start shaking violently when they're standing close to whatever it is they're seeking. Their hands tremble more and more violently as they get closer to it.

Angle Rods

Angle rods are a good tool to start with, as most people are able to work with them. They consist of two L-shaped pieces of metal wire. The longer section that faces forward is about twelve inches long, and the shorter section that is held loosely in the hands is about six inches. The exact measurements are not critical. My first angle rods were made from two wire coat hangers.

Dowsing rods are held in the hands with the longer sections parallel and pointing forward.

You'll find the angle rods easier to use if you place the shorter section inside plastic or wood tubing. This means that the rods can move freely, no matter how tightly you're holding them. The casings of ballpoint pens work well for this.

Some dowsers prefer to use bare rods and hold them loosely in their hands. You'll need to experiment to find out which method works better for you. Some dowsers also rest their thumbs lightly on the top of the bend to steady the rods. This works well for many people, but others say it prevents the rods from moving.

The rods are held in the hands with the longer sections parallel and pointing forward. When the dowser locates whatever it is he or she is looking for, the rods will either cross over each other or move outward. This is known as a "dowsing response."

A few people dowse with just one angle rod that makes a 90-degree movement when it's over the correct location. During the Vietnam War, soldiers dowsed with a single angle rod as they carried a rifle in the other hand.

If you haven't dowsed before, it's a good idea to walk around holding the rods loosely in your fists with the longer section pointing directly ahead. Your hands should be approximately body width apart, but do not tuck your elbows into your sides. The rods should be parallel to each other. As you walk, you may find that the rods move and cross each other. Once you've received a dowsing response, it's time to search for something specific. I usually suggest that people start by dowsing for the water pipe that brings water into their home. It doesn't matter if you already know approximately where this is, as the rods will tell you the exact location.

Take a few deep breaths and tell yourself that you're going to dowse for the water pipe. Keep thinking about this, and maintain a sense of positive expectancy as you're dowsing. Start by walking from one side of the property to the other with your rods pointing directly in front of you. As you get closer to your target, the rods will start moving toward each other, and they'll cross each other when you're standing directly over the water pipe.

Walk across the property again about a yard away from where you walked before. Your angle rods should cross each other again at the same place. Keep your first few experiments short, as dowsing can be mentally and physically draining. Twenty to thirty minutes is about long enough.

Once you've found your own water pipe you might like to walk along your street and locate the water mains of other people.

Don't worry if you fail to receive a dowsing response on your first attempts. You might be holding the rods too tightly or trying too hard. Remember to hold the rods loosely in your hands, or in a sleeve, and hold the rods as horizontal as you can. You might like to turn a tap on in the house and dowse while the water is running. Another possibility is that there's no water pipe in the area you're dowsing in. If you still have no response after several attempts, ask an experienced dowser to rest a hand on your shoulder while you dowse. You'll find you'll be able to dowse successfully while he or she does this, and after experiencing the dowsing response once, you'll have no problems in doing it again.

Divining Rods

Divining rods are the traditional V- or Y-shaped forked sticks cut from a tree. Certain trees, such as hazel, apple, peach, cherry, willow, and birch trees, are preferred, as they keep their flexibility longer. As it's important for the rods to be supple, many diviners cut fresh divining rods every time they dowse. Whenever possible, I prefer to find a fallen branch, rather than cut one from a tree.

The arms of the rod are usually about eighteen inches long, and the angle they create is between 40 and 70 degrees. Again, these measurements are approximate, and you should experiment to see what works best for you. Be aware that your arms will get tired quickly if you're holding rods that are too long.

Hold the rod with your palms upward and grip the rod in such a way that it's under tension and the forks are bent out. Increase the tension to bend the forks slightly outward. I like to have about an inch of the rods protruding from my hands. Keep your elbows close to your sides and the rod pointing very slightly upward. When you locate whatever it is you are dowsing for, the rod will usually turn downward with a strong, almost violent pull. Occasionally, the rod will turn upward, and as the movement is sudden and swift, some dowsers have hit themselves on the head with their divining rods.

Traditional divining rod.

The Pendulum

The pendulum consists of a weight, such as a bead, crystal, or ring, attached to a length of cord or chain. Almost anything that can be suspended this way will work. Some dowsers refuse to work with metal pendulums, while others won't work with anything else. Ideally, the weight should be at least a few ounces. Heavier weights will make your hand and arm tired, and the movements of lighter weights can sometimes be hard to read.

You can buy commercially made pendulums online and in New Age stores. I prefer to buy them at a store, as I can experiment with them before buying. Choose a pendulum that looks attractive and is comfortable to use. My favorite pendulum is a Mermet pendulum. Abbé Mermet was a famous dowser in the early twentieth century. His books are still in print, and are well worth reading. His pendulums are still available, too. A Mermet pendulum can be unscrewed and a small sample of whatever is being dowsed for can be placed inside.

The pendulum is suspended from the thumb and first finger, and the movements it makes are interpreted.

Unlike the angle rods and Y-shaped rods, pendulums are normally used indoors. However, they can be used outdoors as well, and I know a couple of water diviners who use nothing but their pendulums, indoors or out.

The length of the string holding the weight doesn't need to be very long. It's a good idea to start with just a half inch of thread, and hold the rest in the palm of your hand. Hold the pendulum with the cord gripped between your thumb and first finger, and the other fingers pointing downward. Rest the elbow of the same arm that's holding the pendulum on a table. Your hands and legs should be uncrossed. Swing the pendulum back and forth. Gradually release more and more thread until the pendulum starts to move in circles. This is the right length for you. Tie a knot in the thread immediately below your finger and thumb to mark the position.

Once you've done this, you can ask your pendulum a number of questions. Hold the pendulum at the knot you've just tied and ask it what movement means "yes." Be patient. After a while, your pendulum will start moving and give you the answer. It might move backward and forward, from side to side, or in circles, clockwise or counterclockwise. Make a note of the answer, and then ask it to tell you what movement indicates "no."

You can now ask your pendulum any question that can be answered by yes or no. This is probably enough to start with. Once you've become used to working with a pendulum, you'll need two more responses: "I don't know" and "I don't want to answer."

Start by asking the pendulum questions that you already know, such as: "Is my name _____ ?" "Am I _____ years old?" and so on. Your pendulum should give you the right answers. If you're a female and ask, "Am I female?" the pendulum should reply "yes." However, if you're a male, the pendulum should give a negative response to that question.

Once your pendulum has successfully answered questions of this sort, you can start asking it questions that you do not know the answer to. Be cautious with the answers initially, as it takes a while to become experienced at this sort of divination. You also need to be careful when asking questions that you have an emotional involvement with, as it may give you the answer you want to hear, rather than the correct one. It's better, in questions of this sort, to have someone with no emotional involvement in the outcome ask the question for you.

As with the divining rod, some people have difficulties when they first start using a pendulum. If this happens, deliberately swing the pendulum in the four different movements to become familiar with how it feels when the pendulum moves. Practice for about five minutes a day until the pendulum starts moving without any conscious input from you. Initially, the movements will be slight, and you'll have to be observant to notice them. As you gain experience, the movements will become larger and faster. If all else fails, ask someone who is skilled at pendulum dowsing to gently rest a hand on the shoulder of the arm that's holding the pendulum. I have yet to meet anyone who can't use a pendulum. Consequently, it doesn't matter how long it takes to get your pendulum moving initially, once you've managed to do it, you'll have no problems with it ever again.

Every now and again you'll need to ask your pendulum what each movement is, as they can change. Some people keep the same responses forever, while others find it changes almost every time they pick up their pendulum.

A number of people dowse by holding their pendulums over a map. If they're dowsing for water, the pendulum will move when it's suspended over a source of water. Abbé Mermet practiced map dowsing for a variety of purposes, including finding missing people. All he needed was a photograph of the missing person, or a piece of the person's clothing, and a map of the area where the person had gone missing. One of the most sensational examples of this occurred in 1934 when Mermet located the body of a six-year-old Swiss boy who had disappeared from his home. Amazingly, the boy had been carried off by an eagle and was found high up in the mountains far away from his home. His clothes and shoes were undamaged, showing that the boy could not have made his own way to the spot where his body was found. [12]

Suggested Reading

Hitching, Francis. *Pendulum: The Psi Connection*. London: Fontana Books, 1977.

Mermet, Abbé. *Principles and Practice of Radiesthesia*. Trans. by Mark Clement. London: Vincent Stuart Ltd., 1959. Originally published in French, 1935.

Webster, Richard. *Dowsing for Beginners*. St. Paul, MN: Llewellyn Publications, 1996.

Webster, Richard. *Pendulum Magic for Beginners*. Woodbury, MN: Llewellyn Publications, 2002.

Dreams

We all dream. Even people who claim they never have dreams. They simply can't remember them. Virtually everyone dreams at least four times every night. The first dreams of the night are comparatively short, but later dreams can last for more than thirty minutes. The last dream of the night is the one that's usually remembered.

It appears that our dreams help us sort out what we've experienced during the day. If you carefully evaluate any dreams you remember when you wake up, you'll find they usually relate to whatever is going on in your life at the time. Although no one knows why we do it, the fact remains that we need to dream. Scientists are still trying to find out why we dream.

Dreaming may be the oldest divination practice of all. Probably the most famous precognitive dream is recorded in the Bible: Pharaoh's dream of seven fat and seven lean cows and seven healthy ears of corn and seven thin ears of corn. Joseph, who already had a reputation for dream interpretation, was able to interpret this dream for Pharaoh. The fat cows and healthy ears of corn showed that Egypt would enjoy seven years of prosperity, and the thin cows and ears of corn showed that they would be followed by seven years of famine (Genesis 41:1–40).

There are three main types of precognitive dreams.

Warning Dreams

Warning dreams are common, and many people experience them. This may be because they're usually emotional and are consequently remembered when the dreamer wakes up. Warning dreams can be useful. Let's assume you dreamed that you were walking along a street you know well at a particular time on the following day, and an out of control car crossed the street and plunged into you. You

---

12   Hitching 1977, 61.

would probably change this possible future by avoiding that street for the next day or two. However, if you did that, was the warning a genuine warning, or simply a crazy dream? Precognitive dreams give glimpses of possible futures, but you have the ability to change them.

Dreams of illness and death worry many people. There are a few recorded cases of people receiving information about their death in their dreams. Abraham Lincoln is a good example. However, these dreams are usually symbolic and indicate the ending of something in your life. This might well be positive, rather than negative, as we all have to let go of things that have outworn their use.

Possible Futures

Precognitive dreams can sometimes provide information about possible futures. If, for instance, you're unhappy at work and are thinking about a complete change of occupation, you might have a number of dreams, each giving you information about different possibilities. You should think about each of these possibilities and decide which one appeals the most. This doesn't mean the other dreams were wasted, as they give you a glimpse of what might be, rather than what will be.

Important Decisions

If you have an important decision to make, or are at a crossroads in your life, predictive dreams can provide insights to help you make the right decision. Sometimes dreams of this sort occur months, or even years, before the decision or change needs to be made. You may have wondered about the significance of the dream at the time but then forgot it until the situation occurred in reality and you realized it was a predictive dream.

Unfortunately, it's difficult to prove the reality of precognitive dreams. Often the dreamers tell friends and family about their dreams, but because these experiences can't be replicated, they can't be used as conclusive evidence for the phenomenon.

During the 1960s and '70s, the researchers at the Maimonides Dream Laboratory in New York spent a great deal of time studying precognitive dreams. A sender would try to send a randomly selected image to a receiver who was sleeping in another room at least one hundred feet away. When the receiver entered the REM (rapid eye movement) state, with the accompanying brainwave changes that indicated he or she was dreaming, the receiver was woken and asked to describe his or her dream. Independent judges analyzed the results to see if the dreams contained any of the images that had been sent by the sender. Frequently they did. [13]

The researchers at Maimonides also conducted experiments in dream precognition. They did this by having the dreamer try to dream of an image that wasn't selected until after he or she had been woken. The results were well above chance level. There were 15,360 trials conducted with a young English psychic called Malcolm Bessent. He recorded 7,859 successes. The odds of this occurring by chance were approximately five hundred to one. [14]

---

13 Ullman and Krippner 1973, 97–110.

14 Ibid., 180.

It's possible to learn to remember your dreams when you wake up. A good method is to tell yourself shortly before falling asleep that you will remember your dreams when you awake. When you wake up, lie quietly without moving and see what comes into your mind. If you do this on a regular basis, you'll find your ability to remember dreams will improve. It's important to record what you remember as soon as you get up. As you know, dreams fade away quickly and are soon forgotten.

It's not easy to have a precognitive dream on request. However, there's a technique called lucid dreaming that enables you to take your dreams anywhere you wish, even into the future.

Lucid Dreaming

Lucid dreaming occurs when you're dreaming and become aware that you're dreaming. It normally occurs in the middle of a normal dream and the person suddenly realizes that he or she is dreaming. Most people experience this occasionally. The term *lucid dreaming* was coined by Frederik van Eeden, a Dutch psychiatrist, in 1913. However, the phenomenon was known at least three thousand years ago, as it's mentioned in the Indian *Upanishads*, and Aristotle mentioned it in his book *On Dreams*.

Most people are surprised and immediately let go of the dream and wake up when they involuntarily start lucid dreaming. If you don't want to wake up, tell yourself that you know you're in a dream, and want to stay in it. It pays to remain as relaxed as possible and allow the dream to continue while at the same time remaining aware that it's a dream.

Once you've become used to the phenomenon, it's a simple matter to guide the dream wherever you'd like it to go. Consequently, you can go anywhere you wish. You can even visit the Moon if you want to. As you can go both backward and forward in time, lucid dreaming is a useful way to divine the future. You can resolve problems that seemed insurmountable when you were awake. You can rehearse activities you'll need to do the following day. You can visit friends and have an enjoyable conversation with them. You can even improve your health by focusing on areas of disease. You can use it for self-improvement, such as gaining confidence, overcoming phobias, and improving study habits. In fact, you can do everything you've ever wanted to do. Many people use lucid dreams to make their fantasies real.

If you find yourself in a lucid dream that is disturbing or unpleasant, you have the ability to wake yourself up or move the dream in a more positive direction. After all, you're in control when you're lucid dreaming.

How to Lucid Dream

There are many different ways to induce lucid dreaming. We're all different, and there isn't a single method that works for everyone.

1. Spend time thinking about where you'd like to go and what you'd do in a lucid dream. It's important to avoid alcohol and overeating whenever you wish to have a lucid dream. If you're lucid dreaming for a particular purpose, remind yourself of this goal several times during the evening.

2. A simple, but not necessarily easy, method is to tell yourself just before you fall asleep that tonight you'll have a lucid dream, and that you'll remember it when you wake up. There's no need to try to force this thought into your mind. Simply think it, and allow yourself to fall asleep. Continue doing this every night until you find yourself lucid dreaming. Once you've done it once, you'll find it a simple matter to do it again whenever you wish. This method also works well if you happen to wake up during the night and think about lucid dreaming as you return to sleep.

   A more effective method is to immediately try to go to back to sleep again after waking up from a vivid dream. Tell yourself that you'll quickly and easily drift into a lucid dream.

   Another method is to set your alarm clock for one hour before you'd normally get up. Wake up enough to turn the alarm off, and allow yourself to drift back to sleep while telling yourself that you'll go straight into a lucid dream. When you fall asleep, you'll enter into a light REM state, which is when most lucid dreams occur.

3. It's important to keep a record of your dreams. Keeping a dream diary increases the chances of having a lucid dream. This is because it subconsciously tells you that your dreams are important and are consequently worth remembering. It also encourages you to consciously remember your dreams before they disappear from your mind.

   After you've been recording your dreams for a while, you may discover a common image that frequently appears. It might be as simple as seeing your hand, or it might be a location, a favorite item, or a particular friend. Before falling asleep tell yourself that whenever you see whatever it happens to be in your dream, you'll immediately start lucid dreaming.

   If the common image in your dreams happens to be your hand, or another part of your body, you can help the process of lucid dreaming by asking yourself if you're conscious or in a dream. If you do this several times a day, the chances are high that you'll ask yourself the same question in your dreams and be able to use it to experience a lucid dream.

4. Once you've woken up you can think about your lucid dream. Many people find it hard to stay lucid dreaming. They either wake up, or the lucid dream turns into a normal dream. You can overcome both of these problems by taking control of some aspect of the dream. You might make something larger or smaller, for instance. You could add something to the scene you're in. These changes might be small, but they demonstrate that you're directing the proceedings, and they help you move farther into the lucid dream.

Some people wake up after entering a lucid dream as they become excited and want to move ahead too quickly. Take your time as you develop your ability to lucid dream. Every time you enter into a lucid dream you'll be able to progress further than you did before. Work at your own pace and enjoy every stage of your progress.

Into the Future

Most people start out by enjoying the sensation of flying and rarely attempt to direct their lucid dreams into other areas. Some people stay at this level, but others progress and use their lucid dreaming skills for more worthwhile purposes. Exploring the future is a good example of this.

1. Before you go to bed, think about where you want to go in the future. Would you like to see what you'll be doing next week, next month, or maybe five years from now? If you're currently unwell, you might like to move ahead to a time when the illness is behind you. You might want to attend one of your children's twenty-first birthday parties. You might want to see how far you've progressed in your career ten years from now. You might want to find out what sporting or other triumphs are ahead of you. There's no limit to what you can do, but it's a good idea to decide ahead of time where you want to go, rather than leaving it to chance.

2. Remember that you can visit many different possible futures. As you possess free will, you can change any future you're not happy with, and ask to see other possible futures. When you find a future that you're happy with, explore it in a number of lucid dreams.

3. Record your lucid dreams in as much detail as possible. Review this information before your next dream, as you might want to explore aspects of it in greater detail.

4. You can use lucid dreaming to create the future you want. However, there's always a price to pay. Use your dreams to find out what you need to do to reach your goals. If you're prepared to do whatever is necessary for success, get busy and make it happen.

Suggested Reading

Auerbach, Loyd. *Psychic Dreaming: A Parapsychologist's Handbook*. New York: Warner Books, Inc., 1991.

Gachenbach, Jayne and Jane Bosveld. *Control Your Dreams*. New York: Harper & Row, Publishers, 1989.

Green, Celia E. *Lucid Dreams*. London: Hamish Hamilton Limited, 1968.

Holloway, Gillian. *The Complete Dream Book: Discover What Your Dreams Reveal about You and Your Life*. Naperville: Sourcebooks, Inc., 2006.

Ullman, Montague, Stanley Krippner, and Alan Vaughan. *Dream Telepathy: Experiments in Nocturnal ESP*. New York: Macmillan Publishing Company, Inc., 1973.

Egg Divination

Oomancy is the art of divination using an egg. The word comes from two Greek words: *oon*, meaning "an egg," and *manteia*, which means "divination." Egg divination is also called *ovomancy* and *ooscopy*.

My first experience of egg divination was in Glasgow, Scotland, in 1968. It was shortly after my father had died, and my landlady thought it would be helpful for me to have a reading from a psychic reader she went to whenever she needed advice about the future. As this lady lived close by, I walked there, holding the egg she'd told me to bring. The lady asked me to continue holding the egg in my cupped hands while we had a brief conversation that was obviously intended to put me at ease. After this, she took my egg, held it in both hands for about a minute, and then made a small hole in the sharper end of it. She held this over a clear glass bowl half full of warm water and allowed the white of the egg to flow into the bowl. Initially, the white was almost invisible, but gradually shapes appeared and the lady interpreted them for me. I don't remember much about the reading, but it was helpful to me at the time.

Since then I've seen eggs used in a variety of ways for healing, cleansing, and removing the evil eye.

How to Do It

Eggs can be used both for readings, and for removing negative energies. One commonly used method to remove negative energies is to roll the egg over the person's body, including the trunk, head, neck, arms, and legs. The egg is then cracked into a bowl containing water, and the diviner inspects this to determine if all the negativity has left the body. Sometimes the inspection is left until the following day when the white of the egg has had time to clot. The process is repeated if there is any negativity left in the person's body.

A different method is to separate the white from the yolk, and to pour it into hot water. The shapes made by the cooked egg whites are then interpreted. Although it takes longer, a similar method can also be used. The person who wants to know the future rubs the egg over his or her body and then cracks the egg into a glass of tepid water. The glass was left untouched overnight, and in the morning the strands of congealed white of the egg in the water were interpreted. Once the reading was over, the person being read for had to raise the glass in the air, as if giving a toast, and then swallow the contents of the glass.

Egg reading was popular in ancient Greece and Rome. They used it mainly to gain information about unborn babies. A hen's egg was rubbed on a pregnant woman's stomach for a few minutes, and then broken open. A single yolk indicated one child, two yolks indicated twins, and three yolks was a sign of triplets. It was an indication of a difficult birth if the yolk was streaked with red.

Another method involved incubating the egg between the pregnant woman's breasts. The sex of the chick would be the same as that of the unborn child. The Roman biographer Gaius Suetonius Tranquillus (c. 70–122 CE) wrote that when Empress Livia Drusilla (55 BCE–29 CE) was pregnant, she carried a freshly laid chicken's egg in her bosom until it hatched. The chick was male, as was the baby she gave birth to.

There's also a form of oomancy that doesn't involve breaking the egg. Instead, it's hardboiled. Traditionally the name of a god or goddess was written on one end of the egg, and a goal was written on the other. The egg was then rolled down a slope, and an interpretation was made by observing which end was pointing upward and the direction the egg was pointing in. A modern-day variation of this is to draw symbols on different parts of the shell, each indicating possible outcomes to your question. The symbol that's face up after the egg has been rolled reveals the answer.

In parts of South and Southeast Asia eggs are thrown to the ground, and the shapes created are interpreted. The Khasi people of the Assam Hills in northeast India throw an egg onto a wooden board, and the pieces of eggshell are interpreted. [15]

In present-day Guatemala, Mayan diviners use eggs to diagnose illnesses. Several eggs are passed over the patient's body to absorb energy from the illness. The eggs are placed into water, and the diviner takes them to a quiet place where he can interpret them. This process is said to divine both the origin and nature of the problem.

Suggested Reading

Brown, Colette. *How to Read an Egg: Divination for the Easily Bored*. New Alresford, UK: Dodona
  Books, 2014.

Face Reading

Physiognomy, or face reading, is the most frequently used form of divination in the world, as everyone practices it. Even people with no interest in any form of divination use it when they make comments such as, "she has an honest face," and "he has shifty eyes." Usually, their assessments are correct, as although we inherit our facial features, the way we live affects the overall look of the face. Someone who constantly worries, for instance, reveals that to everyone by the stresses and anxieties that are visible on his or her face.

Face reading has been a popular form of divination and character analysis in China, and much of the Far East, for thousands of years. The earliest existing records show that it was being practiced at the time of the Yellow Emperor (2697–2598 BCE). Consequently, this particular form of divination is at least five thousand years old.

Face reading was also practiced in ancient Greece, and Aristotle wrote a treatise on the subject called *Physiognomonica*.

The first book in the West on the subject was written by Albertus Magnus (c.1200–1280). Many more followed, and even John Evelyn, the English essayist, wrote an essay in 1697 called *Digression Concerning Physiognomy*. He believed that spirits of passion lived in the brain and how the person acted on these created the features of the face.

Charles Darwin wrote in his diary that he was almost not allowed to travel on the *HMS Beagle* because the captain, who was interested in physiognomy, didn't like the look of his nose.

---

15   Simoons 1994, 146.

Physiognomy fell out of favor for many years, but became popular again when researchers found that certain character traits, such as integrity and antagonism, can be read in the face.

Facial Shapes

The shape of the face can be categorized in a number of different ways. The most popular of these uses the five elements of wood, fire, metal, water, and earth. In Chinese belief, the interaction of these elements created everything in the universe.

These elements can be arranged in a number of different ways. The most common one of these is the productive cycle. It shows that each element is born from the element that precedes it. Wood burns and produces fire. Fire produces earth. Earth produces metal. Metal can be liquefied to produce "water." Water nurtures and produces wood.

Each element has a large number of associations, such as season, direction, color, and face type.

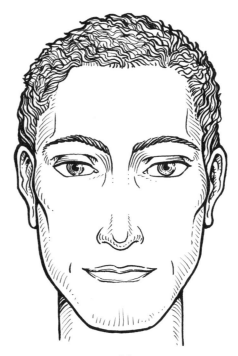

Wood face.

Wood

A wood face is long, slim, and rectangular. The forehead is broad. People with a wood face are enthusiastic, optimistic, progressive, and forward-looking. They are logical, well organized, ambitious, responsible, and hardworking. They show leadership potential and become frustrated whenever they feel held back or restricted. They are also kind and generous.

Fire face.

Fire

A fire face has a wide middle section, with a pointed chin, and a narrow forehead. People with a fire face are courageous, passionate, self-centered, empathic, and restless. The restlessness is often revealed by quick, often nervous, movements of their bodies. They enjoy taking risks and need to be busy and active to be happy.

Earth face.

Earth

An earth face is large, wide, square, or oblong. The jaw is strong and the mouth is wide. People with an earth face are reliable, stable, calm, and practical. They tend to be rigid and stubborn, and dislike change. They are kindly, sympathetic, modest, and friendly. They keep their feet firmly on the ground.

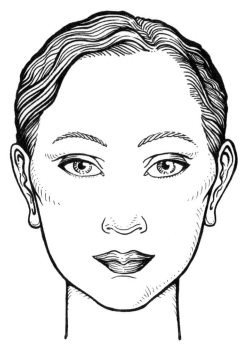

Metal face.

Metal

A metal face is oval, with wide upper cheeks, and a large nose. People with a metal face are sensitive, charming, idealistic, and innovative. They do well in business, and when working for someone else, they usually rise to a position of authority and responsibility. They seek perfection, and can become arrogant, short-tempered, and disappointed when this is not achieved.

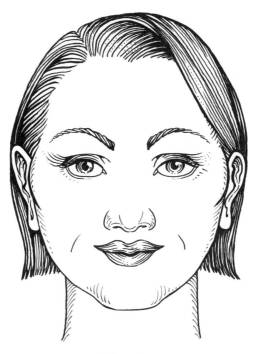

Water face.

Water

A water face is round, usually fleshy, with a broad forehead and prominent chin. People with a water face are flexible, adaptable, sympathetic, emotional, and intuitive. They enjoy helping others, and often choose to work in a humanitarian field. They are also extremely determined and persistent.

Divisions of the Face

Once the type of face has been determined, the next step is to look at the face by mentally dividing it into two halves vertically and three sections horizontally.

The two sides of the face are a good example of the Chinese concept of yin and yang. These are the harmonizing and balancing factors in the universe. Yin and yang are opposite energies and neither can live without the other. Night and day is an example. Without night, there could be no day. Other examples include: male and female, tall and short, black and white, hot and cold, wet and dry, passive and active, hard and soft, and fast and slow.

The left side of your face reveals your private, innermost self, and shows how you relate to family and close friends. It also reveals the major male influence in your life when you were growing up.

The right side of your face reveals your outer personality, the face you show to the world. This is the face that people see when they first meet you or have dealings with you at work. It also reveals the major female influence on you when you were growing up.

Most faces are not symmetrical when vertically split into two halves. The nose may lean toward one side, one ear might be higher or lower than the other, and the eyes might vary in size. The easiest way to determine the differences in each half is to look at various pairs of features, such as the eyes, eyebrows, nostrils, cheekbones, and ears.

The Three Horizontal Zones

The first of the three horizontal zones starts at the hairline, or where it would have been in the case of receding hairlines. It finishes immediately above the eyebrows. This is called the *analytical zone*.

The second zone starts at the top of the eyebrows and finishes immediately below the nose. This is called the *ambition zone*.

The third zone starts immediately below the nose and finishes at the bottom of the chin. It is called the *practical zone*.

Most people have one zone larger than the others. As the differences can be slight, it takes practice to determine which zone is the largest. Some people have two zones larger than the third zone. A few people have all three zones about the same size.

Children's faces develop as they mature. The forehead, for instance, is the dominant part of a baby's face. Over time, the middle section containing the nose develops, and finally, in early adulthood, the third section containing the mouth develops. Consequently, you can't determine the dominant zone of anyone under the age of about twenty.

Analytical Zone

People with strong analytical zones like to think before making a decision. They work logically and enjoy evaluating and analyzing a situation before acting. They have a good imagination and love ideas and abstract thinking.

In traditional Chinese face reading, a large analytical zone indicates a happy childhood and early adulthood. This covers the first twenty-eight years of the person's life.

Ambition Zone

People with strong ambition zones are down-to-earth and willing to work hard to achieve their goals. They enjoy dealing with facts and involve themselves in practical concerns. They enjoy the rewards of their success, and enjoy having the best of everything. They are adventurous when young, but become more cautious as they age.

In traditional Chinese face reading, a large ambition zone indicates success in the middle years (from twenty-nine to fifty).

Practical Zone

People with strong practical zones are well-grounded, secure, capable, and in control. They have a physical, passionate, and sensual approach to life. They rely on their feelings just as much as logic when it comes to making decisions.

In traditional Chinese face reading, a large practical zone indicates a happy later part of the person's life. This runs from the age of fifty-one to death.

The Twelve Palaces

The twelve palaces provide useful indicators about the quality and future of a person's life by looking at different aspects of his or her life. No one knows why this classification is called *Twelve Palaces*, but it might indicate that every part of the face is equally important, and is consequently considered a palace.

Career Palace

The career palace is situated at the center of the forehead. It should be broad, round, and smooth. If this is the case, it's a sign that the person will be ambitious and have the necessary attributes to be successful in his or her chosen career. Any deformities indicate difficulties and slow progress in this area of life.

Parent Palaces

The two parent palaces are located on the sides of the forehead immediately above the temples. These palaces provide information about the health of your parents, their relationship, and your relationship with them. Ideally, this area should be broad and fleshy. Any deformities or irregularities, such as wrinkles and moles, adversely affect the relationship between you and your parents.

Life Palace

The life palace is situated between the eyebrows. It shows how much drive and ambition the person has. It should be wide (at least the width of two fingers), smooth, and clear. This provides opportunities, assistance from others, and a fortunate start in life. A narrow life palace indicates someone who is sociable but lacking in ambition. The broader the life palace is, the more respect, admiration, and power the person will receive. Horizontal lines in this area, or eyebrows that are connected, indicate problems in this area of life.

Travel Palaces

The two travel palaces are situated on the temples. They indicate the amount of travel the person will have, what he or she will gain from the experiences, and the amount of luck he or she has while traveling. The travel palaces should be broad and free of hair. If they are dark, or covered with hair or moles, the person will experience little enjoyment from the travel.

Sibling Palaces

The sibling palaces are located on and immediately above the eyebrows, and provide information about the person's relationships with his or her siblings. If the eyebrows are dark, thick, long, and attractive, the relationships will be harmonious, and the brothers and sisters will be willing to help each other when necessary. If the eyebrows are sparse, short, broken, thin, mismatched, or too close to the eyes, the siblings will find it hard to get along, and will disagree on most matters.

Property Palaces

The eyes are the palaces of property. The palaces of property used to refer to real estate, but nowadays it refers to total assets, such as stocks, business, and other investments, in addition to property. If the eyes are long, with large pupils, clear whites, and a strong, penetrating gaze, the person will ultimately do well financially. People with shifty eyes, red streaks in the whites, or a weak gaze seldom do well financially.

Spouse Palaces

The spouse palaces are situated at the outer tips of the eyes. They should be full, clear, smooth, and free of any abnormalities such as moles, spots, or lines. This is a sign of a long-lasting, harmonious relationship with a happy home and family life. Any irregularities in the spouse palaces create problems in forming and sustaining a good relationship.

Children Palaces

The children palaces are the small semicircles immediately below the eyes. These reveal the quality of the relationships a person has with his or her children. Ideally, the children's palaces should be full, round, smooth, and fleshy. This indicates a harmonious relationship between the parents and their children. When the children grow up, they'll be successful and provide great joy and happiness. If the children palaces are sunken, crisscrossed with lines, or have other imperfections, the parents will receive little respect and happiness from their children.

Health Palace

The health palace is located between the eyes and extends to the bridge of the nose. It provides clues about the person's energy and health, especially during the first thirty years. If the bridge of the nose is high, smooth, and wide, the person will have plenty of energy, courage, and good health. Conversely, if this area is narrow and crooked, the person will experience many minor health problems.

Wealth Palace

The wealth palace covers the lower part of the nose and reveals how good the person is at making, and keeping, money. The perfect moneymaking nose has a large and fleshy tip, with nostrils that are not obvious. The Chinese say that the nose is like a moneybox. If it's wide at the top, plenty of money can come in. A large nose holds more money than a small one. Large, open, highly visible nostrils allow the money to escape. A small, pointed, or upturned nose tip is considered inauspicious and makes it hard for the person to progress financially.

Relations Palace

The relations palace is situated on the mouth and relates to how the person gets on with others. It's a good sign if the mouth is reddish pink, round and full, with well-shaped lips. This denotes harmonious interactions with others and plenty of sexual vigor. It's a negative sign if the mouth is slanting, protruding, and dark. This is said to create misunderstandings with others. The person often speaks before thinking.

Servant Palace

The servant palace used to relate to the times when some people had an army of servants to look after them. Nowadays it indicates authority and the people who work under you. It's a positive sign if the chin is round, fleshy, and slightly protruding. It's a negative indication if it's narrow, short, or thin.

Spheres of Influence

As well as the Twelve Palaces, there are two Spheres of Influence, which also need to be looked at.

Society

How the person relates to society and his or her friends is indicated by the cheeks. If the cheekbones are clearly visible, the person will make good long-lasting friendships and relate well with society as a whole.

Comfort

The person's home life is indicated by the area between the nose and mouth and the area immediately below the mouth. If these areas are smooth and unblemished, the person will enjoy a stable, comfortable home life. He or she will be happy. Any defects indicate problems in the person's home life.

Traits at a Glance

Forehead

- *Forehead slopes back*: impatient, wants quick results
- *Vertical forehead*: patient, good concentration, prefers to make up his or her own mind
- *Rounded forehead*: friendly, people person, enjoys home and family life
- *Square-shaped forehead*: enjoys challenges and new projects, motivated, enthusiastic
- *High forehead*: intellectual, needs mental stimulation
- *Low forehead*: lowbrow tastes, lives in the present

Face

- *Asymmetric face*: rapid mood swings
- *Narrow face*: keen to learn, gains confidence as he or she progresses through life
- *Wide face*: confident, likes to be in control

Ears

- *Protruding ears*: acquisitive, good listener, questions everything
- *Ears flat against side of head*: good spender
- *Large earlobes*: good financial potential
- *High-set ears*: practical, down-to-earth, and easy to get on with
- *Low-set ears*: dreamer, idealistic, lives in own world

Eyebrows

- *High-set*: cool, distant, reserved
- *Low-set, straight eyebrows*: friendly, good conversationalist, good taste
- *Short, oblong eyebrows*: practical, unimaginative, reliable
- *Long, thick eyebrows*: imaginative, sets goals, good worker

Eyes

- *Sparkling eyes*: charismatic, outgoing, responsive
- *Dull eyes*: reluctant to express feelings, disinterested
- *Close-set eyes*: overreacts, lacks tolerance or understanding, enjoys details

- *Wide-set eyes*: tolerant, understanding, easy to get along with

- *Deep-set eyes*: serious approach to life

- *Large pupils*: sympathetic, thoughtful, responsive, emotional

- *Small pupils*: unsympathetic, hard to get to know

- *Crow's feet at corners of eyes*: fun-loving, humorous, positive, optimistic

Nose

- *Turned up nose*: trusting, easily led, spends freely

- *Wide nostrils*: independent, acquisitive

- *Narrow nostrils*: hesitant, lacking in confidence

Mouth

- *Long philtrum* (channel running from nose to top of the lip): intelligent, unusual sense of humor

- *Short philtrum*: sensitive, unsure of him or herself, easily hurt

- *Thick top lip*: imaginative, enjoys talking

- *Thin top lip*: direct, to the point, competent

- *Thick lower lip*: generous, giving nature

- *Thin lower lip*: careful with money, but gives to causes he or she believes in

- *Deep lines from nostrils to side of mouth*: deep thinker, philosophical, enjoys time on own

Chin

- *Pointed chin*: hard to move once mind is made up, stubborn, strong will

- *Square chin*: expresses what he or she believes in, strong sense of justice and fair play

- *Protruding chin*: persistent, obstinate, doesn't give in

- *Receding chin*: avoids confrontation

Into the Future

In face reading, predictions are made based on the characteristics that can be seen on the face. Consequently, someone with a good wealth palace is likely to do well financially. However, he or she must be motivated to seize opportunities and to work hard. Otherwise, despite having a good wealth palace this person is likely to struggle financially. The same thing applies with other indications shown on the person's face.

In addition to this, every year from birth up to ninety-nine is indicated in a particular part of the person's face. If the skin is smooth and healthy-looking in the area of the face that relates to the year the person is in, he or she will enjoy a pleasant, happy, successful year. Any blemishes, such as moles, indentations, or lines, show that the person will have a challenging, difficult, or stressful year.

Following the concept of yin and yang, the positions of the ages are different for men and women, except for the ages running down the center of the face.

Suggested Reading

Lin, Henry B. *What Your Face Reveals: Chinese Secrets of Face Reading*. St. Paul, MN: Llewellyn Publications, 1999.

Webster, Richard. *Face Reading Quick and Easy*. Woodbury, MN: Llewellyn Publications, 2012.

Flower Divination

Floromancy, the art of divining with flowers, was popular in ancient Greece, and many people still practice it today. Flowers are particularly sensitive to the environment they're in. This was demonstrated by an Indian physicist and physiologist named Sir Jagadish Chandra Bose who proved that plants have feelings. Luther Burbank, the American botanist, proved that plants have a central nervous system and respond to kind words and love. In 1972, Dr. V. Pushkin, a Russian scientist, demonstrated that plants have emotions and respond to kind and harsh words.

Most children have blown the seeds off a dandelion while saying, "She loves me, she loves me not." This is a form of floromancy.

In the Far East, it's not uncommon for three carnations on a single stem to be placed in the hair of a young teenager. They're observed until the flowers start wilting. If the uppermost flower dies first, it's a sign that the teenager's later years will be the most difficult. The middle years will be the most difficult if the middle flower wilts first, and the early years will be the most difficult if the bottom flower dies first. It's a sign that the person will enjoy a successful and happy life if the flowers take a long time to die.

The First Flower of Spring

This is an old method to determine what sort of year you're going to have. All you need do is note the day of the week in which you saw the first flower of spring:

- *Sunday*: a year of unexpected pleasures and delights, good fortune
- *Monday*: good luck will follow all year long
- *Tuesday*: a successful year, but you will need to work to achieve it
- *Wednesday*: you, or someone close to you, will get married

- *Thursday*: an enjoyable year, with a slight financial increase

- *Friday*: all the effort you put in pays off handsomely

- *Saturday*: good luck passes you by

How to Do It

Flower reading can be done in a number of different ways. You can ask the person seeking a divination to choose a flower from an assortment of different types and colors of flowers. You can also perform it with a selection of colored photographs of flowers. You can even do it with a pad of paper and colored pencils. Ask the person to draw a flower in as much detail as they can, and interpret that.

Flower reading is based on several aspects of the flower: the theme, shape, color, number of petals, aroma, and stalk.

Theme

The theme is not always apparent, but it can provide valuable information about what the person is thinking about. What would someone be likely thinking about if they selected a red rose? The chances are this person is thinking about love, not his or her mortgage.

Cleansing is the theme of the primrose family. People who choose primrose are reevaluating their lives and looking for a future that's more positive than the past.

Communication and *courage* are the themes of the snapdragon family. People who choose these are good at keeping secrets, and they tend to keep their thoughts to themselves. They find it hard to speak openly.

Confidence, self-esteem, and *security* are the themes of the bluebell family. People who choose these get on well with others.

Energy is the theme of the mint family. People who choose mint are suffering from mental or physical exhaustion. This flower provides them with much needed energy.

Grace and *potential* are the themes of the orchid family. People who choose orchids are looking for love and understanding.

Healing is the theme of the parsley family. People who choose parsley are seeking healing, usually emotional healing.

Hope and *anticipation* are the themes of snowdrops and daffodils. They symbolize new life as they are the first plants to appear in spring. People who choose these are looking forward with great anticipation.

Innocence is the theme of the daisy family. People who choose daisies are searching for patience and inner strength to help them deal with difficult situations. They seek serenity.

Inspiration is the theme of the iris family. Irises promote motivation and inspiration that can be used to produce practical and worthwhile results.

Love is the theme of the rose family. A red rose signifies passion, and a white rose indicates a platonic or idealistic form of love. It also relates to clarity.

Peace and *purity* are the themes of the lily family. People who choose lilies are seeking positive feminine qualities, such as nurturing and comfort. They enjoy caring for others.

Purification is the theme of the eucalyptus family. People who choose eucalyptus want to let go of the past and make a new start.

Sensitivity is the theme of the violet family. People who need protection and psychic healing often choose violets. Violets help them stand up for themselves.

Sexual problems are the theme of the arum family. People who choose arum are experiencing sexual difficulties and are searching for help. They usually need to make changes in this area of their lives.

Stress is the theme of the valerian family. People who choose valerian are undergoing stress and need to make changes in their lives to reduce this. Valerian can help them recognize and work on the underlying reasons behind the stress.

Wisdom is the theme of the jasmine family. People who choose jasmine are searching for knowledge and spiritual growth.

Shape

The shape of the flower reveals the person's emotional state. There are twelve possibilities: bell, cup, jester's hat, trumpet, flame, star, sun, drooping spray, spike, parasol, fountain, and other.

Bell: Bell-shaped flowers, such as fuchsias and bluebells, point downward, indicating the person who chose it finds it hard to express his or her innermost feelings, and needs grounding. It helps them release blockages that have been holding them back and gives them the necessary confidence and self-esteem to enable them start afresh.

Cup: Cup-shaped flowers point upward, indicating the nurturing and caring potential of the people who choose them. This flower helps them realize their true value and worth.

Jester's Hat: The jester's hat is a crescent-shaped flower, such as the nasturtium and tiger lily. People who choose these suppress their emotions and find it hard to express what they really feel.

Trumpet: People who choose trumpet-shaped flowers, such as daffodils and morning glory, want to express themselves in some way, ideally creatively. They also need to learn how to express their true feelings and emotions.

Flame: Flame-shaped flowers, such as mullein and red-hot pokers, provide enthusiasm and energy, but also indicate something needs to be eliminated (burned) or discarded to enable these people to progress.

Star: Star-shaped flowers, such as borage, iris, and St. John's wort, have five or six petals that radiate outward. People who choose these are seeking spiritual growth. They are likely to be sensitive and fearful of the future.

Sun: Flowers that have radiating petals, such as chrysanthemums, daisies, marigolds, sunflowers, and zinnias, look like the sun. People who choose these need to take life less seriously and make good use of their natural confidence and skill at expressing themselves. They may need to express themselves more openly.

Drooping Sprays: Drooping sprays are created by rows of flowers growing along an arching branch. Examples include scotch broom, willow, and wisteria. People who choose these feel overwhelmed with cares and responsibilities. These flowers help them to relax and let go of some of their worries.

Spike: Spike-like flowers are similar to drooping sprays but point up to the sky rather than drooping downward. Examples include aloe, lavender, and sage. People who choose these flowers are self-critical and always feel they could be better than they are. These flowers give them strength.

Parasol: Parasol flowers, such as angelica, feverfew, garlic, and yarrow, are created when a number of stalks spread from a common center. People who choose these are trusting, intuitive, and easily hurt. They need to look after themselves instead of always focusing on the needs of others.

Fountain: Fountain flowers have petals that radiate out from the center in a series of layers. Examples include camellias, hibiscus, peonies, and zinnias. People who choose these are friendly, curious, open-minded, and sometimes shy.

Every so often you'll find flowers that don't fit into the above categories. Columbine and honeysuckle are two examples. People who choose these flowers are searching for emotional freedom and spiritual growth.

Color

People are often attracted to a particular flower because of its color. Their color choices can be interpreted and reveal the qualities the person needs at the time. Many flowers contain more than one color. The main color reveals the person's natural abilities. A different color in the center reveals the person's inner nature. The color of the pistils reveals the person's energy levels. Any additional colors add their influence on the overall picture.

Red is a passionate and enthusiastic color. People who choose this color are independent, energetic people who love life. They are seeking motivation and persistence. Red also relates to the physical aspects of love.

Pink is a cheerful, positive, nurturing, loving color. It relates to innocence, femininity, and positive thoughts about the future. It is also calming and encouraging. People who choose pink want to love and accept themselves.

Orange and *gold* are exciting, stimulating, and happy colors. They symbolize warmth, universal love, tolerance, and prosperity. People who choose these colors are wanting to harmonize and interact well with others.

Yellow is carefree, lighthearted, and full of fun. It relates to creative and verbal communication. People who choose yellow are seeking these qualities.

Green is soothing, peaceful, restful, and nurturing. It is the color of nature and relates to renewal, anticipation, growth, and hope for the future. Green restores the mind, body, and spirit. It symbolizes stability, peace, and healing. People who choose green flowers seek understanding, contentment, and emotional stability.

Blue calms the mind, body, and spirit. It symbolizes honesty, sincerity, self-expression, dependability, and stability. People who choose blue desire these qualities and also want to develop more faith in themselves.

Indigo is peaceful, dignified, idealistic, caring, and considerate. It relates to idealism, wisdom, spirituality, and inner peace. People who choose indigo are searching for inner peace and a spiritual path.

Violet has always been associated with spirituality. Consequently, many people who choose violet will be going through a stage of transformation. They may also be suffering from stress, as violet soothes the mind and emotions. Violet symbolizes inspiration, intuition, transformation, spirituality, and the sacred.

White relates to innocence, purity, forgiveness, trust, and hope. Its purity clears the mind and enables the person to let go of the past and think about the limitless possibilities ahead. People who choose white are, like those who choose violet, undergoing transformation in their lives.

Black is an unusual color for a flower. It relates to sophistication, mystery, and power. People who choose black often have something to hide and are seeking forgiveness.

Number of Petals

The number of petals provide clues about the person's motivation and drive.

One: This is a circle that totally surrounds the flower. People who choose this are honest, loyal, sincere, dependable, ambitious, and determined. They prefer the overall picture and overlook the details.

Two: People who choose flowers with two petals are sympathetic, loving, sensitive, intuitive, caring, tactful, and friendly.

Three: People who choose flowers with three petals are positive, creative, outgoing, and friendly people who make the most of every opportunity. They enjoy experiencing everything life has to offer.

Four: People who choose flowers with four petals are responsible, practical, reliable, controlled, and determined. They enjoy using their particular skills to help others. They prefer a fixed routine and dislike change.

Five: People who choose flowers with five petals seek change, variety, stimulation, travel, wide-open spaces, and freedom. They dislike feeling hemmed in or restricted in any way.

Six: People who choose flowers with six petals are responsible, caring, sympathetic, and idealistic. They enjoy serving and helping family and friends.

Seven: People who choose flowers with seven petals are serious, analytical, idealistic, and spiritual. They enjoy learning and discovering hidden truths.

Eight: People who choose flowers with eight petals are ambitious, reliable, energetic, confident goal-setters. They aim high and are prepared to work hard to achieve their goals.

Nine: People who choose flowers with nine petals are idealistic, romantic, sensitive, creative, and easily hurt. They are natural humanitarians and often choose careers involving helping others.

Ten: People who choose flowers with ten petals are ambitious, focused, persistent, and independent. They're frequently loners and need little input from others to achieve their goals.

More than Ten Petals: People who choose flowers with more than ten petals are charismatic, entertaining, capable, and intelligent. They give and receive universal love.

Aroma

The strength of a flower's perfume provides additional clues. Not surprisingly, a delicate fragrance is more gentle than a stronger, strident, overpowering perfume. People who choose flowers with a strong scent tend to be impatient, hasty, brash, and want instant results.

People who choose flowers with a more delicate scent tend to be gentle, patient, and kind. They're prepared to wait for what they want.

If the flower has no discernible scent, this section is ignored. Naturally, this also happens when you're doing a reading using photographs or drawings.

Stalk

Occasionally, people will hand you a flower without a stalk. Fortunately, this is rare, and most of the time at least part of the stalk will be present. This can be interpreted.

The *bottom third* of the stalk relates to the past and indicates how the flower was removed from the plant. If the flower was cut off the plant, it's a sign that the person's childhood was smooth and happy. However, the opposite applies if the stalk was roughly torn from the plant.

The *middle third* relates to the present. Any knots or other imperfections indicate current problems.

The *top third*, which is closest to the flower, indicates the future. Ideally, this should be as smooth as possible. However, as life always contains its share of ups and downs, sadly, this is rare.

Flower reading is a popular, and highly commercial, form of divination. Because of this, I've always been surprised that so few people practice it.

Numerology of Flowers

The name of the particular flower that someone chooses can be interpreted using basic numerology. (You will need to read the section on numerology, or know something about it, to understand this section.) Here is the number/letter chart that is used to determine the numbers associated with different flowers.

1	2	3	4	5	6	7	8	9
A	B	C	D	E	F	G	H	I
J	K	L	M	N	O	P	Q	R
S	T	U	V	W	X	Y	Z	

Let's look at a couple of examples. Here are the numbers associated with the daffodil:

$4 + 1 + 6 + 6 + 6 + 4 + 9 + 3 = 39$

$3 + 9 = 12$ and $1 + 2 = 3$

According to numerology, the daffodil has an Expression number of 3. Three is the number of joy, fun, laughter, and all the joys of life.

The daffodil also has a Soul Urge number of 7 (from the A, O, and I in the name). This relates to wisdom, analysis, and spirituality.

Consequently, daffodils bring fun and joy into our lives. As well as this, they bring a more serious spiritual element with a desire to grow in knowledge and wisdom.

Here is another example with violet:

$4 + 9 + 6 + 3 + 5 + 2 = 29$

$2 + 9 = 11$

Eleven is a Master Number in numerology and doesn't get reduced down to a 2. Eleven relates to illumination, inspiration, and intuition.

Violet also has a 2 Soul Urge (from the I, O, and E). This relates to friendliness, gentleness, consideration, diplomacy, and adaptability.

Suggested Reading

Telesco, Patricia. *The Victorian Flower Oracle*. St. Paul, MN: Llewellyn Publications, 1995.

Webster, Richard. *Flower and Tree Magic: Discover the Natural Enchantment Around You*. Woodbury, MN: Llewellyn Publications, 2008.

Geomancy

The word *geomancy* comes from the Greek word *geomanteia*. *Geo* means "earth" and *manteia* (-mancy) relates to divination. Therefore, geomancy is the art of divination from the earth. Geomancy is one of the oldest forms of divination, and its origins are a mystery. As is usually the case, there are a number of stories about its origin. The Arabs, for instance, claim that Jibril (Archangel Gabriel) taught geomancy to their prophet, Idris, after he had a dream in which the angel drew a geomantic figure.

Another story says that Idris was drawing figures in the sand and a stranger asked him what he was doing. Idris said he was simply amusing himself. The stranger told Idris that he was actually doing something extremely useful and explained the meanings of the figures Idris had drawn. The stranger asked him to make more figures until he'd drawn all sixteen of the geomantic figures. The stranger taught Idris everything there was to know about geomancy. Before he disappeared, he confided in Idris that he was the angel Jibril.

Historic records show that the ancient Chaldeans practiced geomancy three thousand years ago. [16] In the sixteenth century, geomancy was one of the most popular forms of divination in Europe and the Arab world.

Sixteen Figures

Geomancy uses sixteen figures, each of which has a wide range of associations and meanings. The figures are created by making four rows of small marks on the ground, or on a sheet of paper. The marks are made from the right to the left. As each row needs a random number of marks, the diviner thinks of his or her question while making the marks as quickly as possible, paying as little attention as he or she can to the process.

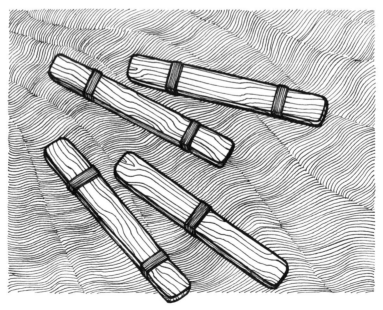

Rune sticks.

16   Gleason 1973.

Once the geomancer has made four rows of marks, the number of marks in each row is counted. An odd number of marks creates a single dot, and an even number creates two dots. Here's an example:

$$\bigcirc \ \bigcirc \ \dots\dots\dots\dots \quad \text{(20 marks)}$$
$$\bigcirc \ \dots\dots\dots\dots \quad \text{(17 marks)}$$
$$\bigcirc \ \bigcirc \ \dots\dots\dots\dots \quad \text{(18 marks)}$$
$$\bigcirc \ \bigcirc \ \dots\dots\dots\dots\text{(22 marks)}$$

A number of methods have been devised to create the figures. In the British Museum in London, I saw a thirteenth-century Islamic divination device that randomly creates figures. During the Renaissance, four geomantic dice were often used. Each die had either one or two marks on each face.

Rune sticks are a quick and convenient way to create the figures. There are four oblong rune sticks in a set. They are usually about three to six inches long and one-half to three-quarters of an inch wide. The sticks contain a single line or a circle on one side and two lines or two circles on the other.

If you use rune sticks you'll also need a casting cloth about eighteen inches square. Mine is made of dark blue velvet. The sticks are held loosely in one hand and mixed while thinking about the question you want answered. Toss the sticks gently as you move your hand from the front of the casting cloth to the back. This tossing is basically a spreading out of the sticks. As soon as they've been cast, cover them with the hand you tossed them with and smooth them out. The casting and smoothing are almost a single movement. Once you've done this, raise your hand to reveal the geomantic figure.

Israel Regardie (1907–1985), the American author and occultist, used a bowl full of pebbles.[17] A handful were grabbed and counted to see if they created an odd or even number. This was done four times to create the figure.

Another method is to toss a die. If an odd number appears face up, one mark is made. Two marks are made if an even number appears face up.

You can even toss a coin. Heads could indicate even, and tails odd. If you used four coins you could create the figure with one toss. In this case, you should gently toss them and immediately cover them with your hand, exactly as you'd do with rune sticks. Arrange them in position with your hand before raising it to reveal the figure.

You can even use the traditional method of making marks in sand or earth. You'll need a shallow box about two feet square. Fill it with sand or dry earth. Use a length of dowel or a pencil to make the rows of dots in the sand or earth. The marks are made from right to left.

---

17   Regardie 1972.

Do not let other people handle your geomantic materials. In geomancy, you must cast the figures yourself, even when reading for someone else.

Sixteen Characters

Via

Via is often a sign that the person has worked out where he or she is going and is moving forward. It usually is a sign that the person is progressing or moving forward, but it can sometimes indicate someone who is still searching for a way to progress. It can sometimes indicate loneliness. This is a highly positive figure if the person wants change. However, it can be mildly negative if the person wants to stay where he or she is. This is also a sign of good people skills and shows the person will use his or her empathy, understanding, and tact to progress.

Caput Draconis, the dragon's head

Caput Draconis is a positive figure that indicates innocence, birth, new starts, and unlimited potential. Interestingly, it becomes more positive when surrounded by other positive figures and less positive when surrounded by negative figures. It often indicates an improvement in the person's circumstances, usually after a difficult start. Caput Draconis also indicates shrewdness and awareness. Even though this person will be willing to help others, he or she will make sure that all his or her personal needs are met at the same time.

Puella, the girl

Puella relates to the traditional female qualities of healing, nurturing, intuition, and wisdom. It enhances all relationships with women and is highly positive for home and family life. For a man, Puella relates to his relationship with his wife and daughters. For a woman, it relates to harmonious relationships with the other women in her family, such as her mother, mother-in-law, and daughters. Puella also indicates happiness in the immediate future.

Fortuna Major, major fortune

Fortuna Major is an extremely positive figure that relates to good luck, success, and security. It's a sign that the good things the person has done in the past will enable him or her to enjoy peace of mind, happiness, and success in the future. It shows that the person possesses enough inner strength to overcome any problem he or she might face in the future. Fortuna Major also relates to possessions and shows that the person will always be generous and have a giving nature.

Puer, the boy

Puer relates to enthusiasm, courage, leadership, responsibility, initiative, and physical activity. Puer is a mixed figure: it is largely positive though it can also be negative. This is because it also relates to recklessness and impulsiveness. The main lesson of Puer is to think before acting.

Acquisito, gain

Acquisitio is a positive figure that indicates the acquisition of possessions and money. It's a sign of worldly success and shows that all the problems and difficulties from the past have been overcome. The person has learned from his or her mistakes and is moving forward again. This person will enjoy the fruits of his or her success.

Carcer, prison

Carcer relates to limitations, restrictions, and confinement. It indicates problems, worries, and indecision. Carcer is a learning experience and shows that the person needs to work hard and wait patiently for conditions to improve. Any negative emotions at this time will only add to the person's existing problems. Carcer can be a positive figure if the question relates to stability, protection, and security.

Tristitia, the sadness

Tristitia is a sign of grief, melancholy, and the possibility of a loss. This is likely to occur without warning, and the person will have to deal with destruction or loss of something that he or she has spent a great deal of time and effort building up. The person will need to learn from the experience, and focus on being kind, charitable, and forgiving.

Cauda Draconis, the dragon's tail

Cauda Draconis is a negative figure that relates to bad luck, disruption, sudden loss, ill fortune, and other calamities. It shows that the person must be prepared to leave the past behind and start all over again. As a result, there'll be a great deal of bitterness and hurt, and the person must learn to let go of these and learn from what has happened. Although Cauda Draconis is a negative figure, it can be positive for anything that is nearing its natural end.

Conjunctio, the union

Conjunctio is an extremely fortunate figure that indicates a joining or partnership. This includes all types of relationships, including friendship, love, and business. It also includes reunions, such as a school reunion. Conjunctio is also a sign of caution. The person should think everything through before moving ahead. Conjunctio is positive for all matters involving dealing with others, but it is mildly negative for solitary activities.

Amissio, the loss

Amissio is a negative figure as it relates to loss. The loss is usually money, but it can be anything, such as the loss of a job or love. Amissio indicates a negative outcome to whatever the person is pursuing. Consequently, the person needs to be absolutely sure that what he or she is doing is in the best interests of everyone concerned. Interestingly, Amissio can also be positive if the desired result is a loss. Someone who was trying to lose weight, for instance, would be delighted to have Amissio as the outcome.

Albus, the white

Albus signifies understanding, harmony, clear thinking, and consideration of others. It's a moderately fortunate figure that shows that the person is successfully balancing the spiritual, mental, and physical areas of life. It's a positive sign for business and career. It indicates slow but steady progress.

Fortuna Minor, minor fortune

Fortuna Minor is a sign of success after a great deal of hard work. The person will feel protected and be willing to learn from everything he or she experiences on the road to success. As Fortuna Minor indicates ultimate success, it will take time for this to happen, and it's often achieved with the help of someone else.

Rubeus, the red

Rubeus is a sign of anger, passion, temper, violence, and danger. It's usually unfavorable, which invariably leaves unhappiness and upheaval in its wake. The person needs to think carefully before starting to move forward again. It's highly likely that the problems were self-inflicted, and the person needs to listen to his or her quiet inner voice before deciding where to go from here.

Laetitia, the joy

Laetitia is the most fortunate figure of all and is a sign of happiness, good fortune, and peace of mind. It also relates to creativity, good health, and further happiness in the future. The person has learned major life lessons and is willing to impart his or her knowledge to others. It shows that he or she has successfully balanced the spiritual and material sides of his or her nature and is continuing to progress in all areas of life.

Populus, the people

Populus represents family, friends, and other groups of people. It's a neutral figure that can be used positively and negatively. If good, honest, and positive thoughts are expressed, the results will be excellent. Negative thoughts will produce the opposite. Populus is a sign that the person will need to learn from experience, and the future depends entirely on the approach he or she adopts.

Simple Questions

You can create a single geomantic figure to answer simple questions. Mentally ask the question as you create the figure.

The outcome will be positive if you create Laetitia, Fortuna Major, Fortuna Minor, or Acquisitio. Conversely, the answer will be negative if you create Amissio, Cauda Draconis, Tristitia, or Carcer. The other figures need to be analyzed carefully to see how they relate to your question.

Rubeus, for instance, might indicate a need to keep your emotions in check to ensure a positive outcome.

Creating a single figure is a quick and easy way to answer a question. It's also a good way to practice and learn what each figure means. However, it's usually better to create a chart, as this enables you to obtain more information than you can from a single figure.

The Geomantic Family

When a question is asked, a chart is created using four Mothers, four Daughters, four Nieces, two Witnesses, and a Judge. The four Mothers are created using one of the methods discussed earlier, and the other figures are derived from them.

The first Mother to be cast is placed on the right, and the other three Mothers are placed in order to her left. Here's an example:

Let's assume the question is, "Should I go into business with Jason?"

The first figure to be cast is Tristitia, followed by Carcer, Via, and Caput Draconis:

The Daughters are made from the Mothers. The first Daughter is made from the top lines of the four Mothers. The second Daughter is created from the second line of the four Mothers. The third and fourth Daughters are created from the third and fourth lines of the Mothers. It can be useful to look at each mother as having a head, neck, body, and feet:

O O Head

O Neck

O O Body

O O Feet

Looking at it this way, the first Daughter is created from the heads of the four Mothers, the second Daughter from the necks, the third Daughter from the bodies, and the fourth Daughter from the feet.

In the example above the four Daughters are Conjunctio, Fortuna Major, Fortuna Major, and Via:

Fourth Daughter	Third Daughter	Second Daughter	First Daughter
O	O O	O O	O O
O	O O	O O	O
O	O	O	O
O	O	O	O O

The next step is to create the four Nieces. The first Niece is created from the first and second Mothers:

First Mother	Second Mother		First Niece
O O	+ O	= (odd)	O
O O	+ O O	= (even)	O O
O O	+ O O	= (even)	O O
O	+ O	= (even)	O O

The second Niece is created from the third and fourth Mothers:

Third Mother	Fourth Mother		Second Niece
O	+ O O	= (odd)	O
O	+ O	= (even)	O O
O	+ O	= (even)	O O
O	+ O	= (even)	O O

The third Niece is created from the first and second Daughters (in the example above, numbers five and six):

First Daughter	Second Daughter		Third Niece
O O	+ O O	= (even)	O O
O	+ O O	= (odd)	O
O	+ O	= (even)	O O
O O	+ O	= (odd)	O

The fourth Niece is created from the third and fourth Mothers:

Third Mother	Fourth Mother		Fourth Niece
O O	+ O	= (odd)	O
O O	+ O	= (odd)	O
O	+ O	= (even)	O O
O	+ O	= (even)	O O

The next stage is to create the two Witnesses. They are created in exactly the same way. The Right Witness (draw the Witness on the right-hand side of your worksheet) is created from the first and second Nieces:

First Niece	Second Niece		Right Witness
O	+ O	= (even)	O O
O O	+ O O	= (even)	O O
O O	+ O O	= (even)	O O
O O	+ O O	= (even)	O O

The Left Witness is created from the third and fourth Nieces:

Third Niece	Fourth Niece		Left Witness
O O	+ O	= (odd)	O
O	+ O	= (even)	O O
O O	+ O O	= (even)	O O
O	+ O O	= (odd)	O

The final figure to be created is the Judge. He is created from the two Witnesses:

Right Witness	Left Witness		Judge
O O	+ O	= (odd)	O
O O	+ O O	= (even)	O O
O O	+ O O	= (even)	O O
O O	+ O	= (odd)	O

The Judge provides the answer to the question. In this example, the question was, "Should I go into business with Jason?" The Judge is Carcer, which means limitations, restrictions, obligations, worries, and other potential problems. It looks as if you should turn down the offer, no matter how tempting it may seem. However, Carcer can be favorable if the question relates to stability and security.

Because of this, you may not feel the question is fully answered by Carcer, and you'll want more information to clarify the situation. The two Witnesses can provide that. The Right Witness represents the person asking the question and also his or her past. The Judge represents the present, and the Left Witness indicates the future. If the Judge is a negative figure created from two negative figures, the outcome will be worse than that indicated by the Judge alone. If one of the Witnesses is positive, and the other negative, the outcome will be mixed. In our example, one Witness is neutral (Populus) and the other negative (Carcer). It's possible that the proposed partnership could work, but there'd be numerous problems along the way.

Occasionally, even more information is necessary to answer the question. When this occurs, another figure called the Reconciler is created by combining the first Mother and the Judge. In our example this creates Laetitia:

First Mother		Judge		Reconciler
O O	+	O	= (odd)	O
O O	+	O O	= (even)	O O
O O	+	O O	= (even)	O O
O	+	O	= (even)	O O

This is highly positive and indicates happiness, good fortune, and contentment. It looks as if the outcome would be good long term, and you'd have to decide whether or not the numerous difficulties you'd experience on the way to success would be too high a price to pay.

Astrological Geomancy

Much more information can be obtained by placing the Mothers, Daughters, and Nieces into the twelve houses of a horoscope chart. The first Mother goes in the first house, and the other figures are placed in order in the other eleven houses. The planets and signs are also added to the chart, enabling the geomancer to examine any question in great depth. Over the years, a number of systems have been devised to create geomancy charts. Gerard of Cremona and Cornelius Agrippa are two notable examples. New systems, such as the one created by Les P. Cross in the United Kingdom, are ensuring that geomancy is still useful and relevant today.

Suggested Reading

Cross, Les P. *Astrogem Geomancy Divination*. Bristol, UK: Les P. Cross, 2012.

Regardie, Israel. *Practical Guide to Geomantic Divination*. London: Aquarian Press, 1972.

Webster, Richard. *Geomancy for Beginners*. Woodbury, MN: Llewellyn Publications, 2011.

Herb Divination

Botanomancy is the technical name for divination with plants and herbs. It's derived from the Greek word *botane*, which means "herb."

My first experience of herb divination occurred when I was nineteen years old. I was at a party in a country home that had a garden that ran down to a river. The garden was beautifully cared for, and at some stage during the afternoon, Jessica, the daughter of the owners, took a group of us on a tour of the garden. I was captivated by the large herb garden.

"It's not all for eating," she told us. "We use herbs for all sorts of things." Without saying any more she gathered some parsley, sage, rosemary, and thyme. I remember the actual herbs well, as the party was held about the time that Marianne Faithful's version of "Scarborough Fair" was released. This was approximately six months before the Simon and Garfunkel version appeared. We went into the kitchen and she chopped the herbs into tiny pieces. She gave several of us a handful of the chopped herbs to hold.

One at a time, we scattered the herbs onto large sheets of paper. "Spread them out a little more," Jessica told us.

Once we'd done that, she looked at each sheet of paper in turn and gave us a reading based on what she "saw." We were all amazed, as none of us had any idea what she was going to do. My reading was all about travel, which wasn't surprising, as I was making plans to travel overseas the following year. I thought about the accuracy of her divination every now and again, but I gave little thought to how she had performed the divination until many years later.

Parsley, sage, rosemary, and thyme are considered divinatory herbs, which is probably why they were the ones Jessica used. However, any herbs, fresh or dried, can be used. Parsley is included, as in medieval times it was eaten to aid digestion and to remove the bitter taste of some meals. Sage symbolizes strength. Rosemary signifies faithfulness, remembrance, and feminine love. Thyme symbolizes courage. No wonder they make a good combination.

Jessica is the only person I've met who had people scatter and spread the herbs. It's more usual for the person being read for to drop the herbs in the center of a sheet of fairly coarse paper. After this, either the diviner or the person being read holds each end of the sheet of paper and gently shakes it. This causes the herbs to move around the sheet of paper, creating a pattern as they do so.

The diviner studies the pattern of herbs and looks for symbols and pictures in it. If this person fails to see anything in the herbs, he or she turns away for thirty seconds and then looks at the herbs again.

This process can be repeated several times in the same divination. The same question can be asked each time, or other questions relating to the same concern can be asked instead.

Daisy Divination

This ancient form of divination is usually considered to be nothing more than a game for young children. Most children have picked a daisy and plucked petals from it while saying, "S/he loves me, s/he loves me not" until one petal remains to provide the answer.

Yes or no questions can also be answered this way. After the question has been asked, petals are removed one at a time while saying yes and no until just one petal is left.

Another version of this can be done with an apple that retains its stalk. Think of a question and twist the stalk. Each time you twist it, say yes or no until the stalk comes off. The word you're saying as the stalk separates from the apple provides the answer.

Dandelion

Another children's game is to take a dandelion that's gone to seed and blow on it while silently asking a question. If all the seeds scatter in one blow, the answer is positive. If a small number of seeds remain, the wish will be positive, but will take time to happen. If the bulk of the seeds remain, the answer is negative.

The version I played as a child was to blow the seeds off, and count each blow until all the seeds were gone. This indicated the number of days, weeks, months, or years that would pass before a certain event happened. I don't know how old I was when I first did this, but remember one occasion when I asked how many years would pass before I kissed a girl.

Apple Divination

Start by peeling an apple so that all the peel comes off in one long strip. Think of your question and toss the strip over your left shoulder. If the peel forms either an O or U, the answer is no. If it forms any other shape, the answer is a resounding yes.

If the peel breaks during the paring, you can eat the apple, but the divination needs to wait for another day.

What Will the Next Twelve Months Be Like?

This is a folk tradition that has spread around the world. You can use it to learn what sort of year you're going to have by noting the day on which you see the first flower of spring.

- *Sunday*: a year of unexpected delights and good fortune.

- *Monday*: you'll enjoy good luck all year.

- *Tuesday*: as long as you apply yourself, you'll have a productive year.

- *Wednesday*: you, or someone close to you, will get married.

- *Thursday*: you'll enjoy a happy year, but with only a modest financial success.

- *Friday*: your hard work and effort will pay off handsomely.

- *Saturday*: good luck will pass you by this year.

Twin Roses

This is a useful way of choosing between two options. Buy two identical rosebuds and place them in long-stemmed glasses somewhere warm, but not too sunny. Both rosebuds should be completely closed. Write down the two possibilities you have to decide between and place one under each vase. The first rose to bloom indicates the choice you should make.

It's possible for the two roses to bloom at exactly the same time. When this happens, you need to see which flower fades more slowly. This indicates the correct choice.

The person who showed me this method of divination used rosebuds, and for a while I thought this was the only way this divination could be performed. However, you can do it with a variety of other herbs and vegetables. The humble onion is a good example. Two onions are planted in identical pots and placed side by side. One indicates a yes response, and the other a no. The first onion to sprout provides the answer. This is an example of cromniomancy, divination with onions.

Cromniomancy

Another version of cromniomancy was popular many years ago when family members traveled far away, and the people who stayed behind had no way of learning how they were. A number of onions were planted, one for every person who was away from home. As soon as they started sprouting, they were observed closely. If they sprouted quickly, it was a sign that the person indicated by that particular onion was happy and in good health.

Even today, people sometimes carve the names of potential suitors onto onions and then wait to see which one sprouts first.

An interesting divination using an onion predicts the weather for the next twelve months. Twelve large, round slices are cut from an onion, and arranged in a row on a wooden tray. A single grain of salt is placed in the middle of each one. The amount of water that appears in each slice indicates the amount of rain or snow that can be expected over the following twelve months.

Herb Pillow

Herb pillows are usually used to help people sleep. However, with a different selection of herbs, they can be useful to encourage prophetic dreams. Fortunately, they're easy to make.

Required

A muslin bag. This bag can vary in size from about six inches square to eighteen or twenty inches square. It can be any shape you wish.

A selection of five or six dried herbs, such as: ash leaves, bay laurel, bay leaves, chamomile, cinnamon, elder, eyebright, hazel, lavender, marigold, mugwort, nutmeg, oak, rose, thyme, wormwood, and yarrow. Experiment until you have a combination that has a fragrance that appeals to you.

Dried orange and lemon peel.

A few ounces of myrrh or frankincense resin. The quantity should be about the same as is used with one of the herbs.

How to Do It

Tear the peel into small pieces, and mix the ingredients in a bowl. Pour them into your muslin bag, sew the top of the bag closed, and place the finished herb pillow into a pillowslip.

When you go to bed, take several slow deep breaths, tell yourself that you're going to enjoy a divinatory dream that will provide insight into whatever matter you're concerned about, and drift off to sleep.

You don't need to sleep with your herb pillow every night, but use it whenever you wish to have a dream about the future.

Suggested Reading

Webster, Richard. *Flower and Tree Magic: Discover the Natural Enchantment Around You.*
Woodbury, MN: Llewellyn Publications, 2008.

I Ching

The I Ching, sometimes known as the Book of Changes, is one of the oldest of all divination systems. It originated thousands of years ago as a Chinese philosophical text called *The Book of Changes*, and it still plays a major role in Chinese folk culture today. The I Ching is by far the best-known Chinese book of divination in the West, and more than thirty different translations are currently available.

Because a number is generated randomly to create the reading, the I Ching has similarities with geomancy and rune stone readings. Historically, sacred yarrow plants were used to generate the number, but today it's more common to use three coins.

Yin and Yang

Yin and yang represent the two opposites that are present in everything. Yin cannot exist without yang, and likewise yang cannot exist without yin. Here are some examples:

- Night and Day
- Hard and Soft
- Hot and Cold
- Wet and Dry
- Male and Female
- Tall and Short
- Start and Finish
- Yin and Yang

Yang corresponds to:

- Male
- Positive
- Fire
- Intense
- Active
- Sun
- Red
- South
- Odd numbers

Yin corresponds to:

- Female
- Negative
- Water
- Gentle
- Passive
- Moon
- Black
- North
- Even numbers

The Trigrams

The trigrams are created from broken and unbroken lines. The broken lines represent yin (female) energy, and the unbroken lines yang (male) energy. Because the lines can be looked at as male or female, it's possible to create a family from the eight trigrams. Here they are, with their natural elements.

Father (Ch'ien—Metal—Creative)

Mother (K'un—Earth—Receptive)

Eldest Son (Chen—Wood—Arousing)

Middle Son (K'an—Water—Abysmal)

Youngest Son (Ken—Earth—Keeping still)

Eldest Daughter (Sun—Wood—Gentle)

Middle Daughter (Li—Fire—Clinging)

Youngest Daughter (Tui—Metal—Joyous)

The father and mother are opposite each other. The father has three unbroken yang lines, while the mother has three broken yin lines. The children are yin (female) or yang (male), and this is determined by the one line that is different to the other two in the trigram. Consequently, the sons all have one unbroken line in their trigrams, and the daughters all have one broken line. The trigrams are constructed from the bottom line to the top. Consequently, the eldest son has an unbroken line at the bottom of his trigram, the middle son has the unbroken trigram in the middle, and the youngest son has the unbroken line at the top. The daughters work in the same way, with the broken line at the bottom of the eldest daughter's trigram, the middle daughter has the broken line in the middle, and the youngest daughter has the broken line at the top.

As well as this, the youngest son and daughter defer to their older sibling of the same gender. The trigram representing the youngest son (unbroken line on top of two broken lines) is the opposite to that of the older son (two broken lines on top of a broken line). The oldest daughter has two unbroken lines on top of a broken line, and the youngest has one broken line on top of two unbroken lines.

Meanings of the Trigrams

Ch'ien (Heaven)
Family Relationship: Father
Element: Metal
Season: Autumn–Winter
Direction: Northwest
Attributes: Strength, creativity, light, yang
Nature: Vigor

K'Un (Earth)
Family Relationship: Mother
Element: Earth
Season: Summer–Autumn
Direction: Southwest
Attributes: Devotion, receptive, yielding, dark, yin
Nature: Submission

Chen (Thunder)
Family Relationship: Eldest son
Element: Wood
Season: Spring
Direction: East
Attributes: Stimulation, arousing, strong, excited
Nature: Movement

K'An (Water)

Family Relationship: Middle son

Element: Water

Season: Winter

Direction: North

Attributes: Dangerous, cunning, negative

Nature: Pausing

Ken (Mountain)

Family Relationship: Youngest son

Element: Water

Season: Winter–Spring

Direction: Northeast

Attributes: Stillness, quiet, stubborn, resting

Nature: Stopping

Sun (Wind/Wood)

Family Relationship: Eldest daughter

Element: Wood

Season: Spring–Summer

Direction: Southeast

Attributes: Gentle, yielding, penetrating

Nature: Thriving

Li (Fire/Sun/Lightning)

Family Relationship: Middle daughter

Element: Fire

Season: Summer

Direction: South

Attributes: Clinging, warm, nervous, light

Nature: Attachment

Tui (Lake)

Family Relationship: Youngest daughter

Element: Metal

Season: Autumn

Direction: West

Attributes: Joyful, laughing, gentle, happiness

Nature: Delight

How to Create a Hexagram

A hexagram consists of two trigrams, and has six lines. You can combine any two trigrams to create a hexagram. The six lines relate to the sequence of events indicated by the particular hexagram. There are sixty-four possible combinations of the eight trigrams, and each one of these has an interpretation that has been developed over thousands of years.

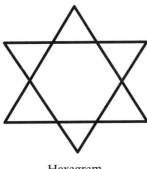

Hexagram.

The bottom, third, and fifth lines represent yang energy, and the second, fourth, and sixth lines from the bottom represent yin energy. It's highly auspicious when yin and yang are in their correct places, and the opposite when they aren't.

To complicate matters slightly, there are actually four trigrams in every hexagram. Lines one, two, and three from the bottom are one, and lines four, five, and six from the bottom are two. However, lines two, three, and four, and lines three, four, and five create two additional trigrams, making a total of four that can be interpreted.

There are several ways to construct a hexagram, and we'll look at the three most common methods—yarrow stalks, coins, and bibliomancy.

Yarrow Stalks

Required: 50 yarrow stalks or rods about 15 inches long. Yarrow stalks were probably chosen as the Chinese considered the yarrow plant to have magical properties. It was associated with fertility and longevity.

Start by saying a prayer and stating your question. Traditionally, incense would be lit after this, and then the yarrow stalks would be passed through the smoke. You should remain focused on your question while doing this.

One of the stalks is to put to one side, leaving 49. (If you wish, you can start with 55 yarrow stalks, and place six to one side, leaving 49.) These 49 stalks are randomly divided into two piles. One stalk is taken from one of these piles and placed to one side.

Using the same pile that you removed the single stalk from, remove four stalks at a time until there are four or less stalks remaining. This is repeated with the other pile. Four stalks at a time are removed until four or less stalks remain. These remaining stalks are placed to one side.

Pick up all the stalks that are in sets of four, and divide them randomly into two groups. Repeat steps four and five. Continue doing this until you have between six and nine groups of four stalks in front of you.

The number of groups remaining tells you whether the bottom line of your hexagram is yin or yang. If you have six groups of four yarrow stalks, you record a yin (broken) line on a sheet of paper. If you have seven groups, you record a yang (unbroken) line. Eight groups is yin, and nine groups is yang. You now have the bottom line of your hexagram.

Repeat this entire process to determine the other five lines in your hexagram.

Changing Lines

Numbers 6 and 9 are called changing lines, as they're transformed into their opposites. Originally 6 was yang, but is turned into yin. Likewise, 9 was originally yin, but is now yang.

This means that if you've produced a hexagram using exclusively 7 and 8, the hexagram you've produced will be the divination and answer your question.

If you've created a hexagram using just one 6 or 9, that line will answer your question.

If more than one line is a 6 or a 9, you create a second hexagram, changing these lines to their opposite. This means you have two hexagrams to determine the answer to your divination. This can be helpful, as the original hexagram determines the first stages of your question, and the second hexagram reveals later stages of your concern.

Here's an example of a hexagram in which the second and fourth lines from the bottom were created by a 6 or a 9:

Coins

Required: 3 coins. Many people use antique Chinese coins, as they look attractive and mysterious, but any coins can be used. The coins you use should be used solely for divination purposes.

- Wash the coins before asking your question. This removes any vibrations left by other people who've handled them. Hold the coins in your hands for about twenty minutes to allow them to absorb your vibrations.

- Pray, and silently ask your question while gently tossing the coins onto a mat or table. Check to see what you have tossed. Heads are given a value of 3, and tails have a value of 2. (If you're using Chinese coins, the side with four figures on it is considered "heads," or yang.)

- You can toss one of four possibilities:

- Three tails. Yin as 3 x 2 = 6

- Two tails and one head. Yang as 2 + 2 + 3 = 7

- Two heads and one tail. Yin as 3 + 3 + 2 = 8

- Three heads. Yang as 3 + 3 + 3 = 9

- Record your total as a broken or unbroken line. Make a note if you tossed three tails (6) or three heads (9), as these are changing lines. In other words, if you toss three tails, yin changes to yang, and with three heads yang changes to yin.

- Think of your question again while tossing your three coins.

- Record the result as your second line from the bottom of your hexagram.

- Continue doing this until you have created all six lines of your hexagram.

- If necessary, construct a second hexagram, changing any lines created by tossing three heads or three tails.

Bibliomancy

Required: A book containing commentaries on each of the 64 hexagrams.

- Hold the book in your hands for several minutes to allow it to become imbued with your energy.

- Hold the book upside down in your left hand with the spine making contact with the palm of your hand.

- Think of your question.

- Using your right thumb, riffle through the pages of the book, and stop whenever it feels right.

- Open the book to see what hexagram you arrived at.

The Hexagrams

Each of the sixty-four hexagrams represents a particular state or situation.

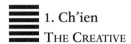 **1. Ch'ien**
THE CREATIVE

Some form of creativity will bring great success, but not immediately. Determination, perseverance, and hard work will provide the desired results.

This is the most powerful hexagram of all, as it symbolizes heaven, the wise man, the leader, and the father. Both trigrams are Ch'ien, providing energy and strength. However, it is important to use your strength wisely.

- *Line 6*: Evaluate carefully, and don't attempt too much.

- *Line 5*: Seek advice from someone you respect.

- *Line 4*: A brief respite before action.

- *Line 3*: Be observant, and think before acting.

- *Line 2*: Seek advice from someone who knows what he or she is doing.

- *Line 1*: Avoid impulsiveness and evaluate the situation before acting.

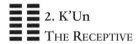 **2. K'Un**
THE RECEPTIVE

Sensitivity and determination lead to great success. Go with the flow. Patient waiting and diplomacy are required. Listen to others, but make up your own mind before acting.

- *Line 6*: Believe in yourself.

- *Line 5*: Luck is on your side.

- *Line 4*: You can accomplish much more than you think.

- *Line 3*: Maintain high ethical standards.

- *Line 2*: Be patient and wait for the right moment to act.

- *Line 1*: Rely on cold, hard logic at this time.

 **3. Chun**
INITIAL DIFFICULTIES

There will be difficulties early on, but everything works out well. Be cautious and allow as much time as necessary. If you persevere you'll achieve success.

- *Line 6*: You may feel disappointed in yourself. This time will pass.

- *Line 5*: A good time to save, but don't be greedy and invest all that you have.

- *Line 4*: If you bide your time, everything will turn out well.

- *Line 3*: Take an expert with you whenever you negotiate.

- *Line 2*: You may feel you're busy, but are achieving little. Progress is slow.

- *Line 1*: Frustrations caused by lack of progress and few results.

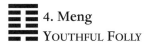 4. Meng
YOUTHFUL FOLLY

You're acting in an immature manner. The I Ching will answer your question once, but if you're unhappy with this answer, and ask again and again, you'll receive no reply. Realize that there's a lot to learn, and be prepared to study. With experience, you'll progress well.

- *Line 6*: Be prepared to help someone who is young and naive.

- *Line 5*: A playful approach pays off.

- *Line 4*: Study and research to achieve the best results.

- *Line 3*: Refuse to be affected by the success of others.

- *Line 2*: Spend time with young people and listen to what they have to say.

- *Line 1*: Allow young people to make mistakes, and help them learn from these experiences.

 5. Hsu
WAITING

As its name indicates, this is a time of waiting. Be patient, and don't push for results. Hard work, honesty, and sincerity lead to success. This is a good time for travel.

- *Line 6*: Treat strangers kindly, as they may provide the seeds of success.

- *Line 5*: Take time out, and return to your work refreshed and invigorated.

- *Line 4*: A good time for a brief vacation in a place where no one knows you.

- *Line 3*: Pay attention to personal security.

- *Line 2*: Avoid gossip and focus on your goal.

- *Line 1*: Wait to see what happens, and then act if the situation is right.

 **6. Sung**
CONFLICT

Something or someone is blocking your progress and you'll be feeling tense. Don't try to force a result. In this situation it's better to stop half way. You'll suffer if you push too hard. Seek advice from someone you admire and respect. This is not a good time for travel.

- *Line 6*: Be careful as others are trying to hurt you and damage your reputation.

- *Line 5*: Initial success with the help of someone in authority.

- *Line 4*: Refuse to argue with others, and make your own path forward.

- *Line 3*: Make sure your goals are shared by others.

- *Line 2*: Progress is stalled. Take time out to restore your energy.

- *Line 1*: Let go of stress and worry. Success is not far away.

 **7. Shih**
THE ARMY

The situation requires strength, perseverance, and good leadership. Honor and loyalty are important. You're likely to need other people's help at this time. The outcome will be successful, and you won't need to compromise your principles.

- *Line 6*: Listen to people in authority.

- *Line 5*: Ask people who are close to you for help and advice.

- *Line 4*: Make sure you and your family are secure.

- *Line 3*: Act now if you want good results.

- *Line 2*: You are in control. Use your power wisely.

- *Line 1*: Work steadily. Be reliable and deliver what you promise.

 8. Pi
UNION

Forming a cooperative alliance or union is beneficial at this time, as it provides harmony, success, and good fortune. People who hesitate and join the union too late will suffer and fail.

- *Line 6*: Be cautious with well-meaning people who don't know what they're talking about.

- *Line 5*: Let others know who you trust.

- *Line 4*: You may need help from someone outside your immediate circle of colleagues.

- *Line 3*: People who say they believe in you may not necessarily be prepared to help.

- *Line 2*: You can trust the people who are closest to you.

- *Line 1*: Employ people who believe in you and what you stand for.

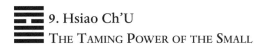

9. Hsiao Ch'U
THE TAMING POWER OF THE SMALL

This is a time to make plans and prepare for future action. It indicates success in the end. Prosperity comes from small incremental steps. In matters concerning love, this hexagram indicates temporary problems that are ultimately resolved.

- *Line 6*: You can start moving ahead again. Evaluate carefully before acting.

- *Line 5*: Express your feelings of friendship, love, and appreciation to others.

- *Line 4*: Refuse to let fear hold you back. This is a time to let others know who you really are.

- *Line 3*: Avoid the blame game. What has happened, has happened.

- *Line 2*: Enjoy the love and support of others, and extend the same feelings to them.

- *Line 1*: You may have little to show for your labor yet, but tomorrow is a new day.

10. Lu
TREADING

Be cautious. The traditional interpretation of this hexagram is stepping on the tail of a tiger, and surviving it. Consequently, you may do something dangerous or reckless, but will get away with it. Success comes from behaving appropriately.

- *Line 6*: Good luck is with you.

- *Line 5*: You can progress quickly now, but there are problems ahead.

- *Line 4*: Step on the tiger's tail cautiously, and you'll get away with it.

- *Line 3*: If you step on the tiger's tail, you won't get away with it.

- *Line 2*: Steady progress pays off.

- *Line 1*: Don't blow your trumpet too loudly. Be humble and modest for best results.

11. T'Ai
PEACE

This is a sign of happiness and good fortune. You are on the right path, and good things are about to come your way. You have the potential for great success.

- *Line 6*: Temporary problems will hold you back.

- *Line 5*: Good luck is smiling on you.

- *Line 4*: Be scrupulously honest, and say what you think.

- *Line 3*: There'll be ups and downs along the way, but enjoy the ride.

- *Line 2*: Keep focused on your goal, and don't let yourself get sidetracked.

- *Line 1*: If you're in control, good fortune smiles on you.

 **12. P'I**
STAGNATION

This indicates a difficult time in which nothing goes your way, no matter how hard you try. Be patient until the situation changes.

- *Line 6*: The situation has changed, and you can move forward again.

- *Line 5*: Think carefully, and then make the necessary changes to enable you to progress again.

- *Line 4*: You may need to compromise to fit in with others.

- *Line 3*: Be grateful for the kind words of others.

- *Line 2*: Someone undermines your efforts and achieves temporary success.

- *Line 1*: Celebrate, as finally everything is going your way.

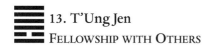 **13. T'Ung Jen**
FELLOWSHIP WITH OTHERS

Spending time with others will provide you with ideas and open doors to success. A trip of some sort will provide good results. You'll achieve success if you continue with a difficult task.

- *Line 6*: Move outside your comfort zone, and make new friends in different fields.

- *Line 5*: Work with others to achieve a worthwhile goal. Take time to relax once the task is done.

- *Line 4*: Be competitive, but allow your opposition room to operate.

- *Line 3*: You are ready and prepared, but need to wait before moving forward.

- *Line 2*: Welcome and accept others to achieve best results.

- *Line 1*: Helping others will enable you to prosper.

 **14. Ta Yu**
ABUNDANCE

Your determination and hard work pay off handsomely, and you'll be able to spend money on good quality possessions.

- *Line 6*: Be grateful for what you have, and expect much more to follow.

- *Line 5*: A true friend helps you on the road to success.

- *Line 4*: Be modest, and resist opportunities to become the center of attention.

- *Line 3*: Appreciate the blessings in your life, and realize that most people are not as fortunate as you.

- *Line 2*: You can expand your business now, but don't overextend yourself.

- *Line 1*: Eliminate whatever is causing the problem, think positively, and move ahead again.

 **15. Ch'ien**
MODESTY

A humble and modest attitude will lead you to success. You'll have the necessary motivation to continue until the task is complete.

- *Line 6*: Be modest and watchful to outwit any potential foes.

- *Line 5*: Speak your mind when dealing with people who won't share their success with loved ones.

- *Line 4*: Remain friendly, open, and modest, and success will shine on you.

- *Line 3*: If you remain modest, you'll have an enjoyable and successful retirement.

- *Line 2*: Good fortune smiles on people who achieve success but remain modest.

- *Line 1*: Remain modest and let your personal influence grow and bring you good fortune.

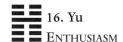 **16. Yu**

ENTHUSIASM

You'll be feeling positive and happy. This is a good time to motivate others to start or continue a worthwhile undertaking.

- *Line 6*: You can relax and enjoy yourself after a good day's work.

- *Line 5*: Seek professional advice if you feel unwell.

- *Line 4*: Share your happiness and success with others.

- *Line 3*: Don't postpone anything that needs to be done, and speak openly and honestly.

- *Line 2*: If you conduct yourself honestly and ethically, you'll succeed.

- *Line 1*: Overindulgence leads to disappointment and loss.

 **17. Sui**

FOLLOWING

You'll have a number of possibilities to choose from. If you follow someone else's footsteps, you'll achieve success. Cooperation and hard work pay off handsomely.

- *Line 6*: Put up with hardship today knowing that success and freedom will follow.

- *Line 5*: Stick to your principles and build your reputation.

- *Line 4*: If you're ethical in all your business dealings, success will come.

- *Line 3*: Your home and family are your number one responsibility always.

- *Line 2*: No matter what happens, don't neglect your responsibilities.

- *Line 1*: Personal benefit will follow when you entertain and are entertained by others.

 18. Ku

DECAY

You'll be successful if you work hard on something that has gone wrong, or is not as it should be. This is a good time to eliminate bad habits and make other necessary changes. Travel will prove worthwhile.

- *Line 6*: Resist any temptation to be dishonest or deceitful.

- *Line 5*: Do what you can to amend any mistakes made by family members.

- *Line 4*: You may feel sad while resolving mistakes made by family members.

- *Line 3*: Despite what you feel, it's a good thing to resolve family mistakes.

- *Line 2*: Listen to all members of the family when resolving family problems.

- *Line 1*: Family support can avert calamity and get the family back on track.

 **19. Lin**
APPROACH

This is a good time to approach others or allow them to approach you. You'll need to work hard and be persistent. However, be prepared for the cycle of yin and yang to come into play. In time (literally "when the eighth month arrives"), the comfortable, enjoyable situation you're now enjoying will change. Enjoy the present, but be prepared for the downturn.

- *Line 6*: Sincere, honest, and open leadership leads on to success.

- *Line 5*: If you wish to lead, learn to use good judgment and wisdom.

- *Line 4*: Be willing to listen to the ideas and concerns of others.

- *Line 3*: No reward comes from exaggeration or distorting the facts.

- *Line 2*: To achieve great success be caring, kind, and compassionate.

- *Line 1*: Long-lasting success comes to leaders who look after the people they work with.

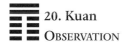 **20. Kuan**
OBSERVATION

This is a time to plan and make preparations for an important change. Be patient, observe, and think before acting.

- *Line 6*: Learn from people of different cultures. Enjoy different points of view.

- *Line 5*: Take time to identify with the people you work with. Recognize their worth.

- *Line 4*: Follow the customs and practices when visiting different places.

- *Line 3*: A good manager listens and observes his staff.

- *Line 2*: Your sincerity is affected every time you listen to rumors or pry into other people's affairs.

- *Line 1*: You're an adult. Childish and immature actions will prevent you from progressing.

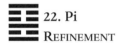 **21. Shih Ho**
SEVERE MEASURES

You will achieve success as long as you ensure everyone involved gets treated fairly. Justice and fair play are the key right now.

- *Line 6*: Your performance is affected if you take on too much responsibility.

- *Line 5*: Be careful, and move ahead cautiously.

- *Line 4*: Remain focused on your goal, no matter what obstacles stand in your way.

- *Line 3*: A temporary health problem could hold you back in the short term.

- *Line 2*: Don't worry if you're trying to do too much, as this situation is only temporary.

- *Line 1*: Someone could be trying to antagonize you. Ignore it, as this person is insignificant.

 **22. Pi**
REFINEMENT

A graceful, elegant approach will help you achieve success. Do not overcomplicate matters. There is value in simplicity. Focus on small goals, rather than large ones, at this time.

- *Line 6*: Wear something white to help you achieve success.

- *Line 5*: Be modest, rather than ostentatious, in your home surroundings.

- *Line 4*: Good luck will follow if you wear something white.

- *Line 3*: Make sure you're well-groomed and tidy to achieve all that you can.

- *Line 2*: This is a good time to beautify your hair.

- *Line 1*: A good time to walk instead of drive.

23. Po
DISINTEGRATION

This is a negative, disruptive time, and it's best to sit quietly until it passes. Be kind and generous to others, but do not try to advance yourself at the moment.

- *Line 6*: Times have been good, but now you need to be cautious.

- *Line 5*: Enjoy your home and family life, and be cautious at work.

- *Line 4*: Make sure you're fully protected at this time.

- *Line 3*: This is a temporary situation, and you'll progress again soon.

- *Line 2*: Be cautious, and take extra precautions.

- *Line 1*: Any disruptions to everyday routine could bring bad luck.

 24. Fu
RETURN

Your fortunes are improving, and success is not far away. You seem to have a magic touch at present, and your friends will encourage and support you. "On the seventh day," new opportunities will manifest.

- *Line 6*: Any problems you have now will be temporary, and you'll soon be back on track.

- *Line 5*: Be prepared to give up your vacation and return home if the need is urgent.

- *Line 4*: Be aware of personal security when traveling, especially when returning home.

- *Line 3*: The needs of home and family are more important than anything else.

- *Line 2*: Take care of whatever is necessary before spending time away from home.

- *Line 1*: Any travel you do at this time will be brief.

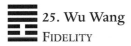 **25. Wu Wang**
FIDELITY

If you go about your life in a natural and positive way, you will achieve success. Hard work and persistence are required. There could be unexpected benefits.

- *Line 6*: Prepare carefully, know what you intend on doing, and then act.

- *Line 5*: Look after yourself to avoid potential health problems.

- *Line 4*: Divination can help you prepare for the future.

- *Line 3*: Unexpected problems may hold you back.

- *Line 2*: Have a specific goal in mind when you travel.

- *Line 1*: You'll experience good luck if you move forward with an open mind.

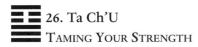 **26. Ta Ch'U**
TAMING YOUR STRENGTH

You need to harness your abilities and strength to make the most of the opportunities that come your way. This is an excellent time for travel.

- *Line 6*: Good fortune is not far away.

- *Line 5*: The best results will come if you discipline yourself and don't push too hard.

- *Line 4*: Work on the positive virtues of love, truth, empathy, and fairness.

- *Line 3*: Travel broadens the mind and provides opportunities.

- *Line 2*: Be forgiving, and avoid overreacting.

- *Line 1*: Follow the divination to avoid problems.

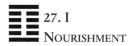 ## 27. I
NOURISHMENT

Hard work pays off. However, you must look after yourself and nourish your body, mind, and soul. Avoid impulsiveness, and think carefully before acting.

- *Line 5*: Be patient, and wait for any difficulties to pass.

- *Line 4*: Quiet contemplation will provide insights into the problem.

- *Line 3*: Be cautious, and think carefully before acting. A time to keep a low profile.

- *Line 2*: Move ahead, but don't aim too high until the situation improves.

- *Line 1*: Potential problems will hold you back. Be vigilant and on your guard.

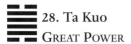 ## 28. Ta Kuo
GREAT POWER

You have almost too much power and energy at your disposal now. You might need to travel to achieve your greatest potential at this time. With hard work, success is assured.

- *Line 6*: A situation you don't fully understand will create temporary difficulties.

- *Line 5*: A happy time with plenty of fun and laughter. This is not a time to move forward or back.

- *Line 4*: A big concern is finished, and you can focus on the future. Think carefully to avoid mistakes.

- *Line 3*: You're trying to do too much. This pressure can cause bad luck.

- *Line 2*: You'll feel full of vitality and energy. You can do anything now.

- *Line 1*: A time to look back and make plans for the future.

 **29. K'An**
WATER

You need to be honest and sincere to achieve peace of mind. Be aware that other people might not be telling you everything you need to know. Honorable thoughts and actions lead to success.

- *Line 6*: You may struggle for the next few years, but you will ultimately triumph.

- *Line 5*: Be patient, and wait for any difficulties to pass.

- *Line 4*: Quiet contemplation will provide insights into the problem.

- *Line 3*: Be cautious, and think carefully before acting. A time to keep a low profile.

- *Line 2*: Move ahead, but don't aim too high until the situation improves.

- *Line 1*: Potential problems will hold you back. Be vigilant and on your guard.

 30. Li
FIRE

You may feel like giving up, but success is assured if you persevere and remain focused on your goal. Honesty pays off handsomely. Cooperate and remain aware of the needs of others.

- *Line 6*: Make sure you deal with the right person when problems arise.

- *Line 5*: You may feel surrounded by problems, but this will soon pass and the way ahead is clear.

- *Line 4*: Someone close to you lacks loyalty and is punished for his or her actions.

- *Line 3*: For the best results, be prepared and act when the time is right.

- *Line 2*: Use the best tools to achieve the results you desire.

- *Line 1*: Prepare carefully when starting anything new.

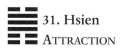 **31. Hsien**
ATTRACTION

Hard work leads to success. Traditionally, Hsien meant it was a good time to marry. This makes this an auspicious time to enter into a partnership, business or otherwise.

- *Line 6*: Reveal your emotions for best results.

- *Line 5*: You may feel your emotions are letting you down, but in reality they're aiding your cause.

- *Line 4*: You'll have to make a decision soon. People close to you are prepared to help.

- *Line 3*: Familiar surroundings benefit you at this time.

- *Line 2*: This is a good time for anything to do with home and family.

- *Line 1*: Be guided by your hunches and feelings.

 ## 32. Heng
STABILITY

This is a good time to move ahead as you're sure to prosper. A short trip would be advantageous.

- *Line 6*: There's no need to be envious at the success of others. Your time will come.

- *Line 5*: Act ethically and you'll achieve success.

- *Line 4*: You may need to travel to find new opportunities.

- *Line 3*: You'll be tempted, but as long as you remain open and honest, you'll come to no harm.

- *Line 2*: Focus on the future rather than the past.

- *Line 1*: Know what you can do and what should be left for others.

 ## 33. Tun
RETREAT

This is a time when you need to take a step back in order to achieve success. It's a temporary situation. You can progress in small undertakings, but even they will entail hard work and effort.

- *Line 6*: This is a good time for a well-earned vacation.

- *Line 5*: You'll be recognized for doing the right thing.

- *Line 4*: You'll benefit from time on your own, but you will find it hard to achieve it.

- *Line 3*: Focus on what's important, and let go off anything that doesn't matter.

- *Line 2*: Your personal beliefs are important, but you should question them every now and then.

- *Line 1*: Be aware of personal security, and avoid risky activities.

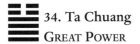 ## 34. Ta Chuang
GREAT POWER

You'll be full of good ideas and creative energy. Your energy and enthusiasm ensure you'll progress at this propitious time. Be responsible, and think before acting.

- Line 6: Persistence and hard work pay off.

- *Line 5*: Stay calm, no matter what situation you find yourself in.

- *Line 4*: Refuse to be diverted, and focus on your goals.

- *Line 3*: Arrogance and egotism will impede others. Honesty, uprightness, and modesty pay off.

- *Line 2*: Be reliable, and do what you say you're going to do for future success.

- *Line 1*: There could be problems, but nothing will hold you back for long.

 ## 35. Chin
PROGRESS

You'll start enjoying the rewards of your dedication and hard work. This marks the start of a productive and successful cycle. Make the most of the good luck you have at this time.

- *Line 6*: You're about to take a big step forward. Problems will simply motivate you to succeed.

- *Line 5*: Let go of any fears and worries. They only hold you back.

- *Line 4*: Haste and impatience for results will be counter-productive.

- *Line 3*: You can move forward now with the support of your loved ones.

- *Line 2*: You have the necessary determination and persistence to make great progress now.

- *Line 1*: Cooperate with others to achieve the best results.

 ## 36. Ming I
DARKENED LIGHT

This is a difficult time, but you can progress, albeit slowly. Be patient, work hard, keep a low profile, but keep your light shining.

- *Line 6*: You are suffering from trying to do too much. Learn from this bad experience.

- *Line 5*: Keep true to yourself, regardless of what other people are doing.

- *Line 4*: Keep away from idle gossip.

- *Line 3*: You have the opportunity to correct something that goes against your principles.

- *Line 2*: You'll need help from others to sustain you at this time.

- *Line 1*: You might find yourself in hot water, despite doing the right thing.

 **37. Chia Jen**
THE FAMILY

Don't try to do everything on your own. A woman's determination and perseverance will help you achieve your goals. These are largely family goals, but it also includes an improvement in the family's financial situation.

- *Line 6*: A good, loving, and supportive home and family life ultimately bring success.

- *Line 5*: It's a positive sign if someone important comes to your home.

- *Line 4*: Good money management pays off long term.

- *Line 3*: You'll have to exert your authority in the home to avoid problems later.

- *Line 2*: Approach any household tasks with enthusiasm to achieve good results.

- *Line 1*: Maintain household security to avoid potential problems.

 **38. K'Uei**
OPPOSITION

Expect some sort of opposition to your hopes and plans. It will be difficult to get everyone involved to agree on a course of action. However, you can still make progress in minor matters.

- *Line 6*: You and your family are secure and safe.

- *Line 5*: Enjoy pleasant social times with family and friends.

- *Line 4*: New friends provide motivation. Select them carefully.

- *Line 3*: You'll learn from other people's mistakes.

- *Line 2*: A chance meeting with an influential person will provide benefits later on.

- *Line 1*: Focus on what's important, and let other people deal with minor concerns.

 **39. Ch'ien**
OBSTRUCTION

This indicates temporary delays. You can expect help from the southwest. Someone you respect and admire will provide good advice if asked. Keep working hard, as you're on the path to success.

- *Line 6*: A short trip pays off, despite problems along the way.

- *Line 5*: You have good friends who are prepared to help and support you if you need it.

- *Line 4*: Travel problems, especially at the start and end of each journey.

- *Line 3*: Return home if you experience antagonism or violence while traveling.

- *Line 2*: Other people will do your worrying for you so you can focus on important matters.

- *Line 1*: Despite all the problems you've endured on the road, you'll be appreciated and thanked.

 **40. Hsieh**
RELEASE

The southwest is a favorable direction right now. If you take a trip in that direction, you'll gain good fortune when you return. If you need to travel in other directions, you'll have to go quickly to achieve good luck.

- *Line 6*: Keep focused on your goal. You can accomplish more than you think.

- *Line 5*: Others will appreciate you for your skills and talents.

- *Line 4*: People you trust will give you good advice. Listen carefully.

- *Line 3*: Pay attention to your personal security.

- *Line 2*: Good fortune is smiling on you.

- *Line 1*: There are no threats or major problems at this time.

 **41. Sun**
SACRIFICE

If you're honest and sincere, you can cut back on something and gain benefit from it. Your fortunes will improve with hard work and perseverance. You may have to put other people's needs ahead of your own. A short trip would be beneficial.

- *Line 6*: This is a good time to travel. You'll receive useful financial advice.

- *Line 5*: You may receive something valuable that will help you prosper.

- *Line 4*: Don't delay seeking medical attention if required.

- *Line 3*: Something will come to an end, but a new start occurs right away.

- *Line 2*: Mind your own business and remain focused on your goal.

- *Line 1*: Any health matters need to be attended to quickly.

 **42. I**
INCREASE

This is a time to act. Determine what you want, think carefully, and act decisively. This is a good time to travel overseas. Great success is possible.

- *Line 6*: If you delay too long, you'll receive nothing.

- *Line 5*: Success comes from helping others along the way.

- *Line 4*: Keep influential people fully informed about potential problems.

- *Line 3*: Be honest and open about your mistakes. If you do, you'll gain respect.

- *Line 2*: Set aside time to fantasize and imagine what you want your future to look like.

- *Line 1*: This is a good time to start anything new.

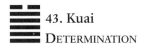 **43. Kuai**
DETERMINATION

There is potential danger, and you could be suffering from stress. Make sure that everyone around you knows what's going on. Keep superiors informed. Avoid anger and violence. Proceed calmly, and you'll progress.

- *Line 6*: Check that insurances and other important bills are paid.

- *Line 5*: Be flexible. A fixed, rigid approach hinders your progress.

- *Line 4*: Learn what you can from rejection, and continue your progress.

- *Line 3*: You may get rejected, but if you don't try you'll never find out.

- *Line 2*: Tell others about problems and other concerns as quickly as you can.

- *Line 1*: Ensure that you're well organized and on top of everything before traveling.

 **44. Kou**
CONTACT

You'll make contact with an influential, forceful woman. Listen to what she has to say, but avoid entering into any kind of partnership or relationship with her. All other one-on-one relationships are favored at this time.

- *Line 6*: Communicate with someone who is deliberately holding you back, and resolve the situation.

- *Line 5*: You'll achieve better results if you work harmoniously with others.

- *Line 4*: Share your problems with family and friends. You have more support than you think.

- *Line 3*: Keep a low profile, and refuse to accept any other tasks or responsibilities.

- *Line 2*: Keep an eye on what is yours. Think carefully about sharing what is yours with others.

- *Line 1*: This is a good time to stay close to home. Relax and unwind.

 **45. Ts'Ui**
GATHERING

Some form of celebration will take place. An influential man provides opportunities to progress. Hard work and determination pay off. Be generous with people less fortunate than you.

- *Line 6*: You may lose a small amount of money or a possession. It's not worth worrying about.

- *Line 5*: If you're honorable and stand for something, others will follow.

- *Line 4*: Something good will happen. Enjoy your success.

- *Line 3*: You'll achieve more with work than you will with play.

- *Line 2*: Appreciate your colleagues for the contribution they make to your life.

- *Line 1*: Bolster your confidence, and move forward.

 **46. Sheng**
ASCENDING

Your fortunes are improving. An influential person will offer advice and help. Your contributions will be appreciated. A trip to the south will pay off handsomely. Work hard and take pride in your achievements.

- *Line 6*: New opportunities are present if you're prepared and vigilant.

- *Line 5*: Your motivation and persistence help you progress.

- *Line 4*: Be patient, as the results will be well worthwhile.

- *Line 3*: Make sure the rewards are worthwhile before agreeing to do it.

- *Line 2*: A good time to celebrate your progress with friends and loved ones.

- *Line 1*: You're in a good position to move forward. Success is not far away.

 **47. K'Un**
OPPRESSION

K'un is one of the four danger hexagrams. You'll experience opposition, but persistence will help you progress. A good man will offer help. People may not believe what you say, but will respect your actions. Believe in yourself.

- *Line 6*: Your thoughts and actions are holding you back. Change your attitude and move forward.

- *Line 5*: Accept the help of others to reduce your workload.

- *Line 4*: You'll feel run down and tired, but this state is only temporary.

- *Line 3*: You're likely to be surrounded with problems and concerns. Take one day at a time.

- *Line 2*: Overindulgence slows you down. Fortunately, you'll soon want to progress again.

- *Line 1*: A situation may be out of control. Do what you can, but don't lose sleep over it.

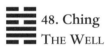 **48. Ching**
THE WELL

Your surroundings might change, but you remain connected to the universal life force. It will be to your detriment to lose contact with it. Appreciate and encourage others. Reevaluate the situation, as you'll have more possibilities than you realize.

- *Line 6*: Refuse to let others take advantage and deplete your creative energy.

- *Line 5*: Sit in the sunlight and accept the blessing and thanks of others.

- *Line 4*: A misconstrued communication causes problems. Communicate with others.

- *Line 3*: You are not fully appreciated at the moment. Bide your time.

- *Line 2*: Do something properly, or not at all. A rushed job won't work.

- *Line 1*: You may feel low. Rest and think about where you want to go from here.

 **49. Ko**
RENEWAL

It won't be long before your ideas are accepted by others and you receive the appreciation and rewards you deserve. Right now you may be wondering if it's worth persevering, but those thoughts will vanish as soon as you get close to your goal.

- *Line 6*: Change is necessary, and you're the person to initiate it.

- *Line 5*: You'll need to call on hidden reserves to make the necessary changes.

- *Line 4*: A good time to make important changes. Think before acting.

- *Line 3*: Evaluate the situation carefully before starting something new.

- *Line 2*: Make plans, and set a date to make the changes and move forward.

- *Line 1*: Change is necessary, but don't make it until you are fully prepared.

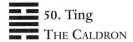 50. Ting
THE CALDRON

This hexagram promises great success and good fortune. Good planning and cooperation with others ensures you'll receive the success you deserve. You should be feeling balanced and in control.

- *Line 6*: You can succeed now while others are going around in circles.

- *Line 5*: You know exactly what you're doing, and are on top of the situation.

- *Line 4*: You'll hold yourself back if you're impulsive and act without thinking.

- *Line 3*: Patience will be rewarded at this time. Wait for the situation to ease.

- *Line 2*: Money flows your way. You'll feel positive about every aspect of your life.

- *Line 1*: This is a good time to evaluate the situation and start again.

 51. Chen
THUNDER

Something that occurs without warning alarms and terrifies others. However, you'll be able to take advantage of the situation and make progress while everyone else is panicking.

- *Line 6*: Remain calm, no matter how stormy the situation becomes.

- *Line 5*: Problems increase, but your calm approach means they won't damage you.

- *Line 4*: Others will be affected, but you remain cool and calm.

- *Line 3*: There'll be plenty of ups and downs, but you'll be prepared to weather it.

- *Line 2*: Something will shock or surprise you. Keep a low profile.

- *Line 1*: An unexpected occurrence surprises you but provides a lesson for the future.

 **52. Ken**
STILLNESS

This is a welcome period for meditation or contemplation. You'll enjoy spending time on your own to develop inwardly. Relax, and gather some strength before moving forward again.

- *Line 6:* You've been keeping your own counsel, but now you have to tell others what you really think.

- *Line 5:* Hold your tongue. You'll be tempted to say more than you should.

- *Line 4:* Take time out to restore your soul. Let go of all your concerns.

- *Line 3:* A good time for a vacation. Go somewhere new and different.

- *Line 2:* A time of enforced waiting. Use it productively and learn as much as you can.

- *Line 1:* You'll feel like time on your own to meditate and think. Keep your thoughts to yourself.

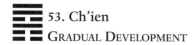 **53. Ch'ien**
GRADUAL DEVELOPMENT

This hexagram is a sign of gradual, steady progress. Be patient and calm. A major commitment may be made. You'll benefit by continuing to work steadily toward your goals.

- *Line 6:* Enjoy what you've achieved so far, and know there is much more success ahead.

- *Line 5:* With hard work and effort, you will become successful.

- *Line 4:* Enjoy your steady progress, but remain aware the situation could change before long.

- *Line 3:* Don't allow others to take credit for what you have done.

- *Line 2:* Take time to enjoy your success with family and friends.

- *Line 1:* If you've made a mistake, admit it at the earliest opportunity. Any damage is temporary.

 **54. Kuei Mei**
MARRYING GIRL

This is a sign of fruition and completion. Pause and wait patiently. If you try to progress at this time, you'll achieve nothing but disharmony and stress. Keep your emotions in check, and avoid impulsiveness.

- *Line 6*: If something sounds too good to be true, it is.

- *Line 5*: Avoid any thoughts of self-aggrandizement. Modesty is a good policy.

- *Line 4*: Expect setbacks and frustrations. Everything will be back on track soon.

- *Line 3*: The praise and compliments you receive are good, but don't help you progress.

- *Line 2*: Move forward cautiously. There's a great deal you don't know.

- *Line 1*: It might be difficult, but you can move forward again now.

55. Feng
GREATNESS

This hexagram is a sign of success. Abundance and prosperity are within reach. Remember to avoid extravagance, and put some aside, just in case you need it.

- *Line 6*: You appear successful to others, but inside you don't always feel that you are.

- *Line 5*: You have the ability to motivate and inspire others with your friendly, giving attitude.

- *Line 4*: A temporary loss of direction. Seek advice from someone you trust.

- *Line 3*: You've become too involved with the details to see the whole picture. Relax and be patient.

- *Line 2*: Look after your health and fitness. Anything done to excess can hurt you now.

- *Line 1*: Someone you admire will share good advice with you.

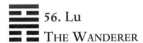

56. Lu
THE WANDERER

This is favorable for people who need to travel for business purposes. Success will come if you continue to work hard and think small. You may feel lonely at times. Refuse to feel sorry for yourself, and enjoy the company of others when you can.

- *Line 6*: Treat others with respect. This is not a time for risk and speculation.

- *Line 5*: A temporary setback will disappoint you, but you are making progress.

- *Line 4*: You may feel unsettled and discontented. This is only temporary.

- *Line 3*: Don't be impetuous, as it could cost you money and friendship.

- *Line 2*: Someone far from your home will offer much needed support.

- *Line 1*: Be kind, generous, and encouraging to others, especially when traveling.

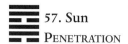 **57. Sun**
PENETRATION

Success will come by thinking small, rather than large. Seek advice from others. It will be to your advantage to travel to consult with someone who can help you.

- *Line 6*: Take care of your assets and avoid any risks or speculation.

- *Line 5*: Even though your progress is slower than you'd like, you are moving forward.

- *Line 4*: You'll be recognized for what you've achieved. Enjoy your success.

- *Line 3*: You can find the answers you need by looking inward.

- *Line 2*: Discuss your future plans with partners and people you respect.

- *Line 1*: Look at the overall picture and pay attention to the details.

 **58. Tui**
JOYFULNESS

A joyful and successful result. It is to your advantage to continue working hard. Social activities will provide happiness and good ideas. People will appreciate your kindness and sincerity.

- *Line 6*: Express yourself, and let everyone see what you're capable of.

- *Line 5*: You may feel alone, despite the company of others. Seek out someone you can rely on.

- *Line 4*: Despite your views on the matter, you have to finish what you started.

- *Line 3*: Don't take too much on trust. Think, consider, and evaluate what you hear.

- *Line 2*: You won't go wrong if you stick to the truth.

- *Line 1*: Enjoy happiness and pleasure with friends and family.

 **59. Huan**
DISPERSION

This is a good time to increase your influence and personal power. Success is possible. Travel is highly advantageous at this time. Someone important is about to make a decision, and you'll make some changes as a result.

- *Line 6*: The difficult times are over. Move ahead strongly.

- *Line 5*: You'll need to evaluate a generous proposition. Take your time.

- *Line 4*: A good time to start moving in a new direction.

- *Line 3*: You might have too much on your plate at present. Do one task at a time.

- *Line 2*: Someone might be holding you back, but despite this you are on the road to success.

- *Line 1*: A problem will be resolved with the help and support of people you care for.

 **60. Chieh**
LIMITATION

Success comes through caution and thrift. Take time, and don't allow others to restrict you or hold you back. You'll need to exercise restraint at times.

- *Line 6*: Take a step back and look at what you're doing from a different perspective.

- *Line 5*: There's no need to hang on to anything that has outworn its use.

- *Line 4*: Keep a close eye on your spending. Cutting back on unnecessary expenses pays off.

- *Line 3*: Be cautious when spending money. The results won't be immediate but pay off long-term.

- *Line 2*: You can start to move ahead again. Be bold and welcome change.

- *Line 1*: Keep a low profile and avoid anything that's controversial, hazardous, or involves investment.

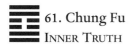 **61. Chung Fu**
INNER TRUTH

Good fortune comes through sincerity, confidence, and harmonious relationships. A trip overseas is beneficial. You're on track and should continue on the path you're now on. Other people will follow your lead.

- *Line 6*: Keep your feet on the ground. Be humble, honest, and realistic.

- *Line 5*: Focus on what you really want, aim high, and take the first steps toward your goal.

- *Line 4*: Be careful, and avoid people who don't share your ideals.

- *Line 3*: A time for reward. Celebrate your success and share it with everyone who's helped you.

- *Line 2*: Express your love to everyone who is close to you. Set aside time for family activities.

- *Line 1*: Take time out to relax and think. An offer or opportunity may surprise you.

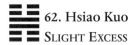 **62. Hsiao Kuo**
SLIGHT EXCESS

Success is likely if you don't raise your sights too high and work diligently. Assess your abilities, and seek the advice of others when required. Keep a low profile at this time, and greater success is possible.

- *Line 6*: Know your limits, and don't try to do too much. Learn to say no.

- *Line 5*: A small success will spur you on to greater success in the future.

- *Line 4*: Work hard, but be aware of possible complications.

- *Line 3*: Moderation is the keyword now. Avoid recklessness and excess.

- *Line 2*: Communication with someone important will bear fruit.

- *Line 1*: Slow, but steady, progress pays off. Read the small print.

 **63. Chi Chi**
COMPLETION

Something is accomplished or completed. Small successes are likely, but don't take anything for granted. However, although everything starts out well, unless you're careful, it might end up in disarray.

- *Line 6*: Without caution you could end up in hot water. Think before acting.

- *Line 5*: Practice what you preach. It will pay greater dividends than you might think.

- *Line 4*: Don't spend too much time on insignificant concerns. Focus on the big picture.

- *Line 3*: You are close to success, but you will need focus, persistence, and hard work to achieve it.

- *Line 2*: A temporary loss. There's no need to worry about it, as the situation is resolved quickly.

- *Line 1*: Minor problems won't hold you back for long. Aim high.

 **64. Wei Chi**
BEFORE COMPLETION

Success is possible, but only if you concentrate and take care until it's achieved. If you fail to do this, the results will be disappointing. Be grateful for the help of others, but don't rely on it, as it may not always be forthcoming.

- *Line 6*: Be modest in your success, and celebrate it wisely.

- *Line 5*: Take time out to celebrate your success with the important people in your life.

- *Line 4*: A long-term project is starting to pay off. What you've achieved may surprise even you.

- *Line 3*: A good time to start anything new. Travel is favored.

- *Line 2*: Take your time and enjoy the journey. Too much haste slows you down.

- *Line 1*: Learn from experience and from observing others.

Once you've created your hexagram, you need to think about your question again and see how you can relate it to the reading the hexagram provides. You also need to look at the two trigrams and relate them to your question. If you've created any moving lines during the casting process, you need to create an additional hexagram by changing the moving lines to their opposite (yin to yang, and vice versa). This new hexagram provides information about the future or the outcome of the question.

This provides valuable information, especially if you also use your intuition while evaluating the readings. This is the system that's used by most I Ching practitioners in the West. If you enjoy working with the I Ching, you should also look at some of the other methods of creating and interpreting this ancient oracle.

Advanced Divination

This is a more advanced form of divination, so it is what you'd be likely to receive if you had an I Ching reading in the East. It goes beyond the standard interpretations of the hexagrams, to answer the question.

1. Possibly the most important part of this divination is to ask the right question. A generalized question will always receive a generalized answer. Include as much detail as possible. If you ask, for instance, "Will I marry Louise?" the oracle might say yes. However, you're not very far ahead, as you don't know if it will happen this year or twenty years from now. Consequently, a better question would be, "Will Louise and I get married in the next twelve months?" Similarly, if you ask, "Will my business trip be successful?" you might receive a yes or no answer, but neither will be particularly helpful. To make it specific you should include where you're going, the purpose of the trip, when you're taking it, and the way in which you want it to be successful. A better question would be, "Will my business trip to see ABC Company in Chicago next week be financially successful?" If part of the purpose of the trip is to create goodwill, you should ask that as a separate question, as each question should be about one particular issue. It's a good idea to write down the question, because you'll need to know the exact words you used when it's time to interpret the hexagram.

For the sake of example, let's assume your question is, "Will I be making good progress in my new job at XYZ Company, three months from now?"

2. Create a hexagram. This is done using one of the methods described earlier. In practice, three coins are usually used. Record the throws as yin or yang lines after each throw. Any lines created from three heads or three tails are the changing lines. They're also the dynamic and active lines. As they indicate where the actions and changes occur, they should be clearly marked. As before, the hexagram is constructed from the bottom line upward.

3. Examine the hexagram. Let's assume that the six throws were 6-8-7-9-9-8. This creates Tui, the fifty-eighth hexagram:

    yin
    yang changing line
    yang changing line
    yang
    yin
    yin changing line

Yang changing lines represent the present or past of the question. Yin changing lines represent the future. The hexagram that is created once the changes have been made represents the outcome once whatever actions are necessary are made.

4. Create a second hexagram from the first one. This is done by changing the necessary lines. In our example this creates:

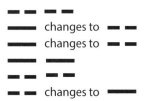

    changes to
    changes to

    changes to

This creates Ming I, the thirty-sixth hexagram.

5. Interpret the two hexagrams and the changing lines.

The question asked was, "Will I be making good progress in my new job at XYZ Company, three months from now?"

In our example, Tui is the present. This indicates that hard work will lead to success. Ming I, representing the future, is a sign of slow progress. The first changing line (line 1) is yin turning to yang. This shows that you might end up in trouble, despite acting appropriately. The fourth changing line (line 4) is yang changing to yin. That shows that you need to avoid idle gossip. The fifth changing line (line 5) is also yang changing to yin. You need to keep true to yourself, regardless of what other people are doing.

It looks as if you're making slow but steady progress in your new job. As long as you avoid gossip and stay true to yourself, you'll do well. However, despite this, it looks as if there will be problems, even though you did the right things.

Many people have spent their entire lives studying the I Ching, and it can be taken much further than we've been able to here. Here's just one example. In the East, the reader looks for seasonality, and uses the five elements of Chinese astrology to compare the strength or weakness of the person's date and time of birth, with the subject or object of the question.

Suggested Reading

Chu, W. K. and W. E Sherrill. *The Astrology of the I Ching*. London: Routledge & Kegan Paul Limited, 1976.

Jou, Tsung Hwa. *The Tao of I Ching: Way to Divination*. Taiwan: Tai Chi Foundation, 1984.

Kiang, Koh Kok. *The I Ching: An Illustrated Guide to the Chinese Art of Divination*. Singapore: Asiapac Books Pte Ltd., 1993.

Legge, James. *The I Ching*. New York: Dover Publications, Inc., 1963. First published by Oxford, UK: Clarendon Press in 1899.

Schoenholtz, Larry. *New Directions in the I Ching: The Yellow River Legacy*. Secaucus, NJ: University Books, Inc., 1975.

Sherrill, W. A. and W. K Chu. *An Anthology of I Ching*. London: Routledge & Kegan Paul Limited, 1977.

Wilhelm, Richard. *I Ching or Book of Changes*. London: Routledge & Kegan Paul Limited, 1951. (The Arkana paperback edition of this book is readily available.)

Ifa Divination

The Yoruba form a large cultural and linguistic group in West Africa. They can be found in Benin, Togo, and southwest Nigeria. The Yoruba practice an ancient form of divination known as Ifa. Ifa is an oral tradition that has been passed down from generation to generation, and the *babalawo*, "fathers of the secrets", or Ifa diviner, still plays an important role in Yoruban life today.

There are five deities in the Ifa tradition. Orunmila is the most important of these, and manifests the heart and soul of Ifa. The second is Ela, a mysterious deity, who is closely linked to Orunmila. Elégba is the trickster deity who carries the gifts and offerings made by people consulting the oracle to the ancestors and gods. Osanyin is the divine healer who helps with medical issues. Olorun, the "owner of the heavens" and creator of Yoruba, is also invoked, but he has no direct role in the divinations as he is far above the interests and preoccupations of humanity.

It takes several years to train a babalawo. He performs his divinations using sixteen palm nuts or a divining chain. The divining chain is more popular, as it's faster and easier, but it is considered less reliable.

The babalawo needs several items to perform his divinations. These are:

1. Sixteen palm nuts from a particular tree (*Elaeis guineensis*). The nuts used for divination have what appear to be four eyes at their base. This means they can symbolically see in every direction.

2. A divining tray. This is made of wood and is usually circular. However, this isn't essential, and sometimes the tray will be square or rectangular. These trays are usually carved around the rim. The carvings include the face of Elégba, which enables the diviner to orient the tray correctly, with Elégba at the far side of the tray, facing him.

3. Wood dust from the *Baphia nitida* tree. This tree is attacked by termites, which creates a fine dust that is sprinkled onto the divining tray.

4. A divining chain with eight seed halves or cowrie shells attached to it. The diviner holds it in the middle, swings it, and casts it onto a mat. The seeds land in a random face up, face down fashion. If the seed lands face up, the babalawo records it on the tray with two marks. If the seed is face down, it is recorded with a single mark.

5. A divining wand, usually made of wood, that is tapped against the divining tray to invoke the deities.

6. A small bowl. In the ritual this contains cold water that is sprinkled over the palm nuts.

7. A shallow bowl to hold the palm nuts at the start of the ritual.

8. A diviner's bag in which he keeps everything necessary for his divinations.

These items all need to be consecrated before they can be used for divination purposes.

The Ifa diviner sits down on a mat facing east, with all the necessary objects in front of him. He sprinkles wood dust onto the tray and then, using the middle finger of his right hand, draws a line in the dust from the top of the tray to the bottom. He creates another line, this time from one side to the other, dividing the tray into quarters. He then picks up his divining wand in his right hand and steadily taps it against the tray while reciting an invocation. After this, he takes water from the bowl and sprinkles it over the palm nuts.

He removes the nuts one at a time and holds them in his left hand. He touches the forehead of his client with one of the nuts while saying a prayer. He replaces this nut in his left hand and covers the nuts with his right hand. He holds the nuts cupped in his hands while touching the four cardinal points he marked on the tray. He follows this by sweeping around the tray in a counterclockwise direction to remove all signs of the cross he'd drawn with the two lines.

He opens his left hand and tries to grasp all the nuts with his right hand. If he succeeds, the nuts are replaced in his left hand. If he grasps all the nuts except for one, he draws a double mark in the dust of the tray. If two are left behind, he draws a single line in the dust. If three or more nuts are left behind, he places all the nuts back into his left hand and starts again. This process is continued until the diviner has drawn eight single or double marks on the tray. There are 256 possible combinations, known as *odu*.

There are a number of verses for each odu, and the diviner knows all of them by heart. They usually consist of stories, myths, and descriptions of occasions in the past when that particular odu was cast.

The person consulting the diviner does not necessarily need to explain his or her concern. If desired, he or she can whisper the question to a coin or a shell that is placed in front of the babalawo.

The consultations vary in length. A short session might simply include a recitation of a few verses after the divining chain has been cast, and the client has to interpret this for him or herself. In longer readings, the diviner will ask a series of questions after the odu has been created. This is to determine if the future is positive or negative, and to find out what can be done to avert any evil that might be surrounding the client. Sometimes an offering is required. This can range from palm oil to food to cloth and even to animal sacrifices. The most frequent offerings are food. After this, the particular verses for the odu that was cast will be recited. It's important that the person being read for provides the offering quickly to keep the gods and the ancestors happy.

A good babalawo will understand what's behind the question and will do whatever is necessary to restore stability and harmony to the client.

Suggested Reading

Epeger, Afolabi A., and Philip John Neimark. *The Sacred Ifa Oracle.* San Francisco: HarperSanFrancisco, 1995.

Gleason, Judith. *A Recitation of Ifa, Oracle of the Yaruba.* New York: Grossman Publishers, 1973.

Mah Jongg

My wife and I received our first, and so far only, mah jongg reading while we were in Honolulu on New Year's Day 2000. We were fortunate enough to be invited to a party at the family home of Jonathan Twidwell, a good friend, and a gifted healer and psychic. During the afternoon, Jon sat on the floor with a cloth bag full of beautiful, old, and extremely large mah jongg tiles. This appeared to be a family tradition, and almost everyone took the opportunity to have a reading. I knew Jon was an experienced I Ching, Chinese astrology, and numerology reader, but I had no idea he was equally as knowledgeable with mah jongg tiles.

In the East, readers don't give advice to their clients. Instead, they use what the mah jongg tiles tell them to create a story, which the client interprets. The reader provides knowledge and insight, rather than advice on what to do or how to do it.

There are 144 colorful, rectangular mah jongg tiles in a set. There are three suits: wheels, bamboos, and characters. There are thirty-six tiles in each suit, numbered one to nine. There are four of each of these in every suit.

The three suits relate to heaven, earth, and man. Heaven is the most important, as it is the ultimate source of everything. Heaven doesn't need anything else to exist. Earth is the second most important suit. It needs heaven to exist. The third suit is man who is between heaven and Earth. Man depends on heaven and earth.

The colors of these suits are blue for heaven, green for earth, and red for man's blood.

The wheels (sometimes called Circles) relate to heavenly luck, the gifts and talents you were born with. They also relate to matters that are outside your control.

Bamboos relate to earth luck, which relates to your surroundings and environment. Bamboos are also associated with money, wealth, and security.

Characters relate to man luck, which is free will, and what you choose to do. Characters also relate to career and education.

There are also twelve dragons (sometimes known as Honors), sixteen winds, four flowers, and four seasons. There are four tiles for each of the three types of dragon. The dragons are known as Green, Red, and White. There are four for each of the four winds, known as East, South, West, and North. There is one tile for each of the four flowers: Plum Blossom, Orchid, Chrysanthemum, and Bamboo. There is one tile for each of the four seasons: Spring, Summer, Autumn, and Winter.

The tiles are mixed face down on a table. This is usually done by spreading them in a counterclockwise direction until they are thoroughly mixed. While still moving the tiles counterclockwise, create a space in the center. Continue moving the tiles and gradually draw thirteen of them into it.

At this stage, the diviner pushes away the three tiles that are farthest away from him or her. This is repeated with the three tiles to his or her right, followed by the three tiles to the left. The three tiles that are closest to the reader are pulled toward him or her, leaving one tile in the center. This tile is interpreted for a quick reading. All thirteen tiles, and their associations to each other, are interpreted for a fuller reading.

One version of this is to consider the center tile as relating to the question. The three tiles to the diviner's right indicate the present. The three tiles to the left indicate any problems or concerns relating to the question. The three tiles closest to the diviner indicate the near future, and the three tiles opposite these indicate further into the future.

The Tiles
Wheels (Heaven)

1. *Pearl*. Financial security, honor, and culture. Enjoys spending money on beautiful things. Often relates to an older woman.

2. *Pine*. A young man who is gentle and dependable. As a pine tree is strong and weathers storms, this provides confidence. When burned, the pine tree creates good charcoal that is used to make ink for writing. Consequently, there's a potential writing talent.

3. *Phoenix*. Happiness, joy, and laughter. Good fortune.

4. *Jade*. As jade holds qi (life force energy), it's more valued than gold. It takes a great deal of skill and insight to create a work of art from this stone. Success through work and self-discipline. Authority figure. Good friends. Long life.

5. *Dragon*. The 5 dragon is at the center of the Wheels order. It provides unexpected good fortune, triumph, and success. This is the good luck tile.

6. *Peach*. Art, culture, good taste. A young woman plays a major role. Peach also relates to extravagance and an interest in creative activities.

7. *Insect*. A quick sudden burst of physical work produces good results.

8. *Tiger*. Inner strength, protection, and assertiveness. An older male, person in authority, police, and people in uniforms.

9. *Unicorn*. Recognition, opportunities, and success against foes. Intuitive powers. The ability to keep one step ahead.

Bamboos (Earth)

1. *Peacock*. This brings success, but be humble. As the peacock is beautiful, watch out for vanity. It can mean a woman. Change direction for best results.

2. *Duck*. Chinese and Koreans say that ducks pair only once. Consequently, their images are always included somewhere in a wedding banquet. Naturally, it means loyalty, love, and an enduring and successful relationship.

3. *Toad*. Recuperation from illness. It could suggest alternative medicine. A long life. Take your time and avoid stress. A negative aspect is overreaching and trying to gain what is unobtainable.

4. *Carp*. Happiness, friendship, and peace of mind. Potential for longevity. The carp doesn't mean that a problem is resolved or disappears, but it shows the querent has made peace with the difficulty.

5. *Lotus*. New starts. Enthusiasm and motivation. Birth of a baby. This tile indicates an improvement in your life. It's as if the Sun has broken through the clouds after a storm.

6. *Water*. Communication and short trips away from home. The tiles around water will provide more information. It's a good sign if it's beside the 7 of Wheels (Insect). The Chinese idiogram of water and insects means a rainbow. It's a sign that a visitor is coming if this tile is in the west.

7. *Tortoise*. Not happy as everything takes too long to happen. As tortoises live for a long time, this tile can also mean wisdom and knowledge. Slow but steady progress produces success.

8. *Fungus*. This is not any fungus, but the Fungus of Immortality. Expect the unexpected. Ethical behavior is essential. Do something different to break away from the old, traditional ways of doing things.

9. *Willow*. The wind blows, but the willow sheds no leaves. Adjust when necessary. Be diplomatic and go with the flow. Difficulties are temporary. Aspirin is obtained from the bark of the willow. There is healing here for sickness or a broken heart.

Characters (Man)

1. *Entering*. New starts favored, as the road ahead is clear.

2. *Double-edged Sword*. Evaluate carefully and then make a decision.

3. *Earth*. All matters involving home, house, real estate, and security are favored.

4. *Lute*. Creativity. The arts, leisure, and pleasure. Retirement, or enjoying the rewards of hard work.

5. *House*. Temporary problems with a property you're involved with. This could be your home, but it may also be a place of business, a school, or an investment property.

6. *Fire*. This indicates a creative person with a keen, quick mind. Be cautious. Problems ahead, with the possibility of loss. You are burning up your resources.

7. *Seven Stars*. The seven stars are an asterism of stars known as the Big Dipper or the Plough. It's the seat of the gods. The seven stars refers to books, writing, and mathematics. Meditate, think, and dream. Learn as much as possible and make plans.

8. *Knot*. Times are changing. Expect confusion and problems that need to be resolved. You're "knotted up." The tiles next to this tile will make the meaning clear.

9. *Heaven*. Success. Ending of one important stage, and the start of something new.

Winds

- *East Wind.* Spring, wood element, and the color green. New starts.

- *South Wind.* Summer, fire element, and the color red. Forward progress.

- *West Wind.* Autumn, metal element, and the color white. Evaluate where you are.

- *North Wind.* Winter, water element, and the color black. Problems. Be patient and wait.

Dragons

- *Red Dragon.* The center. The arrow in the center of the target. Success in all things. Praise, respect, and honor.

- *Green Dragon.* The Chinese character shows a man drawing a bow with an arrow. Let it go! You could say that the lights have turned green. A good time to start anything new. Act now.

- *White Dragon.* A time of confusion and ambiguity. White can also mean paperwork. Double check everything, as there could be a mistake.

Guardians

There are also eight guardian tiles, comprising four occupation tiles and four flower tiles. They provide advice, hidden insights, and have a positive influence on the reading. They each represent one of the four seasons. If you're fortunate enough to draw any of the guardian tiles, you're asked to draw another tile. These two tiles are read together, as each modifies the other.

Seasons—Occupations

- *Spring.* Fisherman, east wind, wood element, plum blossom flower, and the color green. The best position is in the east. Make an effort to get on with everyone. The querent must practice tolerance for doors to open up. Good leadership brings the best out of people, and also makes more money. The fisherman knows that patience is necessary to catch a fish. There may be no fish today, but there will be tomorrow.

- *Summer.* Woodcutter, south wind, fire element, orchid flower, and the color red. The best position is in the south. Action pays off. Opportunity for success. You can get help to start matters moving. Start chopping your way through the problem. Remember, it takes a great deal of heat before you can burn the wood.

- *Autumn.* Farmer, west wind, metal element, chrysanthemum flower, and the color white. The best position is in the west. Enjoy your work for its own sake. Success will come in time through hard work. This often means physical work. (The farmer works hardest during the harvest time. Farmers must get their crops in before they spoil.)

- *Winter*. Scholar, north wind, water element, bamboo flower, and the color black. Be cautious and studious. A time to communicate. Do any paper work now. This is a good time for creativity. Practical knowledge is good, but it will take you only so far. Look around and learn.

Seasons—Flowers

- *Plum Blossom*. Spring and east wind. This is the first flower of spring. The best position to be in is the east. The awakening of life, new starts, and happiness. Good luck. Plenty of energy at your disposal.

- *Orchid*. Summer and south wind. The best position is the south. Beauty, elegance, rare, and precious objects favored. Refinement. Work on improving what you're doing. This guardian protects young girls.

- *Chrysanthemum*. Autumn and the color white. The best direction is west. Autumn is the time of harvest. It is a happy, relaxing time to enjoy the fruits of hard work and pleasure. Sometimes it's good to let your guard down.

- *Bamboo*. Winter and north wind. The best position is in the north. It shows the character you want in a young man. Thinking, studying, gaining knowledge, and writing. You'll also receive help and protection.

Mirror Compass Reading

The Chinese consider south to be an auspicious direction. One reason for this is that they've never been attacked from that direction. Consequently, south, rather than north, is at the top of their maps.

- *East*. The diviner sits in the east position. The east represents the querent and where he is at the present time.

- *South*. South is a fortunate direction that always indicates success. The south wind is always welcomed and influences the tiles in this area.

- *West*. The tiles in the west indicate the obstacles the querent has to face. However, they can indicate another person and can also be a sign of retirement (as the Sun sets in the west).

- *North*. This is the least fortunate direction and represents difficulties, worries, problems with authority, and financial problems. This is not a good time to start anything new.

The chart, or mirror map, used for mirror compass readings is:

Querent

WEST

7 8 9

NORTH   CENTER   SOUTH

10 11 12   (one tile)   4 5 6

EAST

1 2 3

Mirror compass spread.

If possible, the diviner sits in the east, facing west. However, this isn't essential, and the divination will still work if you don't know what direction you're facing.

At the start of the reading, all 144 tiles are face down. They represent the universe and every possibility. The tiles are thoroughly mixed or "washed," and then the querent selects thirteen tiles from the universe, keeping them all facedown. Thirteen tiles are selected as this represents the number of possible lunar months in a year.

The diviner mixes the thirteen tiles, and the querent is asked to "reject" or remove three of the tiles and place them in the west position.

"Why reject these three? They go in the west," he or she says. "They represent your challenges, obstacles, or difficulties to overcome. Now reject three more and place them here." The diviner indicates north. "This is the future, or maybe a possible outcome. It's a possible future, as nothing is written in stone, and you have the power to change it."

"Choose three more tiles. They could represent the near future, or provide insight into your problems." The diviner indicates the south. "Now place one tile in the center. This provides the flavor or direction of the reading. And now, the last three tiles go here in the east. They are about you."

Once this has been done, the diviner starts the reading with the center tile. It provides the direction of the reading.

He or she then turns over tiles 1 and 3 in the east. These cover the querent's personality, how he or she sees the world, and sometimes information about the present situation. Tile 2 (the center of the east) is turned over. This represents the querent's wishes, hopes, and dreams. The diviner then looks at all three tiles and gives another interpretation with all three energies intertwined.

The tiles in the south are turned over one at a time, and explained. They represent the near future, as well as what is being considered or about to occur. Sometimes these tiles hint at a solution.

Tile 7 in the west is turned over. This represents the querent's main obstacle. Tile 9 is turned over to reveal other factors to the problem. The tile between them (tile 8) provides a way to resolve the situation.

Tiles 10 and 11 in the north are turned over. These provide additional insight, as well as clues to the eventual outcome. This is clarified by turning over and interpreting tile 12.

In practice, the meanings of the thirteen tiles change slightly, depending on their position: Center, east, south, west, or north. The seven of Characters (Seven Stars), for instance, indicates a literary person, or a dreamer who fails to act, when it's in the east. It's a sign that your plans should be acted upon when it's in the 8th position in the west. However, your plans are unrealistic if it's positioned in the 7th or 9th positions in the west.

Like astrology, Mah jongg is a fascinating and complex art that can be studied for a lifetime without learning all there is to know.

Suggested Reading

Walters, Derek. *Your Future Revealed by the Mah Jongg.* Wellingborough, UK: The Aquarian Press, 1982.

Numerology

Numerology is the study of the occult meanings of numbers, and is one of the oldest of the divinatory arts. It's so old that it was "modernized" by Pythagoras 2,600 years ago. It has been modernized several times since then, and the numerology that is practiced today bears little resemblance to the methods used by Pythagoras and his school.

Numerology is one of the simplest divinatory arts to learn, but it provides a great deal of information. All you need is someone's date of birth and full name at birth to provide a comprehensive reading.

The Main Numbers

The main numbers in numerology are the Life Path, the Expression, and the Soul Urge. The Life Path is the major lesson to be learned, the central focus in a person's life. The Expression relates to the person's natural abilities, and the Soul Urge shows the person's inner nature—what he or she would like to do or become. The Life Path is the most important of these and represents about 40 percent of the person's makeup. The Expression is about 30 percent, and the Soul Urge 20 percent. The remaining 10 percent is comprised of other factors, especially the person's day of birth.

The Life Path

The Life Path reveals your purpose in life and shows what you have come here to learn. It is derived from the person's full date of birth, reduced down to a single digit. However, as there are two Master Numbers in numerology (11 and 22), the Life Path number must be worked out in a particular way. The first step is to reduce each of the numbers making up the month, day, and year to a single digit or a Master Number. These three numbers are added together and reduced again to a single digit or Master Number.

Here's an example of someone born on April 28, 1980:

Month: April is the fourth month. No reduction is required, giving us a 4.
Day: This person was born on the 28th. 2 + 8 = 10, and 1 + 0 = 1
Year: This person was born in 1980: 1 + 9 + 8 + 0 = 18, and 1 + 8 = 9

The three numbers are added together and reduced to a single digit, or Master Number:

4 + 1 + 9 = 14, and 1 + 4 = 5
This person has a Life Path of 5.

A good friend of mine was born on February 29, 1944:

Month: February, which is the second month: 2
Day: She was born on the 29th: 2 + 9 = 11. As 11 is a Master Number, it isn't reduced further.
Year: She was born in 1944: 1 + 9 + 4 + 4 = 18, and 1 + 8 = 9

The three numbers are added together, and reduced to a single digit or a Master Number:

2 + 11 + 9 = 22
My friend has a Life Path of 22.

If we added her numbers of birth in a line, we'd lose the Master Number:

2 (month) + 2 + 9 (day) + 1 + 9 + 4 + 4 = 31, and 3 + 1 = 4

This is why the Life Path numbers from the person's date of birth have to be worked out in this particular way.

The Numbers
One
Keyword: individualization

One stands for originality, attainment, and independence. Someone on this Life Path needs to "go it alone" and stand on his or her own two feet. Once this person has achieved independence, he or she can progress to attainment by using his or her abilities in an original, creative, pioneering manner. It is the number of the pioneer, the leader, and the striver.

Two

Keyword: adaptability.

Someone with a Life Path of two will be cooperative, diplomatic, and peacemaking. He or she will be considerate, caring, and friendly.

Three

Keywords: creativity and self-expression

Threes are social, fun-loving, creative people who express all the joys of life. The three person is good at expressing him or herself with words: talking, writing, and performing, for instance. A three also freely expresses his or her feelings, love, affection, and friendship.

Four

Keywords: limitation and organization

Four represents self-discipline, hard work, routine, patience, and limitation. We all have limitations, and the lesson of this number is to live in harmony with them, rather than fight against them. By using patience, reliability, organization, and hard work, people with this number ultimately achieve success.

Five

Keywords: freedom and change

People on this Life Path are versatile and talented in a number of areas. The desire for travel is strong, and life will be full and exciting. Freedom, variety, and change play an important role in the life of people on a five Life Path.

Six

Keyword: responsibility

People on this Life Path have the ability to help and comfort others. They enjoy this, but often feel responsible for more than their fair share. People on this Life Path work quietly and efficiently and help adjust inharmonious situations. They send out friendship and love to others and receive it back in full measure. This is a loving, friendly, and rewarding Life Path to be on.

Seven

Keywords: wisdom and understanding

This is a quiet, introverted number, and people on this Life Path enjoy analyzing and searching into hidden truths and mysteries. Many people on this path can be found in technical or scientific occupations. It's a spiritual number, and people on this path often have philosophical, mystical, and spiritual interests. It's a "different" Life Path, as these people have their own special way of doing things.

Eight

Keyword: material freedom

Eight is the number of business, money, and executive ability. People on this Life Path will be concerned with status, power, and success. Their ability to work hard to achieve their goals can make them appear stubborn and single-minded to others. Once they've achieved the success they desire, they can be generous, but they need to satisfy their material needs first.

Nine

Keyword: humanitarianism

People on this Life Path need to learn the satisfaction of giving to others. It's not an easy path, as sometimes the person will have to give up his or her ambitions to help others. The satisfaction comes from helping and giving to others. The giving could be some form of creative expression, such as art or writing.

Eleven

Keywords: illumination and inspiration

People on this Life Path are visionaries and dreamers. They are naturally intuitive and have the potential to inspire others by example. There is always a degree of nervous tension associated with number eleven.

Twenty-two

Keyword: master builder

This number represents the practical idealists who can make their visions a reality. This is a practical, powerful number, and people on this Life Path have the potential to achieve almost anything they desire. Unfortunately, the nervous tension surrounding this number means that few people on this path achieve more than a minute fraction of what they could.

The Negative Side

Sadly, all the numbers have a negative side to them as well. This will be apparent when you're not expressing yourself as you should.

One

Keywords: self and dependence

On the negative path one's can appear to be at everyone's beck and call. They need to overcome this dependence before they can become independent. Alternatively, they may think of themselves, first and last. These people can be self-centered and egotistical, and they are likely to be concealing an inferiority complex.

Two

Keyword: sensitivity

Negative twos can be overly shy, self-effacing, and pessimistic. Sometimes twos fight against the role they've been given and try to become leaders. They might succeed, but they will never excel as they're fighting against their own natures.

Three

Keyword: superficiality

Negative threes are inclined to waste time, frittering their energies away, and scattering their forces in many directions. People on this Life Path need to be constantly aware of this, so they do not become superficial and frivolous.

Four

Keyword: drudgery

Negative fours are so tied down with feelings of limitation and frustration that they find themselves in a rut of their own making. The stubbornness and rigidity that this creates makes it hard for them to realize that they're creating their own misfortune.

Five

Keyword: self-indulgence

Negative fives find it hard to stick at anything for long, as they are surrounded by opportunities everywhere they look. They can also be procrastinators who lose themselves in self-indulgence and sensuality.

Six

Keyword: slave

Fortunately, there are few negative people on this Life Path. Occasionally, sixes will become overwhelmed with responsibilities and be misused by others. Sometimes people on this Life Path can be overly critical and meddle in other people's business.

Seven

Keyword: introspection

Negative sevens can be so withdrawn and self-centered that they retreat from every situation. As they're also likely to be nervous, they find it hard to relate to others, and this holds back their growth and development.

Eight

Keyword: demander

Negative eights want money and power and will do anything to achieve it. They might misuse power and become a tyrant. Because they're impatient they frequently fail to achieve their goals. Even when they do, their accomplishments bring little satisfaction.

Nine

Keyword: egotist

Negative nines are frequently aimless dreamers who live more in their minds than in the real world. They may also be ambitious and refuse to accept the selflessness that is an important part of their development.

Eleven

Keyword: fanatic

Negative elevens are aware of their special capabilities and will use them to gratify their own selfish desires. These people often have delusions of grandeur.

Twenty-two

Keyword: greed

Negative twenty-twos are extremely materialistic. They want to get rich quick, and will do almost anything to achieve it. Although they may succeed in these goals, they'll always be aware that it's not what they could, or should, be doing.

It's impossible to change your Life Path, as it's derived from your date of birth. Most numerologists believe that we're all here to learn certain lessons, and our Life Path can tell us what they are. Many people have told me that they wish they were on a different Life Path to the one they're on. Spiritual people believe that our souls chose our Life Path, and it was consequently decided before we were even born. No matter what you may think about your Life Path, it still represents the central focus of your life.

Some Life Paths sound easier than others. The warmth, friendliness, and the self-expression of the three, and the natural enthusiasm of the five sound more exciting than the introspection and lack of adaptability of the seven or the self-centeredness of the one. However, all is not as it appears. The enthusiasm of the five, for instance, can lead to an inability to stick to anything for long, and the self-centeredness of the one provides the self-belief that is essential for success.

Expression

The second most important number in numerology is the Expression. This reveals the person's potential natural abilities, and it is derived from all the letters in a person's full name at birth, turned into numbers and reduced to a single digit or Master Number. To do this, we use a chart:

1	2	3	4	5	6	7	8	9
A	B	C	D	E	F	G	H	I
J	K	L	M	N	O	P	Q	R
S	T	U	V	W	X	Y	Z	

To work out the Expression number, you need to write the full name down and then write the numerological value of each letter underneath. In practice, it's easier to write down the numbers for the vowels above the name, and the consonants below. This is because the Soul Urge, the number we'll look at next, is derived from the vowels:

Jennifer Jane Harding

	5			9		5		= 1
J	E	N	N	I	F	E	R	
1		5	5		6		9	= 8

	1		5	= 6
J	A	N	E	
1		5		= 6

	1			9			= 1
H	A	R	D	I	N	G	
8		9	4		5	7	= 6

The numbers for each letter, both above and below Jennifer's name, are added together, word by word, and reduced to a single digit. If you look at the numbers above Jennifer's first name, you'll see 5, 9, and 5. If you add them up, you'll have a total of 19, which reduces down to a 1. (5 + 9 + 5 = 19. 1 + 9 = 10, and 1 + 0 = 1). The numbers placed below her first name add up to 8 (1 + 5 + 5 + 6 + 9 = 26, and 2 + 6 = 8). This is repeated with the other numbers above and below her name.

If you add up the final, reduced numbers above and below each name, you'll find that Jennifer's Expression number is 1 as: 1 + 8 + 6 + 6 + 1 + 6 = 28. As 2 + 8 = 10, and 1 + 0 = 1. Jennifer has an Expression number of 1.

Expression Number Meanings

- *One*: People with a one expression are creative thinkers. They're independent and make good leaders, promoters, organizers, and administrators. As they're self-reliant and self-centered, they need to follow their own course. They do well in business and when working for others rise to a position of power and responsibility. They're ambitious and determined and aim directly at anything they want.

- *Two*: People with a two expression are sensitive, sympathetic, modest, diplomatic, tactful, and cooperative. They're friendly and have a natural ability at making people feel at ease. They work well with others and make good facilitators and organizers.

- *Three*: People with a three expression are full of ideas, and as they're good conversationalists, enjoy discussing them with others. They're optimistic, outgoing, friendly, and charming. They enjoy harmony in their lives, have a strong artistic sense, and are frequently creative. They love having fun and can often be the life and soul of the party.

- *Four*: People with a four expression are practical, well-organized, and self-disciplined. They like order and routine and have the ability to bring order to any kind of situation. They are good with details and like to finish everything they start. They are hard workers and enjoy careers that involve practicality, accuracy, concentration, and persistence. They are conscientious and reliable.

- *Five*: People with a five expression are good at working with others. They are versatile and thrive on change, variety, and unexpected happenings. They're enthusiastic and need plenty of stimulation. They quickly tire of anything once it has been mastered. They don't like being hemmed in or restricted, and they need plenty of freedom to operate at their best.

- *Six*: People with a six expression have a strong sense of fairness and justice. They're peaceful by nature but react quickly when anything is unfair to anyone involved. They're helpful, caring, understanding, and responsible. They work well in careers involving helping others. They enjoy home and family life.

- *Seven*: People with a seven expression have a good mind and enjoy researching and analyzing anything that interests them. They have a logical, rational approach, and enjoy specialized and detailed work. They seldom express their emotions.

- *Eight*: People with an eight expression have the potential to succeed in any field that interests them. They use determination, persistence, and stamina to reach their goals. They have good organizational skills, and because they're naturally good at dealing with money and finance, they usually do well financially. They're ambitious, hard-working, and confident about their own abilities.

- *Nine*: People with a nine expression are humanitarians, with a genuine interest and compassion for others. They're creative, idealistic, romantic, and philanthropic. They give a great deal of themselves and frequently make careers in a field where they can help or inspire others.

- *Eleven*: People with an eleven expression are idealistic, intuitive, and inspirational. They have good minds and express themselves well. They are very capable at whatever they turn their minds to. They have good taste and work best in harmonious surrounding. They often possess a creative talent.

- *Twenty-two:* People with a twenty-two expression are exceptionally capable and enjoy working on large scale projects. With their abilities, insights, and energy, they have the potential to achieve more than most. However, a degree of nervous tension is likely to hold them back in their younger years.

Soul Urge

The Soul Urge is the third most important number in a numerology chart. It describes people's inner nature, what they'd like to be doing, and what they really want out of life. It's derived from the vowels, reduced to a single digit (unless they reduce to an 11 or 22).

The letter Y can sometimes act as a vowel. Cathy and Sylvia are two examples of this. When this occurs, the Y is classified as a vowel, rather than a consonant. In the name Yolande, for instance, the Y is classified as a consonant. Yancy is an interesting name, as one Y is a consonant, and the other a vowel.

Soul Urge Number Meanings

- *One*: People with a one Soul Urge want to be independent, original, creative, and witty. They want to be the center of attention, and have a strong desire to lead. They might be impatient with people who don't think or act as quickly as they do. They have a strong desire for success.

- *Two*: People with a two Soul Urge want peace, affection, and love. As they're sensitive, sympathetic, and cooperative, they want to be part of a harmonious group, both at work and at home. They want their ideas to be heard and use tact rather than force to achieve this.

- *Three*: People with a three Soul Urge want to express their creativity and joy in life. They want to be at the center of things where they can express their happiness and radiance to everyone. They want to be popular, and they achieve this with their charm and conversational skills.

- *Four*: People with a four Soul Urge want their hard work to be appreciated. They want to lead orderly, well-defined lives, and dislike changes and unexpected happenings. They want to be involved in projects that utilize their love of details, and their organizational skills.

- *Five*: People with a five Soul Urge want freedom, excitement, and travel. They want plenty of change and variety to keep them stimulated and happy. They're adaptable, enthusiastic, innovative, progressive, and have a fear of being tied down or restricted.

- *Six*: People with a six Soul Urge want harmony, beauty, and color in their lives. They enjoy the love, cares, and responsibilities of home and family life. They're modest, conscientious, and frequently creative. They want opportunities to provide stability for their home and loved ones.

- *Seven*: People with a seven Soul Urge want plenty of time on their own to think, contemplate, observe, and dream. They have a strong desire to learn and understand, especially in scientific, religious, or occult subjects. Most of the time they prefer to stand on the sideline and observe, rather than be a participant.

- *Eight*: People with an eight Soul Urge want wealth and power. They want to be involved in profitable enterprises, and other activities that utilize their good judgment and managerial ability. They have plenty of energy and stamina and enjoy using this to help them reach their goals.

- *Nine*: People with a nine Soul Urge want to give of themselves in philanthropic or creative ways. They're inspired more by ideals than the practicalities of life. They don't find it easy to accomplish their goals, as there's often a conflict between personal ambitions and spiritual aims.

- *Eleven*: People with an eleven Soul Urge want to share their idealistic, intuitive, and humanitarian ideas with others. They want to give of themselves to all humanity, rather than to a single individual. They're not satisfied with the world as it is, and want to create a better future for all humanity.

- *Twenty-two*: People with a twenty-two Soul Urge want to make an important contribution to the world. They want to organize and lead on an international scale. Like people with an eleven Soul Urge, they want to use their talents to help mankind benefit and progress in humanitarian ways.

The Day of Birth

The number of the day of birth has an effect on the Life Path, which it modifies slightly. If, for instance, someone had a Life Path of 3 and was born on the 7th of the month, he or she would be a deeper thinker than would otherwise be the case. The sociability of the three would also be affected by the need for solitude provided by the seven, and the adaptability of the three would be affected by the rigidity of the seven. This is why two people might share the same Life Path but be completely different to each other. In numerology, a number that has an effect upon another number is called a modifier.

Putting It Together

Jennifer Harding, the person is our example, has an expression of 1 and a Soul Urge of 8. If we also assume she was born on April 28, 1980, which we used as an example when working out the Life Path, she has a Life Path of 5, and a birthday of 1. This gives us:

> *Life Path*: 5
> *Expression*: 1
> *Soul Urge*: 8
> *Birthday*: 1

Using these, you could say to Jennifer:

You're versatile, adventurous, positive, and enthusiastic. Unlike many people, you enjoy plenty of change and variety and always need something exciting to look forward to. You'll frequently find yourself doing more than one thing at a time. You become impatient when you feel hemmed in or restricted. You'll always be young at heart (Life Path).

You'd work best in a field where your independence and originality can be utilized. You're ambitious, and you have the potential to do well in any career you choose (Expression).

You have a strong desire to progress in your chosen career and to achieve financial success. Your leadership capabilities and organizational skills will help you progress and achieve your goals (Soul Urge).

You have an interesting relationship between your Life Path and your birthday, as it can work both for and against you. Interestingly, your expression and birthday numbers are both 1, which combined are just as important as your Life Path number of 5. The freedom and variety produced by your Life Path can sometimes help the strong desire of your expression and birthday for achievement and success, particularly if you're self-employed or have a great deal of freedom and autonomy in your work. However, your expression and birthday are independent and goal-oriented, and this can conflict with the strong desire for freedom, variety, and change provided by your Life Path. You'll need to learn to recognize these when they appear so you can make the right decisions and progress toward the financial success indicated by your Soul Urge.

Into the Future

So far, what we've been doing is character analysis. Numerology can also be used to predict the trends of the person's future. In numerology, life is lived in nine-year cycles. This doesn't mean you'll be doing exactly the same things you're doing now in nine year's time. The energies will be the same, but the specifics will be different, as several other numbers modify the year numbers.

The person's personal year number is obtained by adding the current year to his or her day and month of birth, and reducing it down to a single digit.

In Jennifer's case, 2019 is an eight personal year. This is because:

Month: April is the fourth month. This gives us a 4.
Day: Jennifer was born on the 28th. $2 + 8 = 10$, and $1 + 0 = 1$
Current year: in our example 2019. $2 + 0 + 1 + 9 = 12$, and $1 + 2 = 3$
$4 + 1 + 3 = 8$ personal year

The year before (2018) Jennifer was in a seven personal year, and in 2020 she'll be in a nine personal year. The year after that (2021) she'll be starting a new cycle of experience in a one personal year.

Personal Years

Here's what I might say to someone when they're in a particular personal year:

One personal year

This is a year of new starts. You'll have plenty of enthusiasm and energy. You're starting on a whole new cycle of experience. Anything you begin now will last for a long time. You may start twenty new things, but will have enough enthusiasm and energy to keep them all going. There's a potential for an important change this year. This could relate to your career or personal life. Whatever it is, this change will need to be initiated by you.

Two personal year

This is a consolidation year. This year all your different activities are brought back to more manageable proportions. It's a gentler year, too, but you'll need patience. In a one personal year you can push and things will work for you. In a two personal year you need to be patient and allow matters sufficient time to develop. Consequently, it's easy to get frustrated. Spend time with loved ones and also trust and act on your intuition. This is a good year for resolving longstanding difficulties.

Three personal year

This is a lighthearted, carefree year. It would be great if you could have the whole year off to play. It's unlikely that you'll be doing that, though, as there seem to be many pressures upon your time. All the same, your thoughts this year will be focused on pleasant, fun activities, rather than hard work. It's a good year for making new friends and catching up with old ones. It's also a good year for creativity. Do some entertaining or be entertained.

Four personal year

This is a nose to the grindstone sort of year. It's a year of hard work, where you'll probably feel you're simply plodding along. Actually, it's a particularly good year to set a specific goal, as by the end of the year you'll have achieved it. If you have no particular goal, it can be a year where you sink deeper and deeper into the mire. Recognize that this is a year of hard work. After a less serious year, you'll be needing a challenge, and this year provides it in full measure.

Five personal year

This is a year of change and variety. It would be wonderful if you could go on an overseas trip this year as that would provide the necessary stimulation and excitement you crave. If you're not planning anything as momentous as this, at least do something different. If there's something you've always wanted to do, but have never quite got around to doing it, this is the perfect year to make it happen. Expect the unexpected, also. You may have someone call you and suggest you both do something exciting and different. Seize these opportunities. If you're not doing something different or exciting this year, you'll feel unsettled and not really know why.

Six personal year

This is a home and family year. It's the perfect year to get married in. It's also an excellent year for divorce! If relationships are going well, this year brings you closer and closer together. Naturally, if they're not going well, this year takes you further and further apart. You may find that people close to you will need extra help or advice this year. Be understanding and compassionate. You may find you're not able to do all the things you want to do this year because of the needs of others. You'll find it a pleasure to help others in this way.

Seven personal year

This is a quieter, gentler year. You'll have time to smell the flowers as you pass by. It's a year when you'll want more time than usual by yourself to meditate and think about what's going on in your life. You may decide to carry on your education in some way, or you may perhaps experience some sort of spiritual insight. This is a nonmaterialistic year, and it brings its own special rewards. Let other people know when you're planning to spend time by yourself, so they'll understand and leave you alone.

Eight personal year

This is the money year. This is the year you reap the rewards for the work you have put in over the previous decade. Ensure you have some financial goals this year. If you decide you want, say, a new car, you'll find that by the end of the year you'll have it, albeit at some cost. If you have no financial goals, you'll still do okay, but nowhere near as well as you would have if you'd taken the time to set them. This year favors all financial activities, good and bad. It's a good year to buy and sell, and to invest. However, if you owe everyone in town money, this is the year they'll try to collect. Make sure you have a vacation during the year. People are often inclined to overdo things in an eight year, so it's important to take time off every now and again.

Nine personal year

This is the completion year of a whole cycle of experience. Part of you will be looking back and part of you will be looking ahead, planning for the future. This will be a pleasant year, but there'll be odd melancholy moments as you'll have to let go of things that have been around you for some time. It's never easy to let go, but it's necessary as it makes room for the new projects that lie ahead. During the year, you'll get a number of false leads as to where you want to go from here. However, in the final few months of the year it will become blindingly obvious as to where you want to go. You may wonder why you didn't think of it years before, but these things happen when the timing is right, not always when you think the time is right. By the end of this year, you'll have a clear idea of where you want to go, and next year, in the one personal year, you'll be heading toward it. The nine year is a year of planning; the one year is the year of action.

Personal Months and Days

It's a simple matter to determine someone's personal months and days. All you need do is add the personal year to the number of the month, and reduce it down to a single digit. In a three personal year, January would be a four personal month (3 + 1 = 4), February would be a five personal month, March would be a six, and so on. The personal months are not nearly as powerful as the personal years, but have a noticeable effect on them.

A personal day is worked out by adding the day to the personal month, and reducing it down to a single digit. Naturally, this is of minor importance compared to a personal month or year, but it can be useful if you're planning to do something and want to know the best day to do it on. If you're planning to start something, do it on a one personal day.

- *One, two,* and *three* personal days are good for shopping.

- A *four* day is the perfect day to do something you've been putting off.

- A *five* day is a good time to do something fresh or different.

- A *six* day is an excellent day to get married on. It's also a good day for home and family activities.

- A *seven* day is a good time for study or spiritual development.

- You should pay bills and make investment decisions on an *eight* day.

- A *nine* day is a good time to finish projects.

Spiritual Days

Spiritual days are positive, red-letter days when you can move ahead, progress, and undertake important tasks. They're good days to buy a house, take a trip abroad, and even get married on. Many people consider spiritual days to be lucky days, and certainly good things seem to happen on these particular days. Fortunately, you have three or four spiritual days every month.

You start by working out the universal day number. This is done by adding together the year, month, and day, and bringing them down to a single digit. Let's assume we want to find out someone's spiritual days in December 2019. We start by determining the universal day for the first day of the month:

Year: 2019. $2 + 0 + 1 + 9 = 12$, and $1 + 2 = 3$
Month: December: 12, reduces to 3
Day: the 1st = 1
$3 + 3 + 1 = 7$

December 1, 2019, is a 7 universal day. This means December 2 is an 8 universal day, December 3 is a 9 universal day, December 4 is a 1 universal day, and so on. Three or four times every month, your Life Path number will be the same as the universal day number. These are your spiritual days.

Jennifer, our long-suffering example, has a five Life Path number. This means that in December 2019, the following dates will be her spiritual days: 8, 17, and 26.

The Pyramids

The pyramids reveal the trends of the person's entire life. Start by drawing a diagram of an upside down V, known as a pyramid. Inside this pyramid is another pyramid, with two smaller pyramids inside it. The person's full date of birth, with each number reduced to a single digit (unless, of course, it reduces to an 11 or 22) is placed at the base of the two innermost pyramids.

If we continue using our example of someone born on April 28, 1980, Jennifer's month of birth is placed below the left-hand side of the inner pyramid. This is a 4. Place the number of her month of birth below the right-hand side of the same pyramid. This is a 1, as $2 + 8 = 10$, and $1 + 0 = 1$. Finally, place her year of birth (1980, which reduces to a 9) below the right-hand side of the second pyramid.

The other numbers need to be worked out by a process of addition. Add the person's month and day of birth together, and place that at the top of the left-hand inner pyramid. This is 5, as the 4 from the month added to the 1 of the day, totals 5.

Do the same with the other pyramid, adding the person's day and year together. In our example this is 1 and 9, and the total, reduced to a single digit, in this case 1, is placed at the top of the right-hand inner pyramid. Take the two numbers at the top of the small pyramids (5 and 1), add them together and place the total (6 in this example) at the top of the larger inner pyramid.

The final stage of this is to add the month and year numbers together ($4 + 9 = 13$, and $1 + 3 = 4$) at the top of the outermost pyramid.

Time needs to be added to this chart to make it useable. The first important year in the person's life, numerologically speaking, is placed at the top of the first innermost pyramid. The number 5 in our example is in this position. This year shows when the person reaches maturity, again from a numerological point of view. This number is determined by subtracting the person's Life Path number from 36. In this position, 11s and 22s are reduced to a single digit before subtracting it from 36. This means everyone reaches numerological maturity from 27 to 35 years old. In our example, the person reaches maturity at the age of 31, as her Life Path number is 5. Consequently, 31 is written beside the 5 at the top of the first innermost triangle. I usually circle the ages to differentiate them from the other numbers.

As we lead our lives in nine-year cycles, the next important age is nine years after the person has reached numerological maturity. In our example, this is 40, and it is placed next to the 1 at the top of the second innermost triangle. Nine years after this is 49, and this is written next to the 6 at the top of the larger inner pyramid. Then 58 is written next to the 4 at the top of the large outside pyramid.

If you want to carry on beyond this, the next important year (67) is placed next to the month number (4) at the bottom left-hand side of the first inner pyramid. Then 76 is placed next to the day (1), and 85 is placed next to the year number (9). If necessary, you can go around the pyramids again for as long as you wish. In this case, 94 would be placed next to the age where the person reached maturity, and so on.

The pyramids have nothing to do with length of life. They simply mark periods of time. What they do do is show what the person is working toward during each cycle.

All of the ages written on the chart are important in terms of the person's life. They always correspond to the 9 and 1 personal years. The transition from one pyramid to another happens quickly. About three months before one cycle ends, the person starts to feel the influence of the next cycle of experience.

The first cycle of experience is from birth up to the age of maturity. Throughout that time, the person is learning the lesson of the number he or she is heading toward. In our example, this number is 5. That means our long-suffering example, Jennifer, is experiencing a great deal of change and variety and is learning to use her time wisely. During the second cycle, from 31 to 40, she is learning the lesson of 1. This means she's achieving independence, and standing on her own two feet. From 40 to 49, she's heading toward a 6. This means home and family responsibilities. Because of the freedom and variety in her first 31years, she's probably settled down later than most people. From 49 to 58, and then on to 67, she's heading toward a 4. The 4 indicates limitations, restrictions, and hard work. They're going to be busy times in terms of her life. She's heading toward a 1 again in the years from 67 to 76, and experiences 9 for the first time between 76 and 85. Nine is a humanitarian number, and she'll be learning to give of herself to others.

As you can see from this example, it's possible for a lesson to need more than nine years to be learned. Our example person needs eighteen years to learn the lesson of number 4. If you create a chart for someone born on September 9, 1998, you'll see that he or she needs a whole lifetime to learn the lesson of number 9.

It's also possible for someone to learn a lesson during a nine-year period only to have the same number turn up again in a later stage. This means that although the lesson was learned during the first cycle, the knowledge was gradually forgotten, which means the lesson needs to be learned again.

Knowledge of personal years, personal months, personal days, and the pyramids can be extremely helpful in planning for the future and for pursuing goals at the right time. It's easier, and much less stressful, to work with your numbers rather than fight against them.

Tic-Tac-Toe Numerology

The tic-tac-toe system of numerology is frequently called Chinese numerology, as it uses a three-by-three grid of numbers. Numerology, along with Chinese astrology, the I Ching, and feng shui, is said to be derived from a three-by-three square in the markings of a tortoise shell that was found by Wu of Hsia, the first of the five mythical emperors of China, some four thousand years ago. What fascinated Wu and his men was that the numbers in every horizontal, vertical, and diagonal row added up to fifteen:

4	9	2
3	5	7
8	1	6

In addition to this, the number five was regarded highly in ancient China, and this magic square had a five in the central position. No wonder Wu and his advisors were so excited with their discovery.

Chinese numerology was based on their lunar calendar, and at some stage over the years, people discovered that similar types of numerology readings could be done using the Western solar calendar by changing the positions of the numbers:

3	6	9
2	5	8
1	4	7

The rows and columns making up the chart can be looked at in different ways. The top row (3, 6, and 9) can represent a person's head, the middle row (2, 5, and 8) the body, and 1, 4, and 7 the legs and feet.

Consequently, the top row is considered the mental plane, and includes thinking, creating, imagining, and analyzing. The middle row is the emotional plane. The heart, the seat of the emotions, is situated in the body. This plane includes spirituality, intuition, feelings, and emotions. The bottom row is the practical plane. This includes physical labor, manual dexterity, and the ability to be practical in day to day life.

The vertical rows can also be interpreted. The first of these (1, 2, and 3) is the thought plane. This reveals the person's ability at coming up with ideas, and carrying them through to completion. The middle vertical row (4, 5, and 6) is the will plane. This gives the person the necessary persistence and drive to succeed. The third vertical row (7, 8, and 9) is the action plane. It shows the person's ability at putting his or her thoughts into action.

Each number in the person's full date of birth is placed into the appropriate box in the chart. Here's an example of someone born on April 28, 1980:

		9
2		88
1	4	

You'll notice that two 8s (from the 28 and 1980) are placed in the 8 box. Also, zeros are ignored, which is why the zero in 1980 doesn't have a place in the chart.

Here's another example, this time for Britney Spears, who was born on December 2, 1981:

		9
22		8
111		

As it's impossible for any date of birth to fill in every box, everyone is missing at least one number. In fact, someone born on February 20, 2022, would have eight empty boxes.

Arrows of Pythagoras

There are sixteen arrows or lines that can appear in a chart. They are named after Pythagoras, but there's no evidence that he ever used them.

The arrows are complete lines, made up of either numbers or gaps. They can be vertical, horizontal, or diagonal. The example of someone born on April 28, 1980, has one arrow, made up from the absence of the numbers 3, 5, and 7.

Britney Spears has two arrows, both created by the absence of numbers. They are: 3, 5, and 7, and 4, 5, and 6.

Here's an example of someone born on March 25, 1947, who has three arrows made up of numbers:

3		9
2	5	
1	4	7

This is Elton John's date of birth. His chart has three arrows: 3, 5, and 7; 1, 5, and 9; and 1, 4, and 7.

Not everyone has an arrow in his or her chart. Some years ago I read that arrows are essential, as they give the person the necessary ability to capitalize on his or her strengths, and to compensate for any weaknesses. However, this is not the case, as many famous people are missing arrows in their charts. One example is Wolfgang Amadeus Mozart, the famous composer, who was born on January 27, 1756.

The Arrows of Strength

The arrows of strength indicate natural talents or abilities that can be used to help the person progress.

The Arrow of Determination

The arrow of determination is a diagonal arrow: 1, 5, and 9. As its name indicates, it gives people with it plenty of determination and persistence. They're also enterprising, progressive, and patient.

The Arrow of Compassion

The arrow of compassion is also a diagonal arrow: 3, 5, and 7. People with this arrow develop a strong faith and philosophy of life, usually built on the experiences they've gone through. Many people with this arrow are strongly interested in music.

The Arrow of Intellect

The arrow of intellect comprises the horizontal row of 3, 6, and 9. These are the mental numbers, and provide people with this arrow a good mind and an excellent memory. They usually prefer to use their intellect over their emotions. Home and family are important to them.

The Arrow of Emotional Balance

The arrow of emotional balance is made up of 2, 5, and 8. People who have this are compassionate, understanding, empathetic, supportive, and emotionally well-balanced. They are also natural healers.

The Arrow of Practicality

The arrow of practicality comprises all three numbers on the practical plane: 1, 4, and 7. People with this arrow are capable, practical, down-to-earth, and hardworking. They're prepared to work long and hard to achieve their goals.

The Arrow of the Planner

The arrow of the planner consists of the first vertical column: 1, 2, and 3. People with this arrow have at least one number in each of the mental, emotional, and practical planes. They are well organized and enjoy lengthy conversations on matters that interest them. They make good students and can lose themselves totally in what they're studying.

The Arrow of Willpower

The arrow of willpower comprises the numbers 4, 5, and 6. People with this arrow are self-centered, dynamic, forceful, and persistent. They often experience problems in their lives, but remain positive and optimistic. They make good friends.

The Arrow of Activity

The arrow of activity comprises the numbers 7, 8, and 9. People with this arrow need to express themselves with action. The need to be busy, either mentally or physically. They enjoy wide open spaces and hate being hemmed in or restricted.

The Arrows of Weakness

The arrows of weakness indicate the areas of the chart that the person needs to develop. We can all develop as people, and these arrows show where we should start.

The Arrow of Indecision

The arrow of indecision is made up of spaces in boxes 1, 5, and 9. These people find it hard to make decisions, as they want to be liked and do the right thing. As it's impossible to please everyone, they prevaricate until forced to act.

The Arrow of Skepticism

The arrow of skepticism comprises spaces in boxes 3, 5, and 7. People with this arrow want to see things demonstrated or proven, rather than accepting anything on trust. They find it hard to express their feelings and are inclined to be idealistic. They have a conservative approach toward religion.

The Arrow of Poor Memory

The arrow of poor memory is made up of the absence of the numbers 3, 6, and 9. People with this arrow have strong mental faculties but tend to become forgetful and absentminded as the person ages.

The Arrow of Emotional Sensitivity

The arrow of emotional sensitivity is created by the absence of the numbers 2, 5, and 8. This means there are no numbers on the emotional plane. Consequently, people with this arrow are extremely sensitive and easily hurt. They're extremely good at helping and nurturing others. They're usually shy as children.

The Arrow of Impracticality

The arrow of impracticality is an absence of any numbers on the practical plane: 1, 4, and 7. These people are impractical and idealistic and are happiest when using their minds and emotions. They prefer theories over practical application.

The Arrow of Frustrations

The arrow of frustrations is created by the absence of the numbers 4, 5, and 6. This effectively divides the chart in two, with no numbers on the emotional plane. People with this arrow experience more than their share of disappointments, setbacks, and frustrations. They need to learn to accept other people as they are.

The Arrow of Hesitation

The arrow of hesitation is made up of the absence of the numbers 7, 8, and 9. People with this arrow are lateral thinkers but lack drive and motivation. They seldom achieve much until they learn self-discipline, and realize that success comes only through effort.

The Individual Numbers

The individual numbers in the chart are interpreted, too. They provide valuable information about people's character, as well as their strengths and weaknesses.

One 1

This creates people who have difficulty in self-expression. They may be good speakers, but will have problems in expressing their innermost thoughts and feelings to others.

Two 1s

This is considered the ideal number of 1s to have in a chart. People with this have the ability to express themselves clearly and openly. They also possess a broad, sympathetic understanding.

Three 1s

This creates one of two things: people who are nonstop talkers or people who are quiet and reserved. The nonstop talker is the combination usually found, but you can bet on the second being the case if the person also has an Arrow of Skepticism.

Four 1s

People with four 1s find it extremely hard to express themselves verbally. They are quiet, sensitive people, who are easily misunderstood. They find it extremely hard to relax and unwind.

Five or more 1s

The more 1s, the harder it becomes for people to express themselves verbally. This can create sad, aloof, lonely people. People with this combination must learn to express themselves in some way, such as in writing, music, and art.

One 2

People with one 2 are intuitive and sensitive. They're likely to be psychic, and even if they don't call it that, they'll act on their hunches. They're also likely to be easily hurt. They have an incredible gift at detecting insincerity.

Two 2s

People with two 2s possess balanced sensitivity and intuition, coupled with a high intelligence. Their first impressions are invariably correct. They make good use of their intuition.

Three 2s

This creates an imbalance that can lead to hypersensitivity. These people are easily hurt, and suffer inwardly, as they cannot always express their feelings. Three twos usually gives people a lack of confidence early on in life.

Four and five 2s

People with four or more 2s are impatient and inclined to overreact. They're likely to have a bad temper and will try the patience of everyone around them. They usually suffer from self-doubt and low confidence.

One 3

People with one 3 have a good brain and a retentive memory. People with one 3 have contented and happy dispositions. They keep their feet on the ground and have a positive approach to life.

Two 3s

People with two 3s possess vivid imaginations and frequently struggle to keep it under control. They enjoy flouting convention. These people need to learn self-discipline.

Three 3s

People with three 3s possess extremely active imaginations. They find it hard to relate to others, and they become so involved in what's going on in their own minds that they rarely develop close friendships.

Four 3s

This creates worried, timid, fearful, impractical, and confused people. They're hyperactive and possess an excessive imagination. Fortunately, this situation occurs rarely. It's so rare that it occurs on just five days every hundred years. The next time this occurs will be March 3, 2033.

One 4

People with one 4 have a practical outlook on life. They prefer to deal with facts rather than ideas, and can be rather materialistic. They're usually good with their hands.

Two 4s

People with two 4s have good organizational ability and enjoy starting a task at the beginning and carrying it through to the end. They're often talented with their hands. They're conscientious and enjoy doing accurate, careful work. They need to exercise care in choosing friends.

Three or more 4s

People with three or more 4s possess remarkable ability with their hands, but this skill is seldom used to its fullest extent. They enjoy physical activities and enjoy working hard. They need to learn that there is more to life than material possessions.

One 5

Five is the most important number in the chart, and people who have one 5 enjoy emotional stability and a well-balanced approach to life. They have the ability to motivate others, and possess a compassionate, understanding outlook.

Two 5s

People with two 5s can be hard to live with, as they can be overpowering with their tremendous drive and enthusiasm. They find it hard to harness their emotional energies, and this can lead to outbursts that are quickly regretted.

Three or more 5s

Three or more 5s can be extremely difficult for the individual to handle. Their enormous reserves of power and energy must be channeled wisely, and they need to learn to think before speaking. They enjoy adventure and excitement, and they are inclined to take unnecessary risks.

One 6

Six is a creative number that finds its best expression in the home, so these people have a great love of home and family. They enjoy domestic responsibilities, and have a great deal of creative potential. They're usually the person in the family that people come to when things are not going well.

Two 6s

People with two 6s need plenty of rest. They're inclined to worry about loved ones, and they are overly protective and cautious. They have good taste and enjoy creative activities.

Three or more 6s

Three or more 6s increases the degree of worry about loved ones, making for overly protective, possessive parents with a negative approach to life. They must learn that all children grow up and eventually leave home, and they must be willing to let them go. These people can benefit from a creative hobby such as music.

One 7

These people have to learn the hard way and must learn from their mistakes. This doesn't make life easy, especially early on, but ultimately it gives a sound understanding of life. People with one 7 often become involved in spiritual or metaphysical pursuits.

Two 7s

Two 7s increases the degree of lessons that have to be learned, and it usually involves a loss of some sort in the fields of love, health, or money. Many people with this combination become bitter and negative, but when they learn from their disappointments, they ultimately develop a strong philosophy of life, which can include an interest in the psychic world.

Three or more 7s

Three or more 7s often lead sad lives, because of the burden of the heavy losses they must endure. Everything happens with a purpose, and these losses test the strength and fortitude of these people. Once they develop inner strength, these people often attain great vision and wisdom.

One 8

People with one 8 enjoy the details of everything. Consequently, they're usually conscientious and methodical. They enjoy solving problems and possess a strong deductive ability. They often find it hard to finish what they've started.

Two 8s

Two 8s increases the reasoning powers, but these people must ensure that they don't become overbearing. They prefer to experience things for themselves, rather than take too much on trust. They also find it hard to change their minds once a decision has been made.

Three or more 8s

Three or more 8s are conscientious, rigid, and often restless. They usually seek plenty of change and variety early on in life until finally becoming useful, productive citizens once they're in their forties. They usually do well in the business and financial worlds.

One 9

Everyone born in the twentieth century has at least one nine, and it has no significance in their charts. However, for people born in the twenty-first century, it's a sign of humanitarian ideals and concerns.

Two 9s

People with two 9s are idealistic, intelligent, and frequently creative. They enjoy humanitarian type occupations. They must avoid being critical of people who are less intelligent than they are.

Three or more 9s

People with three or more 9s are idealistic, caring, and intelligent. However, they're inclined to exaggerate and can create "mountains out of molehills." They're happiest when involved in mentally stimulating activities, as long as they don't feel confined or restricted. They have strong humanitarian qualities.

Arithmomancy

Many people claim that numerology is descended from arithmomancy. If so, its origins go so far back into prehistory that no one knows how or where it began. No matter how old it may be, parts of arithmomancy are still useful today. Here's an interesting experiment that enables you to answer questions and look at problems and concerns in a different way.

Write your question on a sheet of paper. Cut nine small pieces from another sheet of paper, and make sure they're all as similar as possible. Write the numbers one to nine on these. Mix them thoroughly, and place them, number side down, in a circle surrounding your question.

Sit quietly, contemplating your question. When you feel the time is right, use your left hand to pick up any three of the numbered sheets of paper.

Look at the three numbers you've instinctively chosen, and think about how each one can relate to your question. Once you've done that, add the three numbers together, and then reduce the total to a single digit. This number will answer your question.

Let's assume you asked, "Will we go to Florida on vacation in October?" The three numbers you picked were 1, 4, and 9. The 1 could indicate a new start, which might relate to a vacation that is different to previous ones. As the 4 relates to hard work, you might have to be disciplined enough to take care of all your obligations before you can take the vacation. The 9 relates to completion, showing that the vacation does eventuate. Adding 1, 4, and 9 produces 14, which reduces down to a 5. Then 5 relates to change, variety, and travel. It looks as if you and your family will be enjoying a wonderful vacation in Florida in October.

Another form of arithmomancy is to ask a question and then look around to see what numbers you can find. You might notice a car's number plates or a house number. No matter what they happen to be, add them up and reduce them to a single digit. These are existing numbers that are easily noticed. However, you can take this a step further. You might see 2 dogs playing while 5 birds fly overhead. In this case, you'd interpret the 2 and the 5, and then look at their total (in this case, 7) to determine the answer. It's a fascinating experience to suddenly notice different numbers everywhere you go. A few days ago, while I was out walking on a quiet road, 3 blue cars passed me. As I was thinking about a minor concern at the time, the number 3 gave me something to think about, and effectively resolved the problem.

Suggested Reading

Avery, Kevin Quinn. *The Numbers of Life: The Hidden Power in Numerology*. New York: Freeway Press, 1974.

Goodwin, Matthew Oliver. *Numerology: The Complete Guide*. Two volumes. North Hollywood: Newcastle Publishing Company, Inc., 1981.

Pither, Steven Scott. *The Complete Book of Numbers*. St. Paul, MN: Llewellyn Publications, 2002.

Webster, Richard. *Chinese Numerology.* St. Paul, MN: Llewellyn Publications, 1998.

Webster, Richard. *Discovering Numerology.* Auckland, NZ: Brookfield Press, 1983.

Oghams

	n nuin "ash"		q quert "apple"		r ruis "elder"		i ioho "yew"
	s saille "willow"		c coll "hazel"		z straif "blackthorn"		e eadha "aspen"
	f fearn "alder"		t tinne "holly"		ng ngetal "reed"		u ur "heather"
	l luis "rowan"		d duir "oak"		g gort "ivy"		o ohn "furze"
	b beithe "birch"		h huathe "hawthorn"		m muin "vine"		a ailm "fir"

The ogham (pronounced oh-am) is a secret alphabetic code used by the ancient Celts. Originally there were four groups, each comprising five letters or sounds:

B	L	F	S	N
H	D	T	C	Q
M	G	NG	Z	R
A	O	U	E	I

The key to the code was a simple one. 2:4 would be C, as it's in the second row, fourth along. Likewise, 3:2 is G, as it's three down and two along.

An additional five signs were added in medieval times. These are called *forfedha*, which means "additional letters." The original signs are called *fedha.* They are usually referred to as "fews."

Several hundred ogham inscriptions still survive. Some 360 of these are carved in stone, and the others were carved in wood. About three hundred of these are in Southern Ireland, and the rest are in the United Kingdom.

Although Ogma, son of King Elatha, is credited with inventing oghams in about 600 BCE, the oldest surviving examples date back to the fourth century CE. The ogham script ceased to be popular in the seventh century, but it never entirely disappeared. In the early seventeenth century, the Earl of Glamorgan used ogham to send secret messages to King Charles I of England.

The ogham letters are symbolic, and as each letter has a wide range of correspondences, they form a complete cosmological system.

Not surprisingly, oghams gradually began to be used for divination purposes. No one knows how or when this began. A medieval manuscript called the *Book of Ballymote*, written in about 1390, contains material that was copied from ninth-century texts. It is the main source of information about ogham. This book explains the ogham characters and includes a number of puzzling diagrams that some people believe prove that ogham was used more than a thousand years ago for divination purposes. However, there is no evidence that this ever happened.

The Celtic revival began in the eighteenth century, and this created a new interest in oghams. In the twentieth century, Robert Graves created a second revival of the oghams in his book, *The White Goddess: A Historical Grammar of Poetic Myth*. Oghams have become a popular form of divination, and today ogham cards and ogham fews are readily available at New Age stores and online.

The Original Twenty Oghams

Each ogham relates primarily to a tree, which is then associated with a color, animal, and tree month, followed by a wide variety of other items.

Beithe—Birch
Keyword: Beginnings
Color: White
Animal: Cow
Tree Month: December 24–January 20

Beithe represents new starts, making plans, and taking a major step forward. You have to let go of any negativity from the past before you can move forward. Beithe also indicates change, good luck, and a change of outlook.

Luis—Rowan
Keyword: Insight
Colors: Red and Gray
Animals: Unicorn and Bear
Tree Month: January 21–February 17

Luis relates to spirituality, protection, and the ability to distinguish good from evil. It's a sign that you have the necessary stamina and energy to overcome any potential problems. It provides a warning of any outside problems that might be detrimental. It can also relate to self-doubt.

Fearn—Alder
Keyword: Strength
Color: Crimson
Animals: Red fox, Ram, and Stallion
Tree Month: February 18–March 17

Fearn provides moral and physical strength. It's a sign to be true to oneself, and to refuse to be compromised. The challenge is to know when you should move forward and when to pause and consolidate. Avoid stubbornness and listen to other points of view. Build a strong foundation and move forward.

Saille—Willow
Keyword: Intuition
Color: Fiery
Animals: Hare and Cat
Tree Month: March 18–April 14

Saille relates to creativity, imagination, and intuition. It's associated with the Moon, and can sometimes relate to self-deception. It's a sign that someone you haven't met yet (probably a woman) will teach you something that you need to know. Pay attention to the intuitive side of your nature.

Nuin—Ash
Keyword: Peace
Color: Clear Green
Animal: Snake
Tree Month: April 15–May 12

Nuin is a sign to reevaluate what's going on in your life and to find peace within. You need to learn that things are not always what they seem. You need to strive to grow into the very best that you're capable of becoming. Be honest, and do what you say you will.

Huathe—Hawthorn
Keyword: Restraint
Color: Purple
Animals: Goat and Dragon
Tree Month: May 13–June 9

Huathe indicates a time to be patient and to think carefully before acting. It's a time for learning and inner growth. The challenge is to be disciplined, patient, and to plan ahead before moving forward. Huathe also relates to hope.

Duir—Oak

Keyword: Protection

Colors: Dark Brown and Black

Animals: White Horse, Lion, and Salamander

Tree Month: June 10–July 7

Duir relates to solidity, faithfulness, and protection. It's also a portal into new understandings and spiritual growth. The challenge is to be strong and to stand up for what you know is right. You have the necessary strength and endurance to overcome all the difficulties and negativity that try to hold you back.

Tinne—Holly

Keyword: Balance

Color: Dark Gray

Animal: War Horse

Tree Month: July 8–August 4

Tinne relates to justice, fair play, and right overcoming wrong. It provides unlimited strength and power. If your cause is good and beneficial for everyone involved, you'll ultimately succeed. The challenge is to find a worthwhile goal for yourself.

Coll—Hazel

Keyword: Intuition

Color: Brown

Animal: Salmon

Tree Month: August 5–September 1

Coll represents creativity, poetry, divination, and meditation. It indicates a period of learning and the beginnings of knowledge and wisdom. Logic and intuition are both enhanced by Coll. Listen to your inner voice. The challenge is to avoid holding yourself back with subconscious fears of failure.

Quert—Apple

Keyword: Beauty

Color: Green

Animal: Unicorn

Tree Month: September 2–29

Quert relates to youthfulness and beauty. You should see harmony and perfection in everything you do. You need to live life to the fullest and take advantage of every worthwhile opportunity that presents itself. The challenge is to make the right choice from a range of options. You might be tempted to pursue too many things simultaneously and dilute your chances of success.

Muin—Vine

Keyword: Prophecy

Color: Variegated

Animal: Lizard

Tree Month: September 30–October 27

Muin gives you the opportunity to speak openly and honestly. Pay attention to your intuition. The challenge is to relax and take time out when necessary. Your intuition suffers when you're agitated or stressed. Enjoy the simple things of life.

Gort—Ivy

Keyword: Progress

Color: Sky Blue

Animal: Boar

Tree Month: October 28–November 24

Gort is a sign of change and progress, especially in your career. It's important to keep your eye fixed on your ultimate goal, and to avoid any distractions that might affect that. Persistence pays off. The challenge is to avoid any pitfalls that you meet on the way. People who are jealous of your success might try to cause problems.

Ngetal—Reed

Keyword: Unity

Color: Grass Green

Animals: Dog, Stag, and Rat

Tree Month: November 25–December 23

Ngetal indicates contentment, harmony, unity, and balance. It enables you to adapt to changing conditions and make significant spiritual growth. The challenge is to use your capabilities to their fullest extent. You may suffer from self-doubt and anxiety.

Straif—Blackthorn

Keyword: Fate

Color: Bright Purple

Animals: Wolf, Toad, and Black Cat

Straif is a sign of unexpected changes and a situation that is out of your control. You need to carefully assess the situation and search for a solution. The challenge of Straif is to turn a negative experience around and make it positive. You'll become a much more capable person as a result of this valuable learning experience.

Ruis—Elder

Keyword: Change
Color: Blood Red
Animal: Badger

Ruis relates to the inevitability of change. It represents the ending of something to make way for the new. The challenge of Ruis is to accept the necessity for change. It's natural to hold on and fight change. However, you'll fall behind if you fail to accept it.

Ailm—Fir

Keyword: Power
Color: Pale Blue
Animal: Red Cow

Ailm provides insight and potential. It's a sign that you're making good progress and will soon be able to see the road ahead with much more clarity than ever before. You'll have more self-esteem, confidence, and personal power. The challenge is to spend time working out where you want to go from here. You might be tempted to rush in too quickly.

Ohn—Furze

Keyword: Wisdom
Colors: Yellow and Gold
Animal: Rabbit

Ohn is a sign that you should make use of the knowledge you already possess, or to learn new skills that you can utilize to achieve your goals. The challenge is to avoid scattering your energies. Remain focused on your ultimate goal, and don't become lost in planning and preparation.

Ur—Heather

Keyword: Magnificent Obsession
Color: Purple
Animals: Bee and Lion

Ur is a sign that you should find a suitable goal that will test you to the utmost. Pay attention to your dreams and intuition as you search for this magnificent obsession. The challenge is to act on your dreams with passion and a sense of excitement. They remain nothing more than fantasies until you make them happen.

Eadha—Aspen

Keyword: Endurance

Colors: Silver and Gold

Animal: White Mare

Eadha is a protective sign that shows you possess everything necessary to conquer and overcome any negative situations. It's a sign that you will succeed as long as you remain persistent, determined, and courageous. The challenge is to persist, even when full of doubts, fears, and worries.

Ioho—Yew

Keyword: Immortality

Color: Dark Green

Animal: Spider

Ioho represents transformation and rebirth. It symbolizes what you've inherited from past generations. It provides new strength, enthusiasm, and the ability to understand matters that were previously concealed from you. The challenge is to be able to handle the feelings of loss that are to be expected whenever a transformation takes place.

The Forfedha

The first twenty oghams are the original ones. The final five were not used in premedieval times and were added much later. Because of this, many people refuse to use them for divination purposes. I've included them here for the sake of completeness.

Koad—Sacred Grove

Keyword: Knowledge

Color: Green

Animal: Squirrel

Koad is a sign that hidden knowledge is being revealed, and you'll be able to understand matters that used to puzzle and mystify you in the past. The challenge is that you might be too single-minded and fail to see the overall picture. Take a step or two back and allow enough time for the full understanding to come to you.

Oir—Spindle

Keyword: Inner Peace and Contentment

Color: White

Animal: Owl

Oir represents the feelings of satisfaction and peacefulness you have after achieving a difficult, challenging, and worthwhile goal. The challenge of Oir is that you might find it hard to relax. Take time out to enjoy peace, joy, and true happiness.

Uinllean—Honeysuckle
Keyword: Ancient Wisdom
Color: Pale Yellow
Animal: Mouse

Uinllean is a sign that you'll be able to see through the half truths and self-serving motivations of others, and understand what is true and right. The challenge of Uinllean is to conquer hesitancy and indecision. You'll need confidence in yourself before you can move ahead.

Phogos—Beech
Keyword: Guidance from the Past
Color: Orange
Animal: Deer

Phogos is a sign that answers can be obtained by looking into the past. You may be repeating old mistakes. Fortunately, it's never too late to learn from those mistakes and gain guidance from the past. The challenge is to evaluate information carefully and be willing to learn from the past.

Peine—Pine
Keyword: Illumination
Color: Blue-Green
Animal: Cat

Peine is the final ogham. It's been given many meanings over the years. It's generally considered to relate to illumination and spirituality. It also relates to the mystical, intuitive, and feminine side of your nature. It often relates to travel.

How to Make Your Own Oghams

You can make your own oghams from any material you wish. They're usually made of wood, but I've seen oghams made from cardboard, pebbles, plastic, silver, and modelling clay. I've even met someone who embroidered a set of oghams for herself.

My first oghams were made from cardboard cut into the same size and shape as regular playing cards. They proved extremely helpful while I was learning how to use them. In addition to a drawing of the ogham, I was able to include the name of the few and some of the keywords associated with it.

After a while, I decided to make myself a set of wooden oghams. I found lengths of wood that were about half an inch by one quarter of an inch. I cut these into three-inch lengths and used an artist's engraving tool to carve an ogham character into twenty-five of them. I keep them in an attractive bag with a Celtic design that I found in a New Age store.

I'd love to have a set of oghams created from the tree each character represents. This means that Beithe would be made from a piece of birch, Luis from rowan, and so on. I feel such a set would be particularly powerful.

Even if you intend using only the original twenty ogham characters, it's a good idea to make all twenty-five while you're doing it. This enables you to experiment with both twenty and twenty-five oghams, and you may find the additional oghams helpful.

How to Read the Oghams

How the oghams were originally interpreted is lost in history. Consequently, you have considerable freedom in creating your own layouts. Some layouts use just one few, while others use a dozen or more.

Single-Few Reading

Mix your fews in a bag while thinking about your question or concern. When you feel ready, pull out one few and see how it relates to your question or concern. One-few readings are a useful way to gain insights into minor problems. They're also a good way to learn the fews and to gain experience in using them. Try pulling out a single few every morning. Before going to bed in the evening, reflect on what effect that particular few had on your day.

Three-Fews Reading

This is similar to the one-few reading. The only difference is that you pull out three fews, one at a time. The first few represents the past, the second the present, and the third the future. This enables you to examine the three energies: what energies from the past created the current situation, what energies are currently having an effect on the situation, and what energies are likely to be involved in the future.

Three Columns of Truth Reading

This is a method I came up with more than forty years ago. It has served me well, and I hope it will do the same for you. A question is asked, and nine fews are randomly selected, one at a time. The first few is placed immediately in front of you. The second and third fews are placed above the first few creating a line. This is called the Pillar of Harmony.

The fourth and fifth fews are placed on either side of the first few, the sixth and seventh fews are placed on either side of the second few, and the eighth and ninth fews are placed on either side of the third few. The line of three fews on the left are called the Pillar of the Goddess, and the line of three fews on the right are called the Pillar of the God.

The fews can be interpreted in a number of ways. Each few in the Pillar of Harmony could be interpreted by calling the bottom few the past, the middle few the present, and the top few the future. The fews in the Pillar of the Goddess could indicate the hidden or overlooked situations behind the past, present, and future. The fews in the Pillar of the God could reveal what should have been done in the past and what can be done in the present and future.

Here's an example of a reading using this spread. A lady called Linda asked, "Should I move to Vancouver?" Linda was divorced and living in Phoenix, Arizona. She had met a Canadian man while on vacation and fallen in love. He was urging her to join him in Vancouver.

Start by looking at the fews in the central line, the Pillar of Harmony. The bottom few, representing the past is Tinne. This shows she had to fight for what she believed in. The middle few, the present, is Ur. This shows she's starting to realize that she can allow love and passion to come into her life again. Beithe, in the future position, shows she's going to make a new start. This could indicate a move to another country. Whatever the change is will prove lucky for her.

You continue by looking at the bottom fews of the Pillar of the Goddess and the Pillar of the God. The bottom few of the Pillar of the Goddess is Duir. This shows that Linda had more personal strength than she realized at the time. Muin in the Pillar of the God shows that she should have spoken more openly and honestly than she did.

The middle row, the present, has Ioho in the Pillar of the Goddess. This is a sign of transformation and rebirth. She should embrace the opportunity to start over again. Eadha in the Pillar of the God shows that she needs to be brave. If she does, she'll overcome her negative thoughts and be able to move forward. It's a sign of endurance, which shows she can overcome difficult situations.

The top row represents the future. Fearn is in the Pillar of the Goddess. Linda needs to remain true to herself, make plans for the future, and work toward her goals. Ruis is in the Pillar of the God. Linda will be able to successfully let go of the past and embrace the new life she's about to begin.

It looks as if Linda has been on the right path for a while but wasn't aware of it. It also looks as if she and her new partner will enjoy a good, loving relationship.

Suggested Reading

Graves, Robert. *The White Goddess: A Historical Grammar of Poetic Myth.* London: Faber & Faber, 1948. Revised edition, 1952.

Thorsson, Edred. *The Book of Ogham.* St. Paul, MN: Llewellyn Publications, 1992.

Webster, Richard. *Omens, Oghams & Oracles.* St. Paul, MN: Llewellyn Publications, 1995.

Palmistry

Palmistry probably began in the Stone Age. Pictures of human hands can be found in many of the ancient cave paintings in France, Spain, and Africa. Palm reading probably began in China or India thousands of years ago and gradually spread around the world. Some 2,500 years ago, Aristotle wrote about palmistry in *De Historia Animalium.* Alexander the Great was vitally interested in divination, and some people believe Aristotle wrote a book on palmistry for him.

Palmistry is mentioned at least four times in the Bible. Probably the most famous of these can be found in Job 37:7, "He sealeth up the hand of every man, that all men may know his work."

In the mid-twentieth century, people started using palmistry for psychological analysis. In 1965, the Kennedy-Galton Centre in Harrow, North London, began studying the skin ridge patterns on people's hands for health purposes. Their research is ongoing, and they're able to predict with 80 percent accuracy the chances a newborn baby has of developing a number of illnesses, including cancer, heart disease, diabetes, and mental illness.

Now that scientists are taking a serious interest in the subject, the future of palmistry is assured.

Palmistry is divided into two main areas. The first, called cheiromancy, examines the shape of the hands and fingers. Chirology, the second area, is concerned with the lines, mounts, and skin ridge patterns on the palm.

The Shape of the Hand

There are a number of ways to classify different hand shapes. The one I find most useful is named after the four ancient elements of fire, earth, air, and water and places people's hands into one of four groups.

You start by mentally removing the thumb and fingers and look at the palm to see if it is square or oblong.

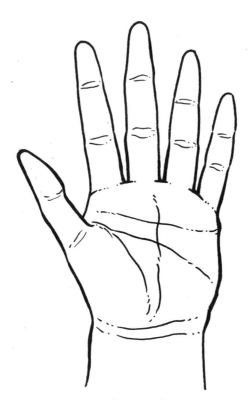

Square palm.

Square-shaped Palms

Square-shaped palms are normally broad. The larger the square happens to be, the more stamina and energy the person has at his or her disposal. People with square-shaped palms are practical, capable, and down-to-earth. They have a positive approach to life and enjoy challenges and hard work.

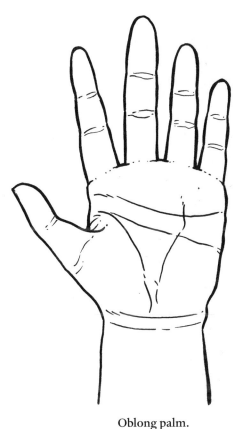

Oblong palm.

Oblong-shaped Palms

Palms that are longer in length than breadth are considered oblong. People with oblong palms are imaginative, intuitive, and frequently creative. They have plenty of ideas, but don't always have the necessary motivation to carry them through to fruition. They get bored easily and need a great deal of variety. The longer the palm is, compared to the breadth, the more obvious these qualities will be.

Every now and again you'll come across someone with a palm that is broad but also slightly oblong. When you look at this palm, you'll find it hard to determine if it's square or oblong. This person will be a practical dreamer.

Finger Length

Fingers are classified into short and long. Often it's obvious which category someone belongs to, as the fingers are obviously short or long. If it's difficult to determine which category a person belongs to, ask him or her to fold the fingers over the palm and see how far down the palm they can reach. If the fingers reach seven-eighths or more down the palm, they're considered long.

This doesn't always work, though, as some people are flexible and others aren't. Fortunately, there is a third category of finger—medium length—which can be used when you can't classify them as short or long.

It's difficult to determine finger length initially, but with practice, you'll be able to classify someone's finger length with just a glance.

Short Fingers

People with short fingers need to be busy and become impatient with details. They're usually better at starting projects than they are at finishing them. This can sometimes be caused by trying to do several things at the same time. They're curious and enjoy learning. However, they usually prefer a broad overview, and tend to overlook the details.

Long Fingers

People with long fingers are good with details and enjoy learning as much as possible about anything that interests them. They're patient and enjoy analyzing and solving problems. They quickly lose interest in anything that's too simple or has little to it.

Medium-length Fingers

People with medium-length fingers are a combination of the short and long types. They're reasonably patient and are good with details when it suits them. However, at other times they can be impulsive and superficial.

Putting It Together

You can now combine the hand and finger shapes to create four types of hand: square palms with short fingers (earth), square palms with long fingers (air), oblong palms with short fingers (fire), and oblong palms with long fingers (water).

The four elements are used in a number of different divination systems. However, they're best known for classifying the twelve signs of the zodiac into four groups. Aries, Leo, and Sagittarius, for instance, are all fire signs. Taurus, Virgo, and Capricorn are earth signs. Gemini, Libra, and Aquarius are all air signs, and Cancer, Scorpio, and Pisces are water signs.

If you have an air hand, though, it doesn't necessarily mean you'll be a Gemini, Libran, or Aquarian. This is because your Sun sign is just one part of your astrological makeup. Consequently, you might be a Capricorn but have four planets in water signs. In this case you'd be likely to possess more of the qualities provided by water signs rather than earth, your Capricorn Sun sign.

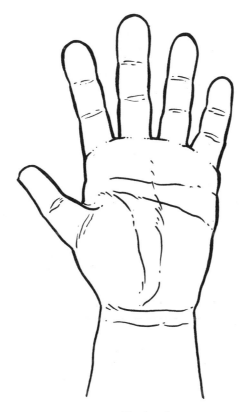

Fire hand.

Fire Hands—Oblong palm with short fingers

Keywords: Enthusiasm, inspiration, excitement, action.

In a fire hand the fingers are always shorter than the palm. Fire heats and warms but can also burn. People with fire hands are very much like this, and they tend to overreact at times. They're enthusiastic, creative, and fun to be around. Their short fingers provide spontaneity and excitement, while the oblong palm provides intuition. People with fire hands are usually extroverts and need plenty of activity to keep them happy. They dislike being told what to do, and work best in occupations where they can use their own initiative. They enjoy physical activities, such as sports, and anything else that stimulates and challenges them.

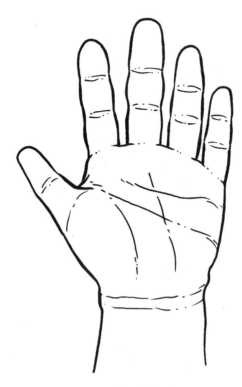

Earth hand.

Earth Hands—Square palm with short fingers

Keywords: Practicality, reliability, dependability, strength.

Earth hands are usually firm and the fingers are stiff. People with earth hands are practical, secure, reliable, and down-to-earth. They enjoy routine and repetitive physical work. They're usually good with their hands. They are hard workers who dislike being rushed. They're possessive, stubborn, steadfast, truthful, and cautious. They seek security. They enjoy being outside, and often seek outdoor work. They are traditionalists who prefer using methods that have stood the test of time.

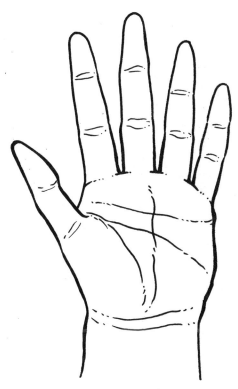

Air hand.

Air Hands—Square palm with long fingers

Keywords: Logical, communicative, quick-thinking, reliable.

People with air hands are practical thinkers, who use logic more than intuition. They express themselves well, and gain great pleasure from all types of communication. They're quick thinkers who need plenty of mental stimulation. If they take something on, they want to learn everything there is to know, and enjoy taking the project all the way to completion. They're thorough, and good with details.

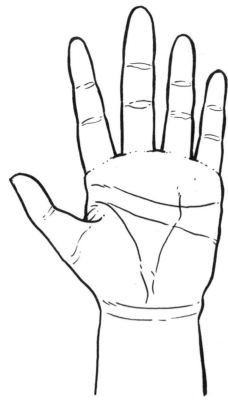

Water hand.

Water Hands—Oblong palm with long fingers

Keywords: Sensitive, emotional, imaginative, intuitive.

Artists enjoy painting water hands as they're long and graceful. People with water hands are gentle, refined, and have good taste. Because they're extremely sensitive, they're easily hurt. They have vivid imaginations, and lead rich inner lives. People with water hands often make a career in a humanitarian field.

The Main Lines

Once you start looking at people's palms, you'll quickly discover that some people have very few lines on their palms while others have what appear to be hundreds of lines. As most lines are caused by worry, someone with just a few lines will usually have an easier life than someone with hundreds. However, someone with just three lines on his or her palms would lead a rather boring, uninteresting life. Consequently, it's better to have hands with a reasonable number of clearly defined lines.

There are four main lines on the hands, though not everyone has all of them. The main lines are the heart, head, destiny, and life lines. They each provide valuable clues about different aspects of the person's life. The heart line reveals the emotional life, the head line shows how the person thinks, the life line reveals the amount of energy and stamina the person has, and the destiny line reveals his or her path through life. These lines should be clear, deep, and easily visible on the palm. The stronger the line is, the more energy the person is prepared to put into that area of his or her life.

The Heart Line

The heart line shows the person's feelings and responses to love and relationships. It is the major line closest to the fingers. It starts on the little finger side of the palm and usually ends between the first and second fingers.

There are two major types of heart lines: mental and physical. The mental heart line crosses the palm in an almost straight line. People with mental heart lines find it hard to express their innermost feelings, especially when they're young. They're sensitive, easily hurt, and need constant reassurance that they're loved. Whenever possible, they avoid public displays of affection.

The physical heart line curves and finishes under the first finger, between the first and second fingers, or under the second finger. If it ends between the first and second fingers, it provides a balance between personal needs and the needs of others. These people have reasonable expectations about their emotional lives and can commit to long-term relationships more easily than people with different ending positions to their heart lines. People who have heart lines that end under the first finger are idealistic, easily hurt, and usually experience a number of emotional disappointments as they go through life. People who have heart lines that end under the second finger often have deep feelings for others, but they make sure that their own personal needs are met first. These people often have strong sexual needs but find it hard to express their innermost feelings.

The heart line should be clear and free of small ovals that look like islands or chains inside the line. These indicate periods of emotional ups and downs. Crosses and breaks in the heart line indicate major emotional losses.

The Head Line

Before looking at the head line, look at the life line. This is the line that encircles the mound at the base of the thumb. The head line starts on the side of the hand below the first finger. It starts either touching the life line, or close to it. It comes across the palm, usually paralleling the heart line for part of its length. The head line either crosses the palm in a reasonably straight line, or curves upward toward the wrist. The head line can be short, long, or anything in between.

The length of the head line indicates how involved and detailed the person's thinking is. Someone with a long head line will think carefully before making a decision. Someone with a short head line will think quickly and then act, while people with long head lines are still thinking about what to do. People with short head lines often do well in business, as they're shrewd and make decisions quickly.

If the head line touches the life line at its start, the person will be cautious and think carefully before acting. If the two lines are close but not touching, the person will enjoy making his or her own decisions on anything that occurs in his or her life. The further away the head line is from the life line, the more independent the person will be. He or she is also likely to be open-minded and impulsive.

There are two major types of head lines: practical and imaginative. The practical head line runs straight across the palm. People with this type of head line are capable, practical, and keep their feet firmly on the ground. They enjoy dealing with facts. They use their imaginations in the real world.

The imaginative head line curves up the palm toward the wrist. This enhances creativity and imagination. These people need a pleasant environment to work in and need a career they consider fulfilling and stimulating.

Some people have a fork at the end of their head lines. People who have this possess qualities of both the imaginative and practical head lines. They can come up with good ideas and then use their practical skills to make them a reality. This fork is called the writer's fork, because writers create stories and then write them down. However, its presence doesn't necessarily give writing skills, and most people who have it use their imaginations to come up with good ideas that they're able to act upon.

The head line should be clear, deep, and unmarked. This shows the person is enthusiastic, positive, and using his or her brain effectively. Islands and chains indicate periods of stress and tension. Breaks in the head line can indicate a time when the person was unconscious or suffering from a brain injury. It is more usual for a break to indicate a time when the person experienced a major change in how he or she viewed life. The period after the break indicates the person's new way of thinking.

The Single Palmar Crease

About one person in thirty has at least one hand in which the head and heart lines are connected and appear to be a single line. Traditionally, this formation was known as a simian crease. However, as the name has negative connotations, palmists are starting to call this formation the single palmar crease. Most people with this crease are intelligent, single-minded, goal-orientated high achievers. They'll listen to all points of view, but once their mind is made up, it's almost impossible to get them to change it.

It's rare to find this crease on both hands. People with this are rigid and unyielding. They're ambitious and achieve their goals with little input from others.

Approximately 40 percent of people with Down syndrome have a single palmar crease.

The Life Line

The life line encircles the thumb. Like the other lines, it should be clear, deep, and well marked. It starts at the edge of the palm on the side of the first finger and forms a semicircle around an area known as the Mount of Venus at the base of the thumb. The life line usually starts about halfway between the first finger and the base of the thumb. It's a sign of ambition if it starts closer to the first finger than the thumb. Naturally, it means the opposite if it starts closer to the thumb than the first finger.

Contrary to common belief, the life line does not indicate when someone will die. A short life line does not mean a short life, and a long life line doesn't indicate a long life. The life line reveals how much energy the person has at his or her disposal, and it also indicates the person's vitality and enthusiasm for life. It should be clear and well marked. It should also come as far across the palm as possible, as the area it encloses indicates how much energy and stamina the person has at his or her disposal. If the life line hugs the thumb, the person will be listless and lacking in energy. If the area it encloses is large, the person will have plenty of energy, enthusiasm, and zest for life.

Some people have a fine line inside the life line that runs parallel to it. It has a protective influence on the person at the time it parallels the life line. This line is called the sister line.

Many people have a number of fine lines radiating out from the base of the thumb toward, and sometimes crossing, the life line. These are called worry lines. Some people have an abundance of these showing that they'll worry about almost everything. Some people have a few, and occasionally you'll find a palm with no worry lines at all. These people worry only when there's major cause.

Breaks in the life line are usually not serious, and often the life line will overlap itself when this occurs. The breaks usually indicate a major change in the person's life.

Squares, islands, and chains are frequently found on the life line. Squares are usually protective and cover a break in the line. A square that covers the line but does not enclose a break is a sign of confinement. This could mean imprisonment, but it usually indicates a time when the person felt hemmed in or restricted.

Islands on the life line indicate low periods in someone's life. It is sometimes a sign of depression. A chain is a sign of potential health problems caused by the person's emotional state.

There are several ways to time events using the life line. The most common method is to measure the length of the life line from where it starts to where it starts to turn around the Mount of Venus at the base of the hand close to the wrist. This is said to equal seventy years. Once you have this measurement, you can work out the time with reasonable accuracy. Half of the length would indicate thirty-five years, for instance, and one-tenth would indicate seven years. Of course, although the life line indicates periods of time, it doesn't measure length of life.

The Destiny Line

Not everyone has a destiny line. It's difficult to describe, as it can start and finish in a variety of places. It can even start, stop, and then start again. It usually begins near the wrist and runs down the palm toward the fingers. A typical destiny line would start in the center of the palm close to the wrist and finish close to the second finger.

It's a positive sign to have a destiny line, as it shows that the person will be able to focus on achieving his or her goals. People without a destiny line take life as it comes. They don't have a strong desire to succeed in a specific field, and they may try a variety of different occupations in the course of their lives.

If the destiny line starts inside the life line, someone, usually a parent or other family member, will have had a strong influence on the person in childhood and adolescence. If the destiny line starts close to the center of the palm, away from the life line, the person will have a strong desire for independence. The further the destiny line is away from the life line, the stronger the desire for independence will be. If the destiny line starts more than halfway across the palm, the person will often seek a career in the public eye.

The ending position can give a clue as to the type of career the person would enjoy. If the destiny line curves slightly and ends beneath the first finger, he or she will be interested in politics, philosophy, and law. If it ends under the second finger or between the second and third fingers, the person is likely to pursue a conventional career. If the destiny line ends under the third (ring) finger, the person will probably choose a career in an aesthetic or creative field. Occasionally, the destiny line will end under the little finger. This person will choose a career that utilizes his or her communication skills.

It's common to find breaks on the destiny line. If the line stops, but another line starts on one side of it, it indicates a change of career or the type of work the person is doing. It's a sign that the person wasn't sure where he or she was going if the line stops and starts again after a gap. Squares on the destiny line are always a sign of protection.

You can time events on the destiny line. The period from the wrist to where it crosses the head line indicates the first thirty-five years. Ages thirty-six to forty-nine are the area between the head and heart lines. The rest of the person's life is the period after the heart line. Many people's destiny lines stop at the heart line. This doesn't mean their destiny stopped. What it does show is that they've reached middle age and have become set in their ways.

The Fingers and Thumb

The fingers are divided into three sections, known as phalanges. The tip phalange, or nail, relates to spirituality and intuition. Someone who has long tip phalanges on each finger will be kind, thoughtful, and have an interest in the spiritual side of life.

The second phalange relates to the person's intellect. People with longer middle phalanges generally do well in business or in their careers.

The base phalange relates to the material aspects of life. If these phalanges are long and puffy, the person will have a strong desire for physical gratification. If these phalanges feel slightly spongy to the touch, the person will enjoy food and may well be a good cook.

Fine vertical lines on the bottom phalange show that the person has been under strain and would benefit from having a few days off. More important than these are stress lines that are fine horizontal lines on the tip phalanges. These show that the person has been under considerable stress for a long period of time. These lines appear slowly and take just as long to disappear. When they appear it shows the person is overdue for a vacation.

Finger Settings

There are four ways in which the fingers can be set on the hand. If the base of the fingers create a gentle curved arch, the person will be conscientious, well-balanced, compassionate, and able to stand up for him or herself.

If the first and little fingers are set lower than the middle fingers, the person will be timid and lacking in confidence.

If the fingers are set in a straight line, the person will be overflowing with confidence, and they will enjoy being the center of attention.

If the fingers are set in a slight curve but the little finger is set noticeably lower than the others, the person will experience a number of setbacks in life. He or she will learn from these, but usually the lessons are learned the hard way. A low-set little finger is called a "dropped" little finger.

Fingertips

The fingertips can also be classified into four types: conic, pointed, square, and spatulate. Conic fingertips are the most common of these, and you'll find them everywhere you go. Conic fingertips are gently rounded. People with these are easygoing, practical, and think quickly.

If the fingertips appear almost pointed, the person will be idealistic, sensitive, and intuitive. He or she will dream of a perfect world and have unrealistic expectations.

If the fingertips appear square, the person will be meticulous, practical, and down-to-earth. He or she will be cautious when it comes to trying out something new or different.

Spatulate fingertips appear to flare out slightly at the ends of the fingers. Someone with these will be restless, imaginative, and unconventional. He or she will need to be busy to be happy.

Mercury Finger (Little Finger)

The Romans named this finger after Mercury, the winged messenger of the gods. Consequently, the Mercury finger is the finger of communication

An average-length little finger reaches up to approximately the first joint of the ring finger. The longer the little finger is, the better the person will be at some form of communication. Good talkers and natural salespeople have long little fingers.

Someone with a short little finger finds it hard to express him- or herself clearly. He or she can also be impulsive and a risk-taker.

The tip phalange is usually the longest. This governs verbal communication. As most people express themselves best by talking, it's not surprising that this phalange is the longest in most people. The middle phalange relates to written communication. It is usually the shortest of the three phalanges. Someone with a long second phalange will be able to express him or herself easily with words on paper. The base phalange relates to the material world. If this phalange is the longest, the person's communication skills will help him or her make money and progress in his or her career.

Apollo Finger (Ring Finger)

The ring finger is named after Apollo, the Greek and Roman god of poetry and music. The Apollo finger relates to beauty and creativity. An average length Apollo finger reaches halfway up the fingernail of the second finger and is about the same length as the first finger.

The three phalanges of this finger are usually equal in length. People with equal length phalanges enjoy surrounding themselves with attractive things, and are happy when their surroundings at home and work are pleasant.

If the tip phalange is the longest, the person has a good imagination and is likely to be creative. If the second phalange is longest, the person will have good taste and would work well in a field that utilized this talent.

It's rare for the base phalange to be the longest. As all the base phalanges relate to physicality, this person's creativity will be expressed physically, possibly by dancing or playing sport.

Saturn Finger (Middle Finger)

Saturn was the rather gloomy, austere Roman god of time. Because of this, the Saturn finger relates to duty, conscientiousness, restrictions, and limitations. The Saturn finger should be the longest finger on the hand. If it's shorter than the Apollo or Jupiter fingers, the person will lack a sense of responsibility and will find it hard to work in a group. He or she would be extremely private and hard to get to know.

The Saturn finger is considered long if at least half of its tip phalange is above the other fingers. This denotes someone who finds it hard to relax and get along with others. He or she is likely to be a loner. This person will also have a strong sense of tradition.

If the tip phalange of this finger is longer than the others, the person will be intelligent and feel superior to others. He or she will also have a strong sense of responsibility.

If the second phalange is the longest, the person will work best in a skilled technical field. He or she will enjoy sharing his views on local and international matters with others.

In the past, the person would be considered interested in agriculture if the base phalange was longer than the others. Keen gardeners often have a long base phalange, but it primarily shows that the person is reliable, honest, and loyal.

Jupiter Finger (First Finger)

The supreme god in Roman mythology is Jupiter. It's not surprising that the first finger is named after him, as it relates to enthusiasm, energy, drive, confidence, and self-esteem.

The Jupiter finger should reach half to two-thirds of the way up the tip phalange of the Saturn finger, and be approximately the same length as the Apollo finger.

Someone with a long Jupiter finger will have plenty of energy and ambition. This person is prepared to work as hard as necessary to achieve success.

If the Jupiter finger is about the same length as the Apollo finger, the person will be ambitious, but will know when to pause and relax. He or she will be realistic about the chances of achieving success.

If the Jupiter finger is shorter than the Apollo finger, the person will lack confidence in the early part of his or her life. He or she is likely to be shy and find it hard to share much of him- or herself with others.

Ideally, the phalanges should all be about the same length. If the tip phalange is longer than the others, the person will become interested in spirituality and philosophy. He or she would be happy working in a humanitarian field.

If the middle phalange is longer than the others, the person will use his or her brain to create good ideas. He or she will enjoy carrying them out, but they will always enjoy the thinking part most.

If the base phalange is the longest, the person will keep busy and enjoy the practical aspects of life. In time, he or she will build up a strong faith or philosophy of life.

The Thumb

The thumb looks as if it contains just two phalanges, but the mound of flesh at the base of the thumb (surrounded by the life line) acts as the third phalange.

The length of the thumb is important. People with large thumbs enjoy greater success than people with small thumbs. This is because they possess more motivation and are more persistent and ambitious than people with smaller thumbs. People with extremely long thumbs are intelligent, decisive, and are likely to have a leadership role in whatever field they're working in.

A medium-length thumb reaches at least halfway up the base phalange of the Jupiter finger. Most people have these. It means they are fair, able to stand up for themselves, and possess common sense.

Ideally, the two main phalanges of the thumb should be equal in length. The first phalange, containing the thumbnail, represents will, and the second phalange represents logic. If both phalanges are equal, the person will possess an equal amount of willpower and logic. This means he or she will be able to come up with a good idea and have the necessary drive and energy to make it happen.

If the first phalange is longer than the second, the person will have more willpower than logic. He or she will make plenty of mistakes, but will get up each time and continue pursuing his or her goals until they're achieved. This person will be determined but may also try to dominate others.

It's much more common for the second phalange to be longer than the first. This means the person has more logic than willpower. He or she will have plenty of ideas, but will lack the motivation to carry them through.

Thumbs can be firm or flexible. It's described as flexible if the thumb bends backward from the joint. Someone with this type of thumb will be optimistic, easygoing, and flexible. He or she will also give in under pressure rather than create a scene.

A firm thumb is stiff and inflexible. Someone with this type of thumb will be reliable, determined, and stubborn. He or she will not give in under pressure.

The Mounts

The mounts are the raised, fleshy areas on the palm. They indicate areas of energy and what the person enjoys doing. They can be read for both quality and quantity. A high mount shows that the person will have plenty of energy in the specific subjects covered by the mount. A wide mount shows the potential of the person's mind in that particular area. Consequently, palmists look for mounts that are both high and wide.

There are eight mounts on the hand. The most obvious one is the Mount of Venus, which is the raised area at the base of the thumb, encircled by the life line. Directly across the palm from this, at the base of the hand, is the Mount of Luna. Between them, also at the base of the hand, is the Mount of Neptune. There are mounts on the palm at the base of each finger. They are named after the particular finger they're under. The Mount of Jupiter, for instance, is below the Jupiter (first) finger, and the Mount of Mercury is below the Mercury (pinky) finger. The final mount is split into two. Between the mounts of Jupiter and Venus is the inner Mount of Mars. It's partially inside the life line. Between the mounts of Mercury and Luna is the outer plain of Mars.

The first step is to determine which mount is being used more than the others. This is not always easy, as some people have mounts that seem average in height and size. Even in these cases, examination will reveal one mount that can be considered the main mount. Press on it to determine how firm it is. If the mount is firm, it's a sign that the person is making use of the knowledge indicated by the mount. If the mount is soft, the person will have learned information, but will not be making any use of it.

If all the mounts are firm and of reasonable height, the person will have plenty of ambition and drive and be motivated to achieve his or her goals. This is called a "lucky hand."

You'll also find hands where it's difficult to locate any of the mounts. Someone with this formation will be lacking in confidence and is usually plagued with doubts and fears. Fortunately, if this person's hand is firm to the touch, he or she will be able to set and achieve goals, but will need to work hard to achieve them.

Each of the mounts under the fingers contains a triangular skin ridge pattern that looks similar to fingerprints. This is called the apex. If the apex is situated directly under the middle of the finger, it's a sign that this mount is the most important mount on the hand. If two or more finger mounts have centrally sited apexes, each mount is of equal importance.

The Mount of Jupiter

The Mount of Jupiter is situated at the base of the first finger. If it is wide and high, the person will possess strong leadership qualities and enjoy taking responsibility and being in charge. He or she will have plenty of initiative and self-esteem. This person will also be ambitious and have more than enough energy to achieve his or her goals.

If this mount is high but appears spongy, rather than firm, the person will be vain and proud. He or she is likely to be greedy and have a tendency to overindulge in anything he or she enjoys.

The Mount of Saturn

The Mount of Saturn is situated below the second (Saturn) finger. Most people have a flat, rather than a raised, area below this finger, as it's the mount that's least likely to be dominant in the hand. This is fortunate, as it means they don't possess the negative qualities usually associated with this mount.

If this mount is well developed, the person will have a gloomy, melancholy approach to life. The word *saturnine* is related to this. This person will enjoy working on his or her own, with little input from others. He or she will be patient, hardworking, responsible, and enjoy working on detailed, involved projects. Although loved by others, he or she will find it hard to express affection and love in return.

The Mount of Apollo

The Mount of Apollo is situated under the ring, or Apollo, finger. A well-developed mount provides enthusiasm, good taste, and the ability to deal well with others. He or she will appreciate beauty and work best in pleasant surroundings. This person will be adaptable, versatile, and shrewd at assessing worthwhile opportunities.

If this mount is soft and spongy, the person will fantasize about great success but lack the motivation to achieve it. If the mount is scarcely visible, the person will be down-to-earth and practical, but lacking in imagination.

The Mount of Mercury

The Mount of Mercury is located under the little finger. People with a well-developed Mercury mount will have a good mind and the ability to think and express themselves clearly. They are quick thinkers who enjoy interacting and communicating with others. They are affectionate and have no problems in expressing their feelings.

People with an undeveloped Mercury mount are impractical, insincere, and lacking in motivation.

The Mount of Venus

The Mount of Venus is at the base of the thumb and is encircled by the life line. This mount relates to love, affection, passion, energy, and compassion.

If this mount is reasonably high and firm, the person will be affectionate, passionate, sympathetic, and make the most of life. He or she will be happiest inside a strong, loving relationship with a partner who is a friend as well as lover.

The higher this mount is, the greater the passion, making this an important factor when checking a couple for compatibility. A low Venus mount denotes the opposite. People with this are lacking in love, sympathy, and compassion. Consequently, there'll be problems in a relationship if one person has a high Venus mount and the other person has a low mount.

If the life line comes well across the palm, the person will have a wide Mount of Venus. This provides the person with enthusiasm, love, and generosity. If the life line stays close to the thumb, the person will be cautious in every aspect of his or her life.

The Mounts of Mars

The two mounts of Mars are on opposite sides of the palm. Inner Mars is just below the base of the thumb and almost entirely inside the life line. If it is firm, the person will possess courage and be prepared to stick up for him- or herself when necessary. If this mount is overdeveloped, the person will be argumentative and aggressive. Conversely, someone with an undeveloped inner Mars will find it difficult to stand up for him- or herself.

Directly across the palm, and usually between the head and heart lines, is the Mount of outer Mars. This relates to self-control, tenacity, and moral courage.

If either of these mounts are strong, the person will be willing to stand up for his or her friends. They also provide staying power, energy, determination, persistence, and aggression, all good qualities for anyone involved in a competitive sport.

The area between these two mounts is called the plain of Mars. This area should be firm as the head, heart, and destiny lines all cross it. A firm plain of Mars helps people make the best use of these lines. If the plain of Mars is weak or spongy, the person will be easily influenced by others.

The Mount of Luna

The Mount of Luna is situated at the base of the palm on the side of the little finger, directly opposite the thumb. This mount relates to creativity, imagination, emotions, and the subconscious mind.

This mount should be firm to the touch, showing that the person has a good imagination and is interested in creative activities. If the Mount of Luna is the predominant mount on the palm, the person will have a tendency to daydream and never get around to pursuing his or her dreams.

The Mount of Neptune

The Mount of Neptune is situated at the base of the hand between the Luna and Venus mounts. When it's firm, it creates a level surface on the palm where the three mounts meet. This is a sign that the person can think quickly on his or her feet and would make a good public speaker, debater, or actor.

If the Mount of Neptune is undeveloped, the person will find it difficult to express his or her deepest feelings.

Minor Lines

Once you start reading palms, you'll find most people will ask questions about marriage, children, money, health, and travel. It's not possible to answer these as accurately as people would like, as we all possess free will. Someone, for instance, might have a large number of children lines on her hand but decide to have only one, or even none. This choice would have been much harder to make a hundred years ago.

Relationship Lines

Relationship lines are fine lines that come up the side of the hand between the start of the heart line and the little finger. These are often called marriage lines, which is incorrect, as they simply indicate a strong relationship that may, or may not, be a sexual one.

Relationship lines should be clear, well marked, and come up the side of the hand onto the palm itself. This indicates a strong, long-lasting relationship. A strong line that doesn't reach the surface of the palm indicates an important relationship that doesn't last.

Relationship lines show potential, rather than the actuality. Someone with three strong relationship lines will not necessarily have three strong relationships. If the first relationship is a successful, long-lasting one, the other lines will remain dormant and unused.

It's possible for relationship lines to disappear from the hand. The subconscious mind of someone who has been in a strong relationship that ended badly can erase the line from the hand. However, the trauma of the relationship will remain evident on the heart line. It's also possible for a new line to form when the person meets someone and starts a new relationship.

Children Lines

The children lines are fine vertical lines immediately below the little finger. These must have been useful in the past, but nowadays most people are able to control the number of children they have and these lines are less important. Consequently, the childrens lines on a lady's palm indicate her potential, rather than the number of children she has. Strong lines often, but not always, indicate the number of children she has.

A man's hand indicates the number of children he's close to. If he has three children, but is close to only two of them, two lines will be visible in his palm. A man can have childrens lines on his palm even if he never fathers children of his own. These are children he's become close to. A friend of mine has had no children of his own, but is close to his nieces and nephews who are clearly visible on his palm.

Travel Lines

Travel lines are fine lines that appear on the side of the palm between the wrist and the heart line on the little finger side of the palm. They indicate a restless side to the person's nature, and a better name for them would be *restlessness lines*. People with these lines on their hands need plenty of change and variety, and travel is a good way to satisfy this desire.

Strong lines indicate important travel. People who travel regularly in the course of their work would not have each individual trip indicated in their hands. However, they'd need to have a number of travel lines on their hands to choose this type of career.

Health Line

The health line, usually called the *hepatica*, runs diagonally across the palm from inside the life line, close to the wrist, and ends close to the start of the heart line. It is not as clearly marked as the four main lines.

Many people do not have this line, and oddly enough, this is extremely fortunate, as it indicates the person will enjoy excellent health and recuperate quickly after any illness. If the line is present, it should be clear and well marked. This is also a sign of good health, and shows that the person is paying attention to his or her physical body.

Usually, health lines have ups and downs in their quality. These indicate times of ill health. This may not necessarily be anything serious. They may simply indicate that the person is suffering from a lack of energy or a prolonged period of minor problems.

Islands on the hepatica are usually a sign of digestive problems, and the person should examine his or her diet. Breaks in this line indicate periods of ill health. It's always good to find a square on the hepatica, as this shows the person is being protected while the line is covered, and will make a full recovery.

Money

Earned money is indicated by a small triangle near the center of the palm. The destiny and head lines form two sides of the triangle, and a small line on the little finger side of the hand on the wrist side of the head line forms the third line. If this third line fails to close the triangle, money will come in, but most of it will escape. A closed triangle shows that the person can keep hold of at least some of the money he or she has made.

Inherited money is indicated by a small line between the third and fourth fingers. It curves part of the way around the third finger. Unfortunately, it's not very helpful as it gives no idea how much money is involved or when the person will receive it.

Easy money, such as a lotto win, is shown by a triangle on the inside of the life line. One line is made up by the life line, and the other two lines are minor lines. It's rare to see these, as they indicate a significant amount of money.

How to Do a Palmistry Reading

If I'm giving someone a quick reading, I'll ask to see his or her dominant hand. Usually, this is the right hand. If the person is left-handed, that is the hand I'll read. If I'm going to give a more detailed reading, I'll examine both hands. The dominant hand reveals what the person is doing with his or her life, and the less dominant hand (left hand for right-handers) reveals what the person is thinking about, as well as inherited traits. The nondominant hand is often the more interesting hand, as it shows what the person would like to be doing if his or her life was different.

No one has palms that are identical. If the palms are similar, the person will be doing, for the most part, what he or she wants to do in life. If the palms are quite different, the person is likely to feel frustrated, as he or she will be thinking and dreaming about one thing, while doing another.

The best way to read a palm is to have a system. This means you won't accidentally leave anything out. When I look at someone's palms, I start by determining the type of hands he or she has (fire, earth, air, or water). I then look at the thumb to determine its size and the degree of logic and willpower the person has. I push gently on the thumb to see if the person can stand up for him or herself. I then look at the four main lines, starting with the heart line, followed by the head line, life line, and destiny line. I then move on to the minor lines, followed by the fingers, thumb, and the mounts.

I like to take a palm print when I give a full reading. It's easier to read the lines from a print, and it creates a useful record of the person's hands at that particular time. If I see the person again, I'll be able to compare the new prints with the earlier one.

Suggested Reading

Benham, William G. *The Laws of Scientific Hand Reading*. New York: Duell, Sloan and Pearce, 1900. Republished as *The Benham Book of Palmistry* by Franklin Lakes: New Page Books, 2006.

Fincham, Johnny. *The Spellbinding Power of Palmistry*. Sutton Mallet, UK: Green Magic, 2005.

Lyon, Sheila, and Mark Sherman. *Palm's Up: A Handy Guide to 21st-Century Palmistry*. New York: The Berkley Publishing Group, 2005.

Webster, Richard. *Revealing Hands*. St. Paul, MN: Llewellyn Publications, 1994.

Webster, Richard. *Palm Reading for Beginners*. Woodbury, MN: Llewellyn Publications, 2007.

Webster, Richard. *You Can Read Palms*. Woodbury, MN: Llewellyn Publications, 2010.

Paper Reading

I was introduced to paper reading by Dr. Joe Slate, emeritus professor of psychology at Athens State University and well-known author of books on esoteric subjects. About twenty years ago, we were both at a book fair in Chicago. We were doing readings for my publisher's clients. He was doing paper readings and I was reading the tarot. When we finished, we had a lengthy discussion about the pros and cons of the different methods we were using. He taught me a great deal about paper reading, and I hope I was able to reciprocate with different ways of reading the tarot. Many years later, I learned that "the wrinkled sheet," as he called it, had been developed by Dr. Slate and his students in the early 1970s at Athens State University in Alabama.

How to Read Paper

Required: A stack of 8½ x 11-inch paper. Regular photocopying paper is ideal, but any type of paper will do.

Ask the person you are going to read for to sign his or her name at the top of the sheet of paper. This enables you to correctly orient the paper when you read it.

"Please crumple the paper now, as if you were going to throw it away. That's good. I'll now unfold it and see what it has to tell us."

Watch the person crumple the paper. If he or she did this quickly and turned it into a small tight ball, you can safely assume that they're independent and assertive. Usually, men make tighter balls of paper than women. However, business women tend to make tight balls, too, making this a valuable clue.

Unfold the paper carefully and smooth it out on the table. The top half of the sheet of paper relates to positive influences, while the bottom half denotes any negative influences. The left-hand side represents the past, and the right hand side the future. This gives us four quadrants:

- *Top left:* positive influences from the past.

- *Top right:* positive influences yet to come (the future).

- *Bottom left*: negative influences from the past.

- *Bottom right:* negative influences yet to appear (the future).

The imaginary center vertical line indicates the present. The farther you move to the left, the farther you travel into the past. The same applies with the right. The far right side of the sheet indicates the more distant future, while just to the right of center indicates the near future.

When you unfold the ball of paper, you'll find a large number of creases and many of these will form shapes, such as triangles, squares, and even hearts. These can all be interpreted.

Triangles indicate problems. The direction the triangle is pointing in indicates how the problem will be resolved. If, for instance, the top point of the triangle is in the lower right hand side of the sheet and is pointing toward the top left, the answer will be found from a positive experience in the person's past. In this case you might say, "This triangle down here indicates difficulties that you will have in the future. However, the solution will be found by looking back into your past, particularly the happier times you've enjoyed. We can all learn from the past, and this triangle indicates a challenging situation. It may not be easy to resolve, but you'll learn and grow as a result."

Squares are also negative and show that the person is hemmed in and restricted. On the left hand side of the sheet these indicate negative experiences that have already happened. On the right hand side, they are yet to come. If they're in the middle of the sheet they're happening in the present.

Stars indicate a psychic talent. The more points the star has, the greater the psychic ability.

Circles indicate good fortune no matter where they appear on the sheet of paper. Usually, this good fortune is associated with career. Consequently, it often indicates a promotion or financial success.

Parallel lines indicate personal relationships. When several are found on the sheet, the person is likely to be highly sociable and have plenty of friends. If few are found, the person is likely to have one special relationship. How long it will last, and how successful it will be, can be determined by the length of these parallel lines and their position on the sheet.

Single lines represent assertiveness. A large number of these indicate someone who is able to stand on his or her own two feet and achieve whatever it is he or she desires.

Straight lines indicate force and momentum. These lines are positive if they go diagonally upward but indicate problems if they go downward. A horizontal line indicates stability, conservatism, and the status quo. Vertical lines indicate a need for stimulation and excitement.

Crossed lines indicate confusion and conflict. Usually the person has hopes and dreams that are proving hard to achieve. Consequently, he or she is in a stalemate until the situation becomes clearer.

Here is a sample reading. Let's assume it's for a young woman in her early twenties. She crumpled the paper tightly and is leaning forward expectantly as you unfold it and place it down on the table.

"You are assertive and ambitious," you might begin (because she crumpled the paper tightly into a small ball). "You should aim high. Ah, this is interesting." You pause and with a finger follow some of the indentations on the paper. "Very good. Before I start, let me explain a couple of things. The left-hand side indicates the past and the right hand side the future. Anything in the middle is in the present. The lower half indicates negative influences and the top half indicates positive.

"Look at this remarkable straight line heading diagonally across the page. It shows you're on the right path. It crosses the center just below the halfway mark, so you're still surrounded by negative influences, but much less now than before. I would say this is people saying you shouldn't do that, be happy with what you've got, don't take risks—all that sort of thing. As you can see, as we go into the future, the line moves into the positive, so you're making good, steady progress. I'm willing to bet that it's not as fast as you'd like it to be, as you tend to want everything today. The hard work pays off in many ways, not least financially. You enjoy making money, and it looks as if you have a great time spending some of it, too.

"You also have three small circles in your future. These are extremely positive and usually relate to career. I think you'll be actively involved in bringing up a family, but you'll be carrying on with your career as well.

"Right in the center you have these two small lines crossing each other. This indicates confusion. There's no need to worry about it. The long straight line shows you're on track. Periodically, you'll pause and reassess things. This is good as it gives you a chance to stand back and look at the situation from the outside. Sometimes we get so involved in what we're doing that we lose sight of the big picture. So there'll be times when you feel confused and uncertain, but fortunately they're not too serious.

"You have parallel lines here in the past. As they're in the top half it indicates a particularly happy relationship. Although it's in the past, I sense it's the sort of relationship that never really dies. Next time you see this person you'll be able to start again exactly where you left off. You have plenty of short parallel lines all over the place. This means that you're outgoing, sociable, and enjoy having a good time. In the near future, you have another major set of parallel lines. As they're largely in the positive quadrant, they denote a particularly happy long-term relationship.

"You're about to start a particularly happy phase in your life."

Suggested Reading

Weschcke, Carl Llewellyn, and Joe H. Slate. *The Llewellyn Complete Book of Psychic Empowerment*. Woodbury, MN: Llewellyn Publications, 2011.

Playing Cards

No one knows where our modern-day playing cards came from. A number of different countries, including Korea, China, India, and Persia, have been suggested. Although the origin of playing cards isn't known, it appears likely they originated in Korea in the sixth century and are related to the Korean divinatory arrow. This is because the original Korean playing cards were similar to the slips of bamboo that were adorned with cock feathers and used as arrows in divinations. These arrows were fired into the air, and where they landed and what direction they indicated provided answers to the shamans' questions. The first cards were similar in shape to the bamboo arrows—about eight inches by half an inch—and were made from oiled silk. The backs were decorated with a heart that looked similar to a feather, and the fronts contained eight different suits.

From there, they gradually spread around the world, reaching Europe in the second half of the fourteenth century. The invention of printing and copper engraving enabled the cards to be produced more quickly, and in better quality, than before. The church strongly disapproved of playing cards, but their condemnation simply increased demand.

Gypsies were probably the first people to use cards for divination, and the first books on the subject appeared in the 1480s.

The meanings of the individual cards has changed over the years. For instance, the king of spades used to indicate either a wicked man or a magistrate, the queen of spades indicated a widow or an evil woman, and the jack of spades indicated a spy or someone pretending to be someone else. Modern-day interpretations are much kinder and caring than they were two hundred years ago.

Why Fifty-Two Cards?

Tarot card readers often ask why the modern-day deck of playing cards contains fifty-two cards (plus the joker), while the minor arcana of the Tarot contains fifty-six. Because there are a number of intriguing numerical correspondences in a deck of playing cards, it seems likely that four cards were intentionally removed.

In a twenty-four hour period we have both night and day. A deck of playing cards contains red and black cards to correspond with this. The four seasons in a year relate to the four suits. The thirteen cycles of the Moon in the course of a year are indicated by the thirteen cards in each suit. There are fifty-two cards in a deck of cards, and these relate to the fifty-two weeks of the year. There are 365 days in a year. If you add up the numerical value of all the cards (four ones, four twos, etc.) you'll find they add up to 364. If you add the joker, you'll have a total of 365. Another interesting fact about playing cards is that when all the cards of a suit are spelled out and added up, they total fifty-two (ace, two, three, four, five, six, seven, eight, nine, ten, jack, queen, king).

How to Do It

There are many different ways in which the cards can be interpreted. This is why you can ask several card readers what a certain card means and receive a variety of different answers. The easiest method I've found is to use keywords for the four suits, combined with numerological keywords for the number cards, and people you know for the court cards.

The Four Suits

Spades indicate change, the unexpected, confusion, mystery, challenges, obstacles, warnings, and the unknown.

Hearts indicate love, romance, marriage, pleasure, friendship, good fortune, and happiness.

Diamonds indicate money, finance, business, success, power, and prestige.

Clubs indicate creativity, energy, hard work, opportunities, and reward.

The Number Cards

These are the standard numerological interpretations for each number. You can find more information on these in the Numerology section of this book.

One (Ace)

Keyword: Independence

Number one relates to new starts and is full of excitement, enthusiasm, and energy. It relates to independence, new ideas, and motivation. It also relates to ultimate attainment.

Two

Keyword: Cooperation

Number two relates to tact, diplomacy, and cooperation. It's gentle, kind, caring, and intuitive. It soothes troubled waters and makes people feel at ease. It's friendly and genuinely interested in the well-being of others.

Three

Keyword: Self-expression

Number three relates to communication and self-expression. It's lighthearted, frivolous, optimistic, and positive. It's creative and enthusiastic, but it is better at starting projects than it is at finishing them. It has a need to express itself in some way.

Four

Keyword: Hard work

Number four relates to hard work, organization, and system and order. It's a sign of the plodder who always gets there in the end. It often relates to feelings of constraint and restriction. It is rigid and serious in outlook.

Five

Keyword: Constructive use of freedom

Number five relates to freedom, variety, and feelings of expansion. Five craves excitement and doesn't want to be held back or restricted in any way. It's enthusiastic and remains forever young. Five is multitalented, and it usually takes many years to decide which interest to pursue.

Six

Keyword: Responsibility

Number six relates to home and family responsibilities. It's loyal, responsible, loving, and hardworking. Six is a sympathetic, understanding, caring, and appreciative number. It has the ability to harmonize and balance potentially difficult situations.

Seven

Keyword: Learning

Number seven relates to learning and growing in knowledge and wisdom. It's an introspective, spiritual, and sometimes solitary number. It enjoys spending time on its own to reflect and contemplate. Seven has an unusual and unique approach to everything it does.

Eight

Keyword: Money

Number eight relates to money and finance and likes being involved in large-scale enterprises. Eight is stubborn, single-minded, and rigid in outlook. Eight is conscious of status and needs to feel successful in order to be happy.

Nine

Keyword: Humanitarianism

Number nine is a humanitarian number. It's concerned with humanity as a whole, rather than helping people one at a time. It's a selfless number and enjoys giving. In fact, nine's greatest pleasure and satisfaction is giving to others.

Ten

Keyword: Attainment

There is no number ten in numerology, as ten is reduced down to a one ($1 + 0 = 1$). A ten has all the qualities of a one, but is more cautious and thoughtful. The enthusiasm and exuberance of the one is more controlled in number ten.

The Court Cards

The court cards relate to specific people in the life of the person who is having his or her cards read. Sometimes, the person indicated is the client.

Jacks

Jacks are young people of either gender. They are naive, eager, brash, and not entirely wise in the ways of the world. Consequently, they make mistakes, and usually learn from them.

Queens

Queens are strong, often powerful women who are closely involved with the person having the reading. If this person is a woman, the queen may well represent her. If the person having a reading is male, the queen is likely to be the dominant female in his life.

Kings

Kings are often mature men of influence and power. They offer good, sound advice. A king sometimes represents a male client and is always a strong male influence in the life of a female client.

Putting It Together

Now that you know the keywords, all you need do is relate the number or court card to the suit. The six of diamonds, for instance, relates to family matters (six) and money (diamonds). This could relate to money being spent on something that will benefit the family. It might be a family investment, such as buying the family home.

The seven of clubs relates to learning and spiritual growth (seven), as well as creativity and hard work. This shows that the person has the potential to work hard and learn something that relates to his or her creative or spiritual growth.

How to Read for Yourself

You can read the cards for yourself. There's an old superstition that says you shouldn't, but that was probably invented by a card reader who wasn't successful. You'll find reading your own cards helpful and insightful. They can also provide clues about where to go from here, and can warn you about potential dangers.

The only disadvantage of reading your own cards is that you might misinterpret cards to make the reading fit what you want, rather than what the cards say. If you feel that would be a problem, you should ask someone else to do the reading for you. You shouldn't read your own cards if you're under stress or have a strong emotional involvement in the outcome.

It's a good idea to write down your questions before starting the reading. Think about just one of them while mixing the cards. The cards you deal will relate to that particular question. Once it's been answered, you can mix the cards and create another spread.

Significator Card

Before starting the reading, you need to choose the court card that best symbolizes you to use as a significator card. Here are the traditional interpretations for the court cards:

- The suit of *spades* symbolizes people with dark hair and dark eyes.

- The suit of *clubs* symbolizes people with brown hair and brown eyes.

- The suit of *hearts* symbolizes people with light-brown hair and gray or blue eyes.

- The suit of *diamonds* symbolizes people with blonde or red hair.

- A *queen* symbolizes an adult woman, and a *king* symbolizes a man. A young person of either gender can be symbolized by a *jack*.

The significator card represents you, and the description does not need to be 100 percent accurate. If you have dark hair and blue eyes, you could choose a spade or a heart to represent you.

The significator card is placed in the center of the area where you're doing the reading.

Card Spreads

There are many different ways in which the cards can be laid out. If you have a simple question, you might mix the cards and take one of them at random to provide the answer. You might use three cards to represent the past, present, and future. The three cards might all be used to answer a particular question. One card might clarify the question, one might indicate the future if you carry on as you are now, and the third card could indicate a course of action to resolve the problem. You might use three cards to represent the next three months.

Past-Present-Future Spread

Instead of using three cards to indicate the past, present, and future, you can increase the number of cards and deal fifteen cards into three piles, each containing five cards. The cards on your left indicate the past, the center pile reveals the present, and the pile to your right provides information about the future.

Start by turning over the five cards in the past pile. Interpret these individually, and then see if it's possible to arrange them into a story that relates to your past. Let's assume that the cards in this pile are the eight of hearts, the three of clubs, the jack of spades, the ten of diamonds, and the six of diamonds.

These cards can be arranged in a number of ways. One of these could be: You started out in life in a happy home where you worked hard, but were appreciated and given opportunities to progress (3C). Although someone younger than you caused problems and challenges (JS) you were able to carefully evaluate possible opportunities to progress financially. You were positive, enthusiastic, and ambitious, and thought before you acted (10D). With hard work and the love and support of a significant other (8H), you achieved success. As a result of this, you were able to create a stable, loving home (6D).

The cards for the present are interpreted in the same way, followed by the five cards that represent the future.

If the cards fail to provide enough information, another fifteen cards can be dealt to explore your inner motivations.

Date of Birth Reading

This method uses your date of birth to locate three cards that can be interpreted. Mix the cards slowly while thinking of your question. When you feel the cards have been thoroughly mixed, deal a pile of cards face down that equals the month of your birth. If you were born in March, for instance, you'd deal three cards in this pile. If you were born in November, you'd deal eleven.

After this, deal a pile of cards that relate to your day of birth. If you were born on the sixth of any month, you'd deal six cards in this pile. If you were born on the thirty-first, you'd deal thirty-one cards.

The final pile relates to your year of birth. You start by turning your year of birth into a single digit. If you were born in 1994, for instance, you'd reduce the total down to 5 ($1 + 9 + 9 + 4 = 23$, and $2 + 3 = 5$). If you were born in 1987, the total would reduce down to 7 ($1 + 9 + 8 + 7 = 25$, and $2 + 5 = 7$). Deal whatever number you arrive at in the final pile.

With this reading, all three cards relate to the next few months, rather than to the past, present, and future.

Interestingly, every possible date can be covered by the fifty-two cards in the deck. Someone born on December 31, 1989, would have twelve cards in the first pile, thirty-one in the second, and nine in the third. That totals fifty-two. No other date adds up to more than this.

You can do the date of birth reading whenever you wish. On the day of your birthday, though, instead of using your year of birth, you can use the current year. The three cards will reveal the trends of the next twelve months.

The Mystic Cross Reading

There are many different versions of the Mystic Cross reading, and they each use a different number of cards. Many years ago in Germany I was taught a version that uses thirteen cards, and as it produces good results, I've never considered changing it.

The cards are mixed while you think of your question. When you're ready you deal seven cards facedown in a horizontal row in front of you. The middle card in this row also acts as the middle card in a vertical row that is created by dealing three cards above the central card and three below. If you wish, you can use your significator card as the middle card. I don't usually do this, but many people do.

By the time you've done this, you'll have a Mystic Cross consisting of thirteen facedown cards. The central card is turned over first, followed by the cards in the vertical row, starting with the bottom card. Finally, the cards in the horizontal row are turned over, starting with the left-hand card.

The cards in the vertical row reveal the present situation and the influences that are surrounding you. These are read in order from the top to the bottom. The cards in the horizontal row modify the reading. The cards to the left of the center card relate to the past. The cards on the right indicate what is going to happen in the near future.

The Wish Cards

This is a useful way to find the answer to a yes or no question. Make a wish while mixing the cards. When you feel ready, hold the cards facedown and deal them face up one at a time. Only two cards are important in this reading: the nine of hearts (the wish card) and the ten of spades (the disappointment card). The first of these to appear determines if the wish will come true. If the nine of hearts appears first, the wish will come true. If the ten of spades appears first, it won't.

If you receive a positive response, you cannot make another wish on the same day. If you receive a negative response, you can make another wish (but it must be totally unrelated to your first wish) and try again.

Solitaire

Solitaire is a game you play on your own. Solitaire reading is a divination that can be done for others, but it is usually used to answer your own questions. Most people know how to play solitaire. Thanks to computers, even people who've never handled a deck of playing cards have probably played the game. Interestingly, the game of solitaire is a particularly good way to answer questions. Not only are the cards mixed by chance (shuffled), the process of playing the game adds your choices and skill into determining the cards that are to be read.

Winning the game isn't necessary, though it denotes an extremely positive outcome to your question when it occurs. Once you've played the game and have taken it as far as you can, you'll have one, two, three, or four cards remaining in each column, and these are interpreted in the usual way.

Six Cards

This method of reading the cards is not used for answering a specific question. It's used for looking at your life and indicating possible directions you can take in the future.

Mix the cards thoroughly and place five cards from the top of the facedown deck to the bottom. The original sixth card is now on top of the face-down pile. Place this card onto the table. Move another five cards, one at a time, from the top of the deck to the bottom, and place the sixth card to the right of the first card you placed on the table. Continue doing this until you have six cards face down in a horizontal row in front of you. Turn over the cards from left to right, and interpret them.

The first card relates to your past. The second card relates to your present situation. The third card indicates your future if you make no major changes, and carry on in exactly the same way you are now. The fourth, fifth, and sixth cards all indicate different futures that could be yours, as long as you're prepared to make whatever changes and sacrifices are necessary to ensure the outcome you desire.

I find it helpful to carry the fourth, fifth, and sixth cards with me for a few days. This enables me to look at them whenever I have a spare moment and decide which of the three possibilities I want to pursue.

Reading for Others

Once you've learned the meanings of the cards and have practiced different spreads, you'll find other people asking you to read for them. You can do readings for others in exactly the same way you do readings for yourself. Try to make them upbeat and positive. Card readings work best when the two people involved engage in conversation. Many readers insist on doing most of the talking. This should not be the case with card reading. The reader is there to interpret the cards, but even with this, he or she should speak no more than the client.

You can practice your card reading skills everywhere you go. Social gatherings of any sort provide wonderful opportunities to practice. Ahead of time, mix two or three decks of cards and place them in a large container. Walk around the room asking everyone to take a card. Hold the container high to make sure that people select a card by chance. Once everyone has a card, you can ask each person in turn what card they selected and give them a quick reading based on their choice. As playing cards are cheap to buy, I let everyone keep their card and suggest they use it as a "lucky card."

Suggested Reading

Dee, Nerys. *Fortune-Telling by Playing Cards*. New York: Sterling Publishing Company, Inc., 1982.

Jones, Marthy. *It's in The Cards*. York Beach, ME: Samuel Weiser, Inc., 1984.

Sophia. *Fortune Telling with Playing Cards*. St. Paul, MN: Llewellyn Publications, 1996.

Webster, Richard. *Playing Card Divination for Beginners*. St. Paul, MN: Llewellyn Publications, 2002.

Runes

The word *rune* means "mystery" or "secret." According to legend, runes are credited to the one-eyed Nordic god Odin. To learn the ancient secret of the runes, he sacrificed himself by hanging upside down for nine days and nights, impaled by his sword, from the Yggdrasill, or World Tree.

Although the runes have always been associated with Nordic countries, it seems likely that they originated in northern Italy. This is because prehistoric rock carvings incorporating runic script have been discovered there. They are known as the Hallristinger script. This script was used primarily by Bronze Age tribes approximately 1300–1200 BCE. In addition to this, the runic alphabet shares a number of characteristics with the ancient Etruscan form of writing, which adds credence to the theory that it began in northern Italy.

Runic letters are composed of straight lines, which made them easier to inscribe on rock and trees. There are no word divisions, but dots were sometimes used between words.

Many different rune alphabets have been created, ranging from the Elder Futhark runes to the Cirth runes that were created by J. R. R. Tolkien for his The Lord of the Rings books. *Futhark* is named after the first six letters of the runic alphabet.

Although the runes were not created for magical or religious purposes, they have always had mystical associations, and people wrote prayers, charms, curses, and blessings using them. Old Norse literature contains many stories involving runes, and the magical associations may have come from them. Runic healing charms were popular, and even the act of writing them was believed to be healing. A runic inscription on a sheep bone, dating from the Viking-age, contains the words "by writing heals the crazy woman." [18]

Unlike our alphabet, every letter in the runic alphabet has a meaning. For instance, the first letter in the runic alphabet is *fehu*, which means "cattle." Over the years there have been three main versions of the runic alphabet:

- The *Elder Futhark* runes were used in northern Europe from about 150 to 800 CE. It has twenty-four letters. As the first six letters sound like f, u, th, a, r, and k, these are frequently known as the Futhark runes.

- *Anglo-Saxon Futhorc* runes were the version used in Britain from the fifth to twelfth century CE. Initially, it had twenty-eight letters, but an additional five letters were added in the early tenth century.

- The *Younger Futhark* runes were used in Scandinavia and Iceland from the eighth to thirteenth centuries. The number of futhark runes was gradually reduced to sixteen. As people converted to Christianity, the runic alphabet was gradually replaced by the Latin alphabet.

Unfortunately, the Church banned runes in 1639, and a great deal of runic lore was lost. Because the Nazi movement was fascinated with runes, interest in the subject almost died out after the second world war. It lay dormant until the 1950s when Professor J. R. R. Tolkien started writing about them in The Lord of the Rings trilogy. In the 1970s and '80s, rune stones gained popularity again as part of the increasing interest in the New Age.

Although runes were written on amulets and charms, there is no evidence that they were used for divination purposes until comparatively recently.

---

18   MacLeod and Mees 2006.

Meanings of the Runes

ᚠ	ᚢ	ᚦ	ᚨ	ᚱ	ᚲ	ᚷ	ᚹ
fehu (cattle) f	uruz (wild ox) u	thurisaz (thorn) th	ansuz (god) a	raiðo (chariot) r	kaunaz (torch) k	gifu (gift) g	wunjo (glory) w
ᚺ	ᚾ	ᛁ	ᛃ	ᛇ	ᛈ	ᛉ	ᛊ
hagalaz (hail) h	nauthiz (need, necessity) n	isa (ice) i	jera (harvest) j	eihwaz (yew) y	perth (chance) p	algiz (elk) z	sygel (sun) s
ᛏ	ᛒ	ᛖ	ᛗ	ᛚ	ᛝ	ᛞ	ᛟ
tyr (justice) t	beorc (birch) b	ehwaz (horse) e	mannaz (mankind) m	laguz (water) l	ingwaz (Ing— god) ng	ðagaz (day) d	othel (home) o

The runes that are usually used for divination are the twenty-four Elder Futhark runes. They are divided into three groups of eight stones named after Norse deities: Freya, the goddess of love and fertility, Heimdallr, who kept the keys to heaven, and Tyr, the god of battle and glory:

- *Freya's Eight*: F, U, Th, A, R, K, G, W

- *Heimdallr's Eight*: H, N, I, J, Y, P, Z, S

- *Tyr's Eight*: T, B, E, M, L, Ng, D, O

Freya's Eight

Fehu (Cattle)

Keyword: Fertility

Cattle used to be a measure of someone's prosperity. Consequently, Fehu relates to abundance, possessions, material gain, and wealth, as well as fertility and good health. Share your love and abundance with others. Be willing to pay a fair price for anything you buy.

Uruz (Wild Ox)

Keyword: Strength

Uruz relates to power, strength, stamina, passion, and sexuality. It's a sign that something is about to begin or something is coming to an end. It's also an indication of good luck, as long as you don't allow yourself to be adversely influenced by others.

Thurisaz (Thorn)

Keyword: Protection

Thurisaz relates to Thor, the god of protection. It shows you must be focused and work single-mindedly toward your most important goal. This is a powerful rune, but there are likely to be challenges and difficulties to overcome before you can move ahead. You'll need to be patient.

Ansuz (A God)

Keyword: Messenger

Ansuz relates to communication, self-expression, ultimate wisdom, inspiration, thinking before speaking, and listening to others. You'll receive good advice if you're prepared to be patient and listen. Ansuz also relates to creativity.

Raido (Chariot)

Keyword: Movement

Raido shows that it's time to let go and start afresh. It can relate to travel, journeys, or change. These changes will be positive, though you may not think so initially. Make sure you attend to everything that needs to be done before you move on.

Kaunaz (Torch)

Keyword: Enlightenment

Kaunaz relates to the element of fire. It indicates love, illumination, inspiration, guidance, careful evaluation, and listening to all points of view. It also relates to inner strength.

Gifu (Gift)

Keyword: Blessings

Gifu relates to generosity, giving, and unconditional love. It's a positive rune that indicates good fortune in both love and career. It's good for all kinds of exchanges and is extremely harmonious for all close relationships.

Wunjo (Joy)

Keyword: Reward

Wunjo relates to success, contentment, and happiness. You'll be rewarded for all your efforts. Matters that were hard to understand before will seem obvious now.

Heimdallr's Eight

Hagalaz (Hail)

Keyword: Disruptions

Hagalaz relates to delays, upheavals, losses, and major changes. You need to learn from these experiences and maintain a positive attitude. Once they're over, you'll have a much clearer idea of where you want to go.

Nauthiz (Need)

Keyword: Constraints

Nauthiz relates to frustrations, jealousy, obstacles, delays, and restraint. Be prepared for any problems or difficulties that impede your progress, and remain positive. It also relates to independence and passion.

Isa (Ice)

Keyword: Delays

Isa indicates that all matters in your life are held back, or restricted. In effect, they're temporarily embedded in ice and you're at a standstill and can't move. Use this downtime to your advantage by studying, learning, and evaluating.

Jera (Harvest)

Keyword: Productivity

Jera relates to receiving your just rewards for your actions. There's likely to be an ending, but this is positive, too, as you're entering a new stage of life. Jera relates to the seasons of a person's life. Ultimately, you reap what you sow.

Eihwaz (Yew)

Keyword: Endurance

Eihwaz is a sign that you must plan ahead and protect yourself against potential problems. Make sure your insurances are up to date, and do any necessary home and car maintenance. Be cautious, and evaluate every situation before acting.

Perth (Chance)

Keyword: Instinct

Perth indicates that something important is coming up, and you'll need to use your instinct or psychic abilities to make the right choice. There could be an initiation of some sort. It's a time to make decisions and act on them.

Algiz (Elk)

Keyword: Surprises

Algiz tells you to expect the unexpected. Look at the situation logically rather than emotionally, and work your way through it. Use gentle persuasion, rather than force. Algiz is one of the protective runes.

Sygel (Sun)

Keyword: Light

Sygel shows that you can see things more clearly than ever before. It's as if a light has been turned on. You'll be able to overcome problems with ease, and achieve the success you deserve. Sygel is a rune of good fortune.

Tyr's Eight

Tyr (Justice)

Keyword: Truth

Tyr relates to strength, discipline, selflessness, and conquering your fears. Honesty is the best policy, and one that pays off now. You may be called upon to demonstrate your leadership skills. As Tyr is the god of war, success may not come easily, but in the end justice prevails.

Beorc (Birch)

Keyword: Family

Beorc relates to fertility, children, the mother, nurturing, and family accomplishments. It's a sign that some good news is coming that relates to you, your parents, or children. You'll likely to be offered a new opportunity. Beorc also relates to regeneration and healing.

Ehwaz (Horse)

Keyword: Progress

Ehwaz is a sign of positive change and forward movement if you put in the necessary effort. The changes come slowly, but steadily, and help will be available when you need it. Ehwaz also provides harmony, loyalty, and peace of mind.

Mannaz (Mankind)

Keyword: Experience

Mannaz shows that you should rely on your knowledge and experience to progress. As a member of the human race, you can analyze, think, and communicate. Use these skills to your best advantage. Mannaz reveals the unlimited potential of the human intellect.

Laguz (Water)

Keyword: Go with the flow

Laguz shows that you shouldn't try to force anything now. If you take whatever time is necessary, and accept the situation, luck will follow. It also relates to the subconscious and intuition. Laguz indicates new starts and the ebb and flow of life. Be adaptable.

Ingwaz (Ing, the god of fertility)

Keyword: Power

Ingwaz shows that despite obstacles and setbacks, you'll ultimately be victorious. Let go of the past, live in the present, and make plans for the future. You might need to withdraw temporarily until you've worked out what you want to do. Ingwaz is a protective rune.

Dagaz (Day)

Keyword: Enlightenment

Dagaz indicates spiritual growth and development. You'll develop inner strength, awareness, and positivity. Daylight is coming and you'll be able to see the road ahead clearly. Dagaz attracts luck and good fortune. This is a highly positive rune.

Othel (Home)

Keyword: Material possessions

Othel relates to property and other important possessions, especially possessions you can buy. It also relates to stability and responsibility. This rune can be both positive and negative. It shows that ultimately family are the most important possession you'll ever have.

Some sets of rune stones contain a blank rune, known as the stone of destiny. In some ways this twenty-fifth rune relates to the joker in a deck of playing cards. It relates to your potential and what you do with the opportunities you find. Many readers use a blank rune. I prefer reading with the original twenty-four runes, and use Perthro as my destiny stone.

How to Read the Runes

The runes can be used to answer both simple and detailed questions. If the question is simple, or you need a quick answer, mix the runes in their bag and take one out at random. A more detailed reading can be performed by removing three runes, one at a time while thinking of your question. The first rune indicates the past, the second the present, and the third rune the future.

A more involved method uses nine runes. Nine is considered the ideal number as it took Odin nine days and nights to receive the secrets of the runes. You'll need a casting cloth with a circle marked on it. The circle can be any size you wish up to about three feet in diameter. If you're doing the reading outdoors, you can mark a circle on the ground with a stick or use a number of small objects to indicate the circumference of the circle.

Think of your question, and without looking, take three runes from your bag. Toss them into the circle. Repeat this process twice more so you'll have nine runes inside, or close to, the circle. Return any runes that landed outside the circle to your rune bag.

Occasionally, most, or even all, of the runes will land outside the circle. If all the runes are outside the circle, you should put them away and perform the divination again on another day. Ideally, the more stones that land inside the circle the better, but you can do a reading with just one stone if that's the only one remaining inside the circle.

The first thing to look for is how the runes are sited inside the circle. A group of runes that are touching or overlapping each other are extremely important, as they relate to the immediate concerns of the person having the reading. It's of lesser importance if two or three runes land together. However, they should also be read together. Runes that are sitting on their own also have a bearing on the reading, but their influence is minor compared to the runes that are in groups.

Starting at the twelve o'clock position, and moving around the circle in a clockwise direction, read all the face-up runes in turn. Repeat by turning over the face-down runes and reading them. Face-down runes indicate matters that the person being read for is not consciously aware of. They are usually a sign of delays before the situation can be resolved. Patience is required if all the runes in the circle are face down.

A slightly different version of the nine stone reading is to place all of the runes facedown on a table and mix them. The person who is having the reading selects nine of them, mixes them in his or her hands while thinking of a question, and then gently tosses them into the circle.

Another way to read the runes is to mix them in their bag while thinking of a question. Turn the bag over and let all the runes fall out. Interpret the stones that land face up.

A Sample Reading

Not long ago, a woman asked me for a rune stone reading. Before she married and had a family, she'd been a successful businesswoman. She'd given that up to become a full-time mom for her three children. Now that they were grown up, she wanted to return to the workforce, but felt she was lacking in both confidence and the skills necessary in business today. I asked her to randomly choose three runes. They were Beorc (past), Perth (present), and Othel (future).

"Beorc relates to the past. Interestingly, this is the rune that relates specifically to home and family. It shows you were a good mother, your children have done well, and you've been looking for a new opportunity for quite a while. Perth, in the present, shows that something important is about to come up, and you'll have to decide what to do using both logic and your intuition. You may even find yourself doing something you hadn't considered before. Obviously you'll have to do some fast learning to equip yourself for this new role, but I see you're prepared to do that. You have Othel in the future. This relates to stability and security. It looks as if your fortunes will improve because of the decision you're about to make. However, even though the additional income will be useful, you'll never forget that your greatest asset is your family."

How to Make Your Own Runes

Runes are readily available at New Age stores and online, but many people, myself included, prefer to make their own. By doing this you're imbuing your own personality into the runes as you work on them. Fortunately, as the runic symbols consist entirely of straight lines, you don't need any artistic talent to make an attractive set of runes.

You can make your own runes from any natural material. Stones, wood, and clay are the ones most commonly used. The objects you use should look as alike as possible. I enjoy picking up small stones whenever I'm beside a river or lake, and it doesn't take long to collect a couple of dozen stones that are almost identical.

Traditionally, wooden runes were made from ash, as this was the tree that Odin hanged himself from. However, any type of wood will work well. Instead of using oblong, square, or round pieces of wood, you might prefer to make runic staves using twenty-four twigs of the same size and shape. Runic staves range in length from six to twelve inches long. Cut away a section of the bark, and inscribe the runic symbols on them.

Make sure there's nothing that will identify the rune on the reverse side, as you don't want to know what the rune is until you turn it over.

Use a permanent marker or acrylic paint to inscribe the rune symbols on each stone or piece of wood. Traditionally, the symbols are created in red, but black and blue can also be used. You might prefer to use an engraving tool to carve the runic symbols.

Once you've made your own set of runes, keep them in a bag made from any natural material, such as cotton or linen.

Suggested Reading

Aswynn, Freya. *Northern Mysteries and Magic*. St. Paul, MN: Llewellyn Publications, 2002.

Mountfort, Paul Rhys. *Nordic Runes: Understanding, Casting, and Interpreting the Ancient Viking Oracle*. Destiny Books, 2003.

Peschel, Lisa. *A Practical Guide to the Runes*. St. Paul, MN: Llewellyn Publications, 1989.

Thorsson, Edred. *Futhark: A Handbook of Rune Magic*. New York: Samuel Weiser, Inc., 1984.

Sand Reading

My good friend, the late Karrell Fox, introduced me to sand reading in 1992 at a convention in Minneapolis where we were both lecturing. Although he wasn't able to demonstrate the art to me, he gave me enough information to start experimenting with it when I returned home.

How to Do It

Required: A small, round tray, approximately ten inches in diameter, a chopstick, and a small bag containing fine river sand.

The person wanting a reading and the reader sit opposite each other with the empty tray resting on a table between them. The reader gently pours the sand into the tray and smoothes it with a chopstick. The person requesting the reading places his or her left palm and fingers firmly on the sand. When the hand is raised again, an imprint of the hand remains on the sand. The reader uses the chopstick to gradually remove the handprint as he or she gives the reading. By the time the reading is over, the sand is smooth again.

A reading of this sort is done largely using telepathy and clairvoyance. However, the palm print also provides the reader with information. Using basic palmistry, the reader can interpret the shape of the hand and the length of the fingers and thumb. An introverted person will hold his or her fingers together while making the imprint on the sand. A more extroverted person will spread his or her fingers before pressing them onto the sand.

Much more detail can be obtained if the sand is slightly moistened before the reading. It's often possible to see the person's major lines and the raised sections of the hand (the mounts) when doing this. Unfortunately, I'm rarely able to do this, as most of my sand readings are done for groups of people, rather than individuals.

Some people make deeper impressions than others. Forceful, confident people usually press down firmly and create a deeper print than people who are timid and lacking in confidence.

Dr. Joe Slate uses numerology as well as the handprint when doing sand reading. After the handprint has been made, he asks the person having the reading to randomly write any number from one to nine on the sand beside the palm print. This number is interpreted as the person's present circumstances.

Another version of this uses a form of automatic writing. You need the shallow tray, sand, and a stick or pencil to make marks in the sand. The sand should be slightly damp.

The person you're reading for should sit opposite you with the container of sand resting on a table between you. Ask the person to tell you whatever question is uppermost on his or her mind. Once this has been done, smooth the sand with the side of the pencil.

Extend both of your hands palms upward, and ask the questioner to rest his or her face down palms on yours. Gaze into the person's eyes for at least sixty seconds. If you think kind, gentle thoughts, this will be reflected in your gaze.

When you feel ready, remove your hands and put on a blindfold or close your eyes. Hold the pencil in your writing hand, place your wrist against the container holding the sand, and ask the person to focus on his or her question. Think about the person and the question. After a minute or two, the pencil will start moving and make marks in the sand. Keep your eyes closed, and allow the pencil to continue moving until it comes to a stop.

Remove your blindfold, or open your eyes. Look at the markings the pen has made in the sand, and see what impressions come into your mind.

Suggested Reading

Slate, Dr. Joe H. *Psychic Empowerment*. St. Paul, MN: Llewellyn Publications, 1995.

Weschcke, Carl Llewellyn, and Joe H. Slate. *The Llewellyn Complete Book of Psychic Empowerment*. Woodbury, MN: Llewellyn Publications, 2011.

Scrying

Scrying is the art of divination by receiving visions while gazing at a shiny surface, such as a crystal ball, mirror, or the smooth surface of a still body of water. The word *scrying* comes from the Middle English word *descry*, which means "to catch sight of."

How to Do It

It's important to be in the right state of mind before scrying. It's impossible to scry if you're angry, stressed, or intoxicated. It's better not to scry immediately after eating a meal. You also shouldn't scry when you're overly tired, as you need to remain alert.

Required

A speculum. This is the name that is used for any object that's being used for scrying purposes, such as a crystal ball, a mirror, a large piece of crystal, a bowl of water, or even a glass of dark red wine.

A stand to hold the speculum.

A dark-colored cloth. Black velvet is perfect.

A room where you won't be interrupted for at least twenty minutes.

Two or more candles.

A container of water. Hopefully this will never be needed. It's a precaution you should use whenever you're performing divinations using candles.

Method

The easiest time to scry is at night in a darkened room lit by a few candles. You don't want any bright lights. This is because you're going to be using your psychic vision, rather than your eyes, to clairvoyantly "see" a vision in the object you're gazing at. You can also scry during the daytime. Darken the room, if possible, by closing any curtains and turning off any sources of bright light. If you can't block light coming from a window, sit with your back to it.

The room should be reasonably warm, as you need to be as comfortable as possible. If you wish, you can scent the room with incense and play background music.

- Start by relaxing as much as possible. You might meditate for a while or perform a progressive relaxation exercise. If you're asking a specific question, think about it in general terms during this relaxation stage. Remain detached, even if the question is emotional and is affecting you greatly.

- Place your ball (or whatever you're using) resting on the cloth onto a table, and place a candle on either side of it. Light the candles and make sure they're not being reflected in your scrying instrument.

- Sit down comfortably in front of the object you'll be scrying with. Spend a few minutes relaxing your body and becoming familiar with your surroundings.

- When you feel ready, take five slow, deep breaths and focus on your speculum. You might like to pick up your crystal ball or mirror. If you do this, pick up the velvet cloth as well. This can be used to prevent your hands from touching the ball directly. Make sure that the candlelight remains behind or to the sides of your ball. If you don't pick the speculum up, put your hands on either side of it. Gaze into your speculum. It's best if you're looking downward into it. Allow your eyes to relax and become slightly out of focus. There's no need to concentrate or stare. You can also let your thoughts roam freely. Every now and again bring them back to what you're doing. Blink when necessary.

- After a while, you'll notice a fine, milky gray mist between you and the ball. This is a sign that you've entered the desired state and will soon see visions. These visions may be visible in the ball or the mirror, but are more likely to appear in your mind's eye. They're likely to be indistinct at first. Remain quiet, passive, and expectant. If you're fortunate, they'll gradually become clearer. Any attempts to force them to become more visible will make them fade away.

- Continue doing this for about ten minutes. You may not experience anything the first few times you try this, but results will come with practice. Everyone is different. Some people start seeing visions right away, while others need practice before they can see anything.

- When you sense it's time to stop, close your eyes and take five slow, deep breaths. Open your eyes, get up and move around. Have something to eat and drink before carrying on with your evening.

- Record your results and date them. This is important, as it provides documentary evidence if what you saw in the crystal ball happens later on. You should record everything you experience, even if it is nothing more than a milky gray mist or a flash of color. You should record any thoughts that occurred to you while you were scrying. You might like to also record the question you asked, if any, the kind of light in the room, and how you felt before and after the session.

Short, regular sessions are best when you're learning how to scry. Five or ten minutes every evening will produce better results than sixty minutes once a week.

You'll see either images or symbols in your speculum. Most of the time the images you see will be obvious and won't need to be interpreted. If anything is hard to understand, sleep on it. When you wake up in the morning, you're likely to have the answers in your mind. Symbols will need to be interpreted, and you'll sometimes need to use your imagination to work out what they mean. Most will be fairly easy to interpret. A gun or a spear, for instance, means danger. A bird's nest indicates domestic harmony. If there are any babies in the nest, it could indicate a happy event in the near future. A coffin is likely to indicate a death. A ladder could indicate that you're climbing the ladder to success. Travel could be indicated by a flying bird, an airplane, or a ship. A horseshoe or a letter are signs of good news. With practice, you'll develop your skills at reading symbols and be able to interpret them instantly.

Even expert crystal gazers find it difficult to see or sense anything on occasions. Stress is a common cause of this, especially when there's a strong need for the divination. Overtiredness, alcohol and drugs all affect the person's ability to scry.

I've found it helpful to close my eyes and take several slow deep breaths whenever I fail to receive anything. Breathe in while silently counting to five, and exhale the same way.

Another method is to imagine a *bindu* in the center of your speculum. A bindu is a small dot used as a concentration point in the center of a mandala. Visualize the bindu as clearly as you can, and then allow it to grow larger and larger until it entirely fills your speculum. It doesn't matter what color you imagine your bindu to be, but once it entirely fills your speculum, allow it to turn milky white. Continue gazing at it while taking three slow, deep breaths, and wait for information to come to you. If nothing happens after three to five minutes, thank your speculum, and put it away. There's no need to worry when this occurs, and you'll find it will continue to work for you after you've had a good night's sleep.

It's important to keep your scrying implements clean and use them solely for scrying purposes. They need to be treated with care and respect. Keep them in a black bag when you're not using them.

While you're gaining experience, it's best to practice your scrying on your own. Once you're able to scry whenever you wish, without problems, you can allow other people to watch as you gaze into the ball. They can ask questions, as long as they're serious. It's difficult to scry when people are laughing and joking about the process.

I don't allow my clients to touch or hold my crystal ball, as I don't want it to be affected by other people's energies. However, some crystal ball readers do the opposite and ask their clients to hold the ball for a minute or two before starting the reading. They then take the ball back, place it on a base covered with a black velvet cloth, and start the reading.

Once you've mastered the art of scrying, you should use it only when you need to. The speculum is a focusing device, and there's no point in gazing at it with nothing in mind.

You may also find yourself scrying spontaneously. You may, for instance, pick up a glass of water to drink and happen to see a symbol or picture in it. You might glance at a mirror and see a vision in it.

Many years ago, I saw a vision in a pond. It was memorable, as my children and I had visited this pond dozens of times previously to feed the ducks. The last thing I expected to see was a message. There are many documented cases of this phenomenon, but they usually occur only to experienced scryers.

An interesting example of this was reported in *The Journal of the Society of Psychical Research* in December 1903. A woman woke up during the night and picked up a glass of water. Before she drank from it she saw the image of a moving train in the water. As she watched, one carriage crashed into another. A couple of hours later, her husband returned home and told her of an accident that had occurred at his work. It was exactly what she had seen in the glass. He told her that the brakeman had been badly injured.

Crystal balls made of rock crystal or clear quartz are extremely expensive. Crystal balls made of leaded glass are much cheaper, and for even less money you can buy balls made of acrylic. However, attractive and impressive though they may be, they're not essential. You can scry just as well using a wine glass full of water, a small pool of black ink, a large, shallow bowl of water, a fishbowl full of water, a crystal, or a piece of glass that has been painted black on the underside. You can scry beside a body of clear water, such as a spring, pond, or lake. You can also use your thumbnail if necessary. It's a good idea to experiment with some of these before investing in a crystal ball.

Crystal balls can be ordered over the Internet. However, if you can, experiment with a ball before buying it. You'll find some balls will work better for you than others. I have several crystal balls, and my favorites are the two that were given to me. The first ball I was given was tiny, but worked extremely well. Many years later, someone gave me a full-size ball, which I've used ever since. I've bought the other balls over the years as I received a good response from all of them.

Suggested Reading

Besterman, Theodore. *Crystal-Gazing: A Study in the History, Distribution, Theory, and Practice of Scrying*. London: William Rider & Son Limited, 1924.

Silbey, Uma. *Crystal Ball Gazing: The Complete Guide to Choosing and Reading Your Crystal Ball*. New York: Touchstone Books, 1998.

Tyson, Donald. *Scrying for Beginners*. St. Paul, MN: Llewellyn Publications, 1997.

Tea Leaf Reading

Tasseomancy, also known as tasseography, is the art of reading the shapes and symbols created by tea leaves after the cup of tea has been drunk. Tea has been consumed in the Far East for at least five thousand years, and it seems that tea leaves have been used for divination purposes for almost as long. Over a period of time, tea cultivation spread to India and Sri Lanka. Tea was introduced to Europe in the early seventeenth century. Until Victorian times, it was a luxury and consumed only by the well-to-do.

Tea leaf readers fall into two groups. People in the first group learn the meanings of the shapes that can be created by tea leaves. This provides instant results, and the different shapes can be looked up in any popular book on tea leaf reading. People in the other group use their imagination and intuition to interpret what they see. Many people start by learning the meanings and then gradually move into the second group as they gain knowledge and experience. When this happens, the shapes become symbols that are interpreted by their subconscious minds.

All you need to read tea leaves is a suitable cup, some good quality loose leaf tea, a teapot, and a paper napkin. The best cup is made from bone china, is plain white inside, and has a wide rim. The ideal cup is roughly twice as wide at the top as it is at the bottom. It's important that the cup has no ridges or patterns on the inside.

As I enjoy drinking green tea, whenever possible I use either Chinese or Japanese green sencha tea. When this isn't available, I use Darjeeling, Earl Grey, or English breakfast. The tea needs to contain reasonable sized leaves, which is why you shouldn't use a cheap tea, ground tea, or leaves taken from a tea bag.

How to Do It

- Place a paper napkin onto the saucer. This is to absorb any excess water when you place the cup onto it.

- Put cold water into the kettle or jug, and while waiting for it to boil, warm the teapot with hot water. Pour this out, and put a spoonful of tea into the pot for each person. With black tea you might like to add an extra spoonful for the pot. When the water boils, bring the teapot to the jug, and pour the water into it. Allow the tea to steep for three or four minutes before pouring cups of tea. For the best taste, the water should be boiling when using black tea, but be slightly less than boiling when using green tea. If milk is required, pour it into the cup before adding the tea. While all of this is going on, the person having the reading should think about his or her question.

- The person having the reading should drink the tea until about a teaspoonful remains. This person should then make a wish.

- If the person is right-handed, he or she holds the cup in the left hand and swirls the cup in a counterclockwise direction a number of times, and then, without interrupting the swirling action, turns the cup upside down onto the saucer. If the person is left-handed, he or she should hold the cup in the right hand and swirl the cup in a clockwise direction. I've met readers who say ladies should swirl the cup counterclockwise, and men should swirl it clockwise. I've experimented with both, and prefer the right-handed and left-handed method. Try them both and use the method that feels right for you.

- Tea leaf readers also differ on the exact number of times to swirl the cup. Most say three times, but some say seven. I use the person's numerological Life Path number. This is determined by adding together the month, day, and year of the person's birth, and reducing the total to a single digit. For instance, if someone was born on May 30, 1986, the Life Path number would be 5, as 5 (month) + 3 + 0 (day) + 1 + 9 + 8 + 6 (year) = 32, and 3 + 2 = 5. In numerology, 11 and 22 are considered Master Numbers, and do not get reduced. However, for tea leaf reading, they are reduced to 2 and 4. If the person has a Life Path number of 1 or 2, the cup should be swirled three times.

- Some people like to turn the cup three times while it's face down. This is done using the left hand: three times clockwise for men, and three times counterclockwise for women. Again you should experiment to determine whether or not this final touch is necessary.

- Once the cup has been placed upside down on the saucer, leave it for a few seconds to drain. Some people count up to seven slowly. After this, pick up the cup, hold it with the handle facing you, and examine the leaves. Don't hurry this stage, as it's important that the leaves make some sort of impression on your mind. Move the cup around and look at the leaves from different angles, as this sometimes helps you gain additional insights.

How to Interpret the Tea Leaves

The handle of the cup represents the person's home and family life. If the person isn't living at home, it represents where he or she is living at the time the reading is being done. The area directly across from the handle indicates work colleagues, acquaintances, and strangers.

Events in the past are shown by leaves on the left-hand side of the handle when the handle is pointing toward the person giving the reading. Events in the present and future are indicated on the right-hand side of the handle. The sides of the cup between the handle and the opposite side indicate approximately six months. This means you can go back in the past by examining the area on the left side of the handle and up to six months in the future by looking at the right.

Leaves at the bottom of the cup indicate events that are more than six months away.

Letters are seen frequently in tea leaves. These indicate people who are connected to the person who's having the reading. The larger the letter happens to be, the more important it is. If you're giving the reading to someone else, ask him or her who the person represented by the letter is.

Numbers are important, too. The number four, for instance, might mean four days, four weeks, four months, or even four years. You need to look at where the number is in the cup to determine which one of these is correct. If it's close to the rim of the cup, it could be four days or four weeks. If it's close to, or on, the bottom, it would indicate four years.

You also need to examine what's close to or surrounding the number. If a number is isolated and is on its own, it's interpreted using the nine keywords for the numbers in numerology:

1. This indicates individuality and shows that the person will achieve independence and success.

2. This indicates adaptability and shows the person will achieve better results by gentle persuasion, rather than force.

3. This shows the person will express him or herself well and enjoy close relationships with others. This can also indicate short journeys.

4. This indicates skill, service, and reliability. It's a happy sign to see in a cup as it shows a long, happy, and healthy old age.

5. This indicates eloquence in speech and thought. It also shows a great deal of variety and the lesson that the person needs to use his or her time wisely.

6. This represents love, home ideals, and loyalty. It's a sign of generosity and helping others. It can indicate empathy with animals.

7. This indicates sacrifice and inspiration. It involves solitary time thinking and meditating. It can indicate considerable wisdom.

8. This indicates slow, steady progress. However, the potential for financial reward is strong, and the person will achieve success.

9. This provides leadership qualities, along with a strong desire to help others. It can also indicate spiritual progress.

Lines formed by tea leaves indicate paths and journeys. If the line is strong, clear, and straight, it indicates rapid progress toward the person's goals. A weak, wavering line indicates delays, obstacles, and complications. A clear, winding line indicates a pleasant, leisurely journey.

Tea Leaf Symbols

Here are some of the symbols you're likely to find inside a tea cup. Don't limit yourself to my definitions. If you have a feeling that a certain object represents something completely different, follow your feelings, as your definition will be right for you.

- *Ace*: The ace of clubs indicates that good luck and happiness is not far away. The ace of hearts indicates happiness in love, marriage, and in the home. It can also indicate the birth of a child. The ace of diamonds indicates a business proposition and the potential for financial reward. The ace of spades indicates setbacks and disappointments.

- *Acorn*: Good health and an improvement in health if the person has been unwell.

- *Airplane*: Long distance travel. If it's pointing toward the handle, it's a sign of visitors.

- *Anchor*: Love and peace of mind.

- *Angel*: Good news. It's also a symbol of protection. Some people say that the presence of an angel eliminates any negative indications that might be in the cup.

- *Anvil*: Work opportunities. This could indicate a promotion, new responsibilities, or possibly a job offer.

- *Apple*: A major achievement.

- *Arch*: Overseas travel.

- *Arrow*: Unpleasant news.

- *Baby*: A new arrival in the family. Also the start of a new venture.

- *Balloon*: Sudden financial improvement.

- *Basket*: A pleasant surprise.

- *Bed*: Peace of mind and contentment.

- *Beehive*: Expect an important invitation.

- *Bird*: Good news and prosperity ahead. A number of birds indicate overseas travel.

- *Book*: An open book indicates important news from an unexpected source. A closed book indicates caution and restraint.

- *Bottle*: A sign that you should pour your energies into something worthwhile and important.

- *Bouquet*: An extremely lucky sign. Dreams will come true, and prosperity is assured.

- *Broom*: Changes need to be made before a new start can be undertaken.

- *Bull*: Unknown enemies. Be cautious.

- *Butterfly*: Brief moments of pleasure. Need for a more mature outlook.

- *Cage*: You're being held back, either by your own thoughts, or the activities of others.

- *Cake*: A celebration. A hurdle overcome.

- *Camel*: If you persevere you'll achieve your goal.

- *Car*: Change, power, and sexuality. Avoid being tempted by superficial glamour.

- *Castle*: A classic indication of success and prosperity.

- *Cat*: A seated cat indicates comfort and harmony. A jumping cat is a sign of disagreements and false friends.

- *Chain*: Complete one task before starting another.

- *Chair*: Take some time out to relax and unwind.

- *Child*: An extremely fortunate sign indicating new beginnings.

- *Circle*: Money or a gift is on its way. Joined circles are a sign of commitment.

- *Clock*: Don't waste too much time. If unwell, this indicates a quick recovery.

- *Clouds*: Frustrations and confusions. Think carefully before acting.

- *Clover*: A three-leaf clover indicates good fortune. A four-leaf clover is a sign of success in all things.

- *Coffin*: End of something to make way for the new.

- *Cornucopia*: Peace of mind, happiness, and abundance.

- *Crab*: Patience and persistence are required.

- *Crescent*: A good omen, especially if the points are facing left. If the points face right, delays will be experienced before success occurs.

- *Cross*: Trouble and bad news.

- *Crown*: A sign that your efforts will be rewarded.

- *Cup*: A successful conclusion. Especially good for romantic matters.

- *Dagger*: Danger and unknown enemies. Be alert.

- *Dice*: A good time to take a calculated risk.

- *Dog*: A good and faithful friend.

- *Donkey*: A sign of patience.

- *Dots*: A cluster of dots indicates money-making opportunities.

- *Duck*: A sign that you can keep your head above water. Usually a sign that financial problems are over. It can also indicate international travel.

- *Egg*: New beginnings. Change of outlook.

- *Elephant*: Good health and financial stability.

- *Face*: A friendly face indicates a new friendship. Be cautious if the face is sad or angry.

- *Fan*: Someone will try to flatter you. Be careful.

- *Fish*: Good fortune in all matters, including financial.

- *Flowers*: Traditionally, this is sign of a happy marriage. A single flower is a sign of love.

- *Fountain*: Joy and happiness.

- *Fox*: Someone is lying to you.

- *Frog*: Symbolizes fertility, good health, and longevity.

- *Goat*: An inopportune time to travel.

- *Guitar*: Romance is possible. Fun times with good friends.

- *Gun*: Keep calm, and avoid antagonizing anyone.

- *Gypsy*: An important opportunity that needs to be evaluated carefully.

- *Hammer*: You'll need to be persistent and determined to succeed. Temporary setbacks.

- *Hat*: An important new interest.

- *Heart*: Affection, love, and a good relationship with a kind, considerate person.

- *Hen*: A sign of a family reunion and happiness within the home.

- *Holly*: Good things will happen at Christmastime.

- *Horse*: Good news and potential travel. A rider on horseback indicates important news.

- *Horseshoe*: An important indication of protection and good luck.

- *House*: A change of home, or repairs to an existing home.

- *Igloo*: Temporary accommodation. Time to think about where to go from here.

- *Key*: Unexpected, puzzling, or unwanted changes.

- *King*: A strong, intelligent, and highly supportive man. An authority figure.

- *Ladder*: An improvement in the family's fortunes. There'll be ups and downs along the way if the ladder is incomplete.

- *Lamb*: A sign of happy times ahead.

- *Lizard*: A sign of unknown enemies.

- *Mermaid*: A warning to avoid all get-rich-quick schemes.

- *Monk/Nun*: A spiritual path. A time to grow in knowledge and wisdom.

- *Monkey*: Avoid gossip, and be aware that people will flatter you to achieve their own ends.

- *Mountains*: You don't have the energy, determination, or skills to succeed at the time indicated in the cup. Study, listen, and learn before acting.

- *Mouse*: Someone will try to steal an object or an idea from you. Don't be timid, and stand up for yourself.

- *Nest*: A bird's nest is a sign of security and protection.

- *Nurse*: A sign of ill health for you, or someone close to you.

- *Oak*: A symbol of long life and prosperity.

- *Octopus*: A versatile person with many talents. Opportunity to learn something new.

- *Owl*: A wise person will provide good advice.

- *Padlock*: A symbol of privacy. You may need to be more discreet.

- *Parrot*: Be careful in what you say and how you act. Avoid gossip.

- *Peacock*: A sign of a long, successful, and prosperous marriage.

- *Pig*: Avoid greed and gluttony. Don't seek more than your fair share. Overindulgence.

- *Pipe*: Daydreaming could provide an idea that leads on to success. However, the rewards will come only after a period of hard work.

- *Policeman*: Help will be available if required.

- *Purse*: You'll manage to get through a difficult financial situation. If surrounded by dots, you'll end up better off than you were before the situation began.

- *Pyramid*: Solid achievements built on a good foundation. A strong sign of success.

- *Queen*: An understanding, loving woman. An authority figure. This often indicates a mother.

- *Question Mark*: Time of self-doubt and uncertainty. Don't make any important decisions until the time indicated by the question mark is over.

- *Rabbit*: Start of a joyful, happy time.

- *Rainbow*: An indication of exciting and unusual happenings.

- *Rocket*: An indication that rapid changes will bring increased happiness.

- *Rose*: A symbol of joy and lasting happiness. An extremely fortunate sign.

- *Sausages*: A string of sausages indicates success in a variety of areas.

- *Scissors*: A good omen, but normally preceded by a brief period of bad luck. It indicates promising opportunities for success.

- *Shark*: Someone will try to provoke and antagonize you. Ignore them and they'll go away.

- *Ship*: Traditionally, this is a sign that money is on its way to you.

- *Shoe*: Take time to enjoy your success.

- *Snail*: This is a sign that you're trying to forge ahead too quickly. Slow down, and enjoy the pleasures of home, family, and good friends.

- *Snake*: A warning that someone is not who he or she purports to be.

- *Spectacles*: An indication that strangers will play an unexpected role in your life.

- *Square*: A strong sign of protection that overpowers any negativity that might be surrounding you.

- *Stairs*: This indicates a steady path upward to happiness and success.

- *Star*: This is an extremely good omen. It indicates good health, happiness, love, and prosperity.

- *Sword*: This is a sign of strife and discord. Tact and diplomacy will ensure it doesn't last for long.

- *Tortoise*: Slow, but steady, progress.

- *Tree*: This is one of the most positive symbols to see in a teacup. It indicates good health, longevity, and abundance.

- *Triangle*: This is a positive sign if the triangle is pointing upward or toward the handle of the cup. A downward pointing triangle is a sign of opportunities that should be seized before it's too late.

- *Trident*: A sign that an important decision needs to be made.

- *Trumpet*: An important announcement will come at the time indicated in the cup.

- *Umbrella*: It's always good to see an umbrella in the leaves as it's an important symbol of protection.

- *Violin*: Indicates enjoyable entertainment with good company. It's also a symbol of success for musicians.

- *Walking Stick*: This indicates the arrival of a male visitor.

- *Watch*: You must act and stop wasting time.

- *Wedding Cake*: This indicates news about an impending marriage.

- *Weeping Willow*: A sign of disappointment. It frequently indicates the end of a promising relationship.

- *Whale*: A large scale undertaking that has huge potential. Plan carefully before acting.

- *Wheel*: A symbol of progress and achievement. It can also indicate travel.

- *Windmill*: A sign of many fluctuations in your fortunes before you achieve success.

- *Wineglass*: A well-deserved celebration. Enjoy the moment.

- *Yacht*: A sign that you no longer need to strive for success, and now have time to pursue hobbies and other interests.

- *Zodiac*: Signs of the zodiac in the cup indicate people you'll be in contact with. A bull, for instance, indicates a Taurean, and scales indicate a Libran.

After the Reading

Do you remember telling the person having the reading to make a wish when he or she had almost finished drinking the cup of tea? At the end of the reading, indicate any good luck signs you see in the cup, and tell the person that as long as he or she approaches the future with a positive outlook, his or her wish will be granted.

Superstitions about Tea

There are a number of superstitions about tea. In my experience, the people you read for will expect you to know these and will enjoy telling them to you.

A tea leaf floating on the surface of a cup of tea after it's been poured is a sign that a visitor will arrive. You can tell when this will occur by placing the tea leaf on the back of your left hand. You then hit the hand repeatedly using your fist or two fingers of your right hand until the leaf falls off. Count the number of times you have to hit the hand before the leaf falls off, as this indicates the number of days until the visitor arrives.

Another superstition says that a single leaf floating on the surface is a sign you'll be coming into money. That might be a more appealing scenario than the arrival of a visitor.

A single stalk floating on top of the tea indicates the arrival of a stranger. It will be a man if the stalk is hard, and a woman if it's soft.

You should never stir a teapot. This stirs up trouble and causes friction between friends.

You shouldn't stir someone else's cup of tea for the same reason.

It's bad luck to break a teapot. It's also bad luck to pour tea back into the teapot.

If the lid of the teapot is accidentally left off, you'll receive a visit from a stranger.

Children shouldn't drink tea, as it will stunt their growth.

A single woman will never find a husband if she adds milk to her tea before the sugar.

A single woman will fall for any man who pours her more than one cup of tea from the same teapot.

If two women pour tea from the same pot, one of them will become pregnant within a year.

It's good luck to spill some tea leaves when placing them in the pot.

If you find bubbles in your cup of tea, you'll shortly be kissed.

It's a sign that someone close to you will become ill if a teaspoon is accidentally placed upside down on the saucer.

It's a sign of twins if two teaspoons are accidentally put onto the same saucer.

Rather than disposing of used tea leaves, you should scatter them onto the ground in front of your home, as this repels evil spirits.

Suggested Reading

Dow, Caroline. *Tea Leaf Reading for Beginners*. Woodbury, MN: Llewellyn Publications, 2011.

Struthers, Jane. *The Art of Tea Leaf Reading*. London, UK: Godsfield Press, 2005.

Webster, Richard. *How to Read Tea Leaves*. Auckland, NZ: Brookfield Press, 1982.

Tarot

When people think of divination, the tarot is usually the first method that comes into their minds. There are many different stories about its origins. Although some people claim tarot cards date back to ancient Egypt, the first existing records of them date back to the Renaissance, and tarot cards were recorded in Ferrara, northern Italy, in 1422. Playing cards had been introduced to Europe about fifty years earlier, and it seems that the tarot deck was invented to play tarocchi, a game not dissimilar to bridge, which some people still play today. The tarot wasn't associated with the occult or used for any kind of fortune-telling for at least a century after that, making the tarot a comparatively recent form of divination.

In 1909, Arthur Edward Waite, a leading member of the Hermetic Order of the Golden Dawn, created a tarot deck that is still by far the most popular deck used today. The artist was Pamela Colman Smith, who captured the symbolism Arthur Waite wanted extremely well. This deck used to be called the Rider-Waite tarot, as Rider and Company were the original publishers of it. Nowadays, it's usually known as the Waite-Smith tarot deck. The Waite-Smith deck was the first one to include a picture on every card, making it easier to read than the cards that preceded it. Nowadays, almost every tarot deck follows this system.

How to Do It

The tarot deck contains two sections: the major arcana and the minor arcana. The word *arcana* means "secrets" or "mysteries." The twenty-two cards in the major arcana relate to the major events in our lives. The fifty-six cards of the minor arcana relate to events that can be changed if we're not happy with what they tell us. The minor arcana cards are divided into four suits: cups, wands, swords, and pentacles. These relate to the suits of hearts, clubs, spades, and diamonds in a deck of playing cards. Each suit contains fourteen cards: the ace through to 10, plus the page, knight, queen, and king. Regular playing cards eliminated the knight, and the page changed his name to jack.

The powerful symbolism of the cards represents the cycles and experiences that we all encounter as we progress through life.

The Major Arcana

The cards of the major arcana relate to the important events in our lives, such as births, deaths, marriages, triumphs, and disasters. They represent the important turning points of life and consequently have a profound influence on the reading.

0 THE FOOL

Keywords: Joy, change, adventure, new starts, potential, spontaneity, enthusiasm, and excitement

As it's numbered zero, the Fool can be placed at either the first or last position in the major arcana. The Fool is usually depicted as a young man setting off on a journey with his dog. He's about to step off a cliff. This card shows that the person having the reading is about to start something new. In a reading, the cards surrounding the Fool will indicate if this is a good or a bad idea.

1 THE MAGICIAN

Keywords: Imagination, creativity, originality, potential, magic, spirituality, and enlightenment

In most decks, the Magician is shown standing behind a table holding up a wand. The other three suits of the tarot deck—cups, swords, and pentacles—are resting on the table. This card indicates clear thought, opportunities, and the quest for wisdom and success.

2 THE HIGH PRIESTESS

Keywords: Intuition, psychic, mystery, and spiritual growth

In the Waite deck, the High Priestess sits on a throne with pillars on both sides. The pillars, and the book she's holding, signify wisdom, especially insights gained through intuition and feelings. The message of this card is to search within yourself and trust your hunches and feelings.

3 The Empress

Keywords: Fertility, mother, birth, domesticity, and happiness

The Empress card shows a young woman wearing a crown and sitting on a throne. In many decks, she is obviously pregnant. She is surrounded by trees and flowers that symbolize fertility and renewal. This card indicates creativity, nurturing, and the birth of something new.

4 THE EMPEROR

Keywords: Power, strength, authority, security, father, and protection

The Emperor shows a mature bearded man with a crown on his head and sitting on a throne. This card shows that you must use your personal influence to help matters move in the direction you want them to go. If you do this, you'll achieve success.

5 THE HIEROPHANT

Keywords: Wisdom, advice, tradition, compassion, rituals, and strength

The Hierophant is a mature man wearing a crown. He is standing between two pilars inside a temple. He holds a staff in his left hand and gives a blessing with his right. It shows that you should seek wisdom from someone who is more experienced, and possibly wiser, than you.

6 THE LOVERS

Keywords: Love, relationships, sex, matters of the heart, and choice

The Lovers usually shows a young couple who are obviously in love. Some decks depict one man and two women, showing that some emotional decisions will have to be made. Although this card indicates love, it can also mean nonromantic partnerships, too.

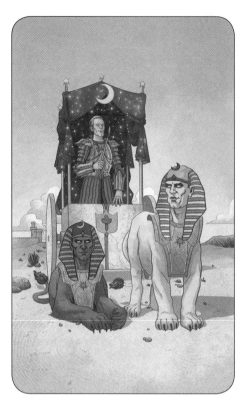

7 THE CHARIOT

Keywords: Success, victory, rewards, and travel

The Chariot depicts a young man riding a chariot that is usually pulled by two horses heading in different directions. This card is a sign of success after problems and difficulties have been overcome. The horses have harnessed opposing energies and triumphed over significant odds. Because this card depicts a chariot, it can also relate to travel.

8 STRENGTH

Keywords: Courage, power, and overcoming negativity

Strength is usually depicted by a woman holding open the jaws of a lion. It's a sign that you possess the necessary courage and perseverance to overcome any obstacle. It's often an indication of hidden strengths that have been forced into play.

Arthur Edward Waite transposed the Strength and Justice cards. Consequently, with some tarot decks you'll find Justice in this position, and Strength will become the eleventh card.

9 THE HERMIT

Keywords: Solitude, meditation, contemplation, renewal, and time out

The Hermit is depicted as a wise old man holding a lamp. The lamp signifies his quest for wisdom, knowledge, and truth. This card shows you need to seek answers to your questions inside yourself. You'll need solitude and time on your own to think matters through.

10 THE WHEEL OF FORTUNE

Keywords: Cycles, choice, luck, change, and opportunities

The Wheel of Fortune card usually contains a large wheel that shows that time doesn't stand still and is constantly moving. Fortune can be both good and bad.

11 JUSTICE

Keywords: Balance, justice, fair play, law, principles, honesty, and integrity

Justice is depicted by a crowned woman with a raised sword in her right hand and a scale in her left. A decision needs to be made, and you should weigh up the various options (the scales) before making a decision. Whatever the outcome, justice will be done.

12 THE HANGED MAN

Keywords: Suspension, transition, renewal, and sacrifice

The Hanged Man is represented by a man hanging upside down by a rope tied to his ankle. Despite this, he's not unhappy. This card indicates a time of patient waiting. It can indicate a temporary loss that helps you to achieve a greater gain. Even though this may seem unlikely at the time, a sacrifice can ultimately be worth making.

13 DEATH

Keywords: Transformation, regeneration, change, and new starts

Death is usually depicted by a skeleton. In the Waite deck, the skeleton is wearing armor and riding a horse. Death is inevitable, and this card signifies the ending of something to make room for a new beginning. It's a good time to make decisions that have been put off for some reason.

14 TEMPERANCE

Keywords: Patience, serenity, harmony, peace, moderation, and understanding

Temperance is depicted by an angel pouring water from one container to another. This card signifies balance and the necessity to sometimes allow matters to take their own course, and take as long as necessary, to reach a conclusion.

15 THE DEVIL

Keywords: Temptation, excess, caution, dishonesty, lies, and deceit

The Devil is usually depicted by a horned devil. It shows that you, like everyone else, experience negative thoughts and feelings that need to be acknowledged and accepted. It's a time to be cautious and to examine the potential consequences before acting.

16 THE TOWER

Keywords: Disruption, unexpected disaster, arrogance, pride, devastation, and danger

The Tower is depicted by a large tower being struck by lightning. It's a sign of destruction and shows there are outside influences present that you cannot control. Despite the apparent negativity of this card, it provides the opportunity to start again from a much stronger foundation.

17 THE STAR

Keywords: Hope, wishes, renewal, opportunities, and positivity

The Star shows a young woman pouring water from two containers on a starry night. This is the card of hope and a sign that good things are ahead for you. It also shows that you need to work out what it is you want to do (make a wish) and then go out and make it happen.

18 THE MOON

Keywords: Dreams, illusion, emotions, mystery, intuition, and insight

The Moon card shows the Moon in the sky. It normally contains a human face that looks downward to the earth. This card can indicate illusion and fooling yourself. It's a time to trust your intuition, rather than making decisions based solely on logic. Things are not always what they seem.

19 THE SUN

Keywords: Progress, growth, excitement, energy, happiness, and success

The Sun card contains a human-faced Sun sending its life-giving rays to earth. On the ground are one or two children close to a wall that they can easily climb over. The Sun card is always positive and symbolizes all the good things life has to offer. This is the perfect time to start something new and enjoy the fruits of your success.

20 JUDGEMENT

Keywords: Fairness, accountability, responsibility, and karma

Judgement is depicted by an angel blowing a trumpet. This is usually assumed to be Gabriel blowing the trumpet on judgment day. Judgement is a sign to reevaluate what's important to you, and to realize that you are responsible for everything you think, say, and do. You need to use your experience to avoid making mistakes in the future.

21 THE WORLD

Keywords: Success, happiness, fulfilment, and happiness

The World card is usually depicted by an almost naked woman holding two wands. She is surrounded by a wreath that symbolizes cycles, as well as completion and success. This is an extremely positive card that shows it's time to celebrate your achievements and enjoy your success before moving on to another cycle of experience.

The Minor Arcana
The Four Suits

The fifty-six cards of the minor arcana are divided into four suits that relate to different areas of life. The cups relate to friendship, love, and relationships. The wands relate to ambitions and activities. Pentacles relate to work, money, career, security, and stability. Pentacles also relate to home, family, and possessions. Swords relate to overcoming conflicts and problems.

ACE OF WANDS

The Number Cards

- *Aces*: Aces relate to starting something new or different. This can be an unexpected occurrence. The aces are positive cards and often provide good luck.

- *Twos*: Twos relate to partnerships and choices that will have to be made in the near future. They can also mean a reunion or get together.

- *Threes*: Threes relate to cooperation, communication, group activities, and friendships.

- *Fours*: Fours relate to manifestation and security. Hard work and good organization help create a strong foundation for future progress.

- *Fives*: Fives relate to changes, challenges, and difficulties.

- *Sixes*: Sixes relate to harmony, contentment, and happiness. You'll have the right mental attitude to enable you to overcome past difficulties with ease.

- *Sevens*: Sevens relate to choices. It's a time of deep thinking and contemplation that will ultimately provide you with wisdom and self-knowledge.

- *Eights*: Eights relate to experience, hard work, and manifestation.

- *Nines*: Nines relate to determination, completion, and satisfaction. You'll be in the final stages of something important.

- *Tens*: Tens relate to fulfilment and completion of a cycle of experience. An issue from the past will have to be attended to before new starts can be made.

PAGE OF CUPS

The Court Cards

- *Pages*: Pages relate to children and young people of either gender. They also relate to communication.

- *Knights*: Knights represent young adults who set goals and go out and achieve them. As knights are messengers, they frequently relate to news that can be good or bad.

- *Queens*: Queens relate to the traditional feminine qualities, such as emotions, compassion, intuition, and home and family life. Queens represent the important women in the life of the person having the reading.

- *Kings*: Kings relate to influential and powerful men. They relate to assertion, confidence, leadership, responsibility, power, and energy.

Sometimes a queen can represent a man and a king symbolize a woman. A powerful, influential woman might be represented by a king, and a caring, compassionate, emotional man might be symbolized by a queen.

The court cards do not necessarily depict a specific person. They can also relate to how you, or someone else, is handling a particular situation. In cases of that sort, you need to relate the court cards to the cards surrounding them.

If you use the key words for the suits, number cards, and court cards you can work out the meaning of every card in the minor arcana.

TWO OF CUPS

The Suit of Cups

- *Ace of Cups* indicates the start of a new relationship. It's not necessarily a romantic relationship. It's also is a sign of happiness, abundance, and fertility.

- *Two of Cups* indicates that a relationship between two people is getting closer and stronger. It also indicates cooperation, partnerships, friendship, and love.

- *Three of Cups* indicates a celebration and harmonious relationships between family members and friends.

- *Four of Cups* indicates growing dissatisfaction with the status quo, boredom, and a desire for excitement.

- *Five of Cups* indicates a setback or disappointment, which is not as major as first feared.

- *Six of Cups* indicates a time of nostalgia, recalling happy times from the past.

- *Seven of Cups* indicates the need to make a choice from a number of possibilities. Be cautious, as everything may not be as it appears.

- *Eight of Cups* indicates a time to take a step back and wait for the situation to improve. You may need to let something go.

- *Nine of Cups* indicates feelings of confidence, assurance, and well-being. You've almost achieved your goal.

- *Ten of Cups* indicates contentment, happiness, and close relationships with the people you love.

- *Page of Cups* indicates a young person who is sensitive, sympathetic, and easily hurt.

- *Knight of Cups* indicates someone who is stimulating, enthusiastic, and exciting.

- *Queen of Cups* indicates a caring, intuitive, and sensual woman.

- *King of Cups* indicates a kindhearted, generous man who sees the best in everyone.

FOUR OF WANDS

The Suit of Wands

- *Ace of Wands* indicates a positive move or change is about to occur.

- *Two of Wands* indicates careful thought is needed before making an important choice.

- *Three of Wands* indicates the time of waiting is almost over, and new horizons beckon. It also reveals the potential for success.

- *Four of Wands* indicates success and temporary happiness before finding a new challenge. Enjoy home and family life.

- *Five of Wands* indicates a need to stand up for yourself and what you believe in.

- *Six of Wands* indicates a realization that you're on the right path, and success is ahead.

- *Seven of Wands* indicates a need to be resourceful and steadfast, no matter what others are suggesting.

- *Eight of Wands* indicates a sudden move forward after a delay or setback. This is a good time to progress toward your goals.

- *Nine of Wands* indicates that you've almost achieved your goal, but more persistence is required. Stand up for yourself.

- *Ten of Wands* shows you're trying to do too much. Fortunately, a heavy load is about to be lifted off your shoulders, and you'll be moving forward again.

- *Page of Wands* indicates a young person who is imaginative, curious, and enthusiastic, but also naive. He or she is keen to learn.

- *Knight of Wands* indicates someone who is good at starting projects but seldom finishes them.

- *Queen of Wands* indicates a wise, creative, intuitive woman who is good at organizing others.

- *King of Wands* indicates an enthusiastic, intelligent, motivating man who enjoys sharing his knowledge and insights with others.

SIX OF SWORDS

The Suit of Swords

- *Ace of Swords* indicates a new start and new opportunities after frustrations and delays.

- *Two of Swords* indicates that logic is required to make an important choice.

- *Three of Swords* indicates problems with relationships. You may have to let go in order to progress again.

- *Four of Swords* indicates fears, doubts, and worries that need to be overcome to move ahead. If possible, take time off to rest and regain your strength.

- *Five of Swords* indicates a short-term gain in difficult circumstances. Honesty pays off.

- *Six of Swords* indicates moving toward greener pastures, and leaving the past behind without regret.

- *Seven of Swords* indicates potential dishonesty. Be cautious and on your guard.

- *Eight of Swords* indicates the need to let go of baggage from the past. Fears are holding you back.

- *Nine of Swords* indicates groundless fears that can be overcome with courage and effort.

- *Ten of Swords* indicates sadness that something important has ended. Take the necessary time to mourn and be sad, and then start moving forward again.

- *Page of Swords* indicates a young person who is smart and mature in some ways but unintentionally hurts other people's feelings by not thinking before speaking.

- *Knight of Swords* indicates a strong person who is dedicated to justice and fairness.

- *Queen of Swords* indicates someone who finds it hard to express her feelings and can be harsh and overly critical as a result.

- *King of Swords* indicates a strong authority figure who uses logic and persistence to achieve his aims.

EIGHT OF PENTACLES

The Suit of Pentacles

- *Ace of Pentacles* indicates the start of something new that has the potential to be profitable.

- *Two of Pentacles* indicates the need to balance home and family commitments with career and investment opportunities.

- *Three of Pentacles* indicates that your efforts have been noticed, and you'll ultimately benefit financially.

- *Four of Pentacles* indicates the need for generosity, rather than hanging tightly onto what has already been gained. You'll need to be flexible and prepared to compromise.

- *Five of Pentacles* indicates a financial loss or uncertainty concerning money matters. Help will come from an unlikely source.

- *Six of Pentacles* indicates the giving or receiving of money or advice. Seek help from others when necessary.

- *Seven of Pentacles* indicates financial difficulties. You'll need to wait patiently until your fortunes start increasing again.

- *Eight of Pentacles* indicates making money from a particular skill or talent.

- *Nine of Pentacles* indicates financial security achieved through your own hard work. Enjoy your success.

- *Ten of Pentacles* indicates a happy family life, free of financial stress.

- *Page of Pentacles* indicates a young person who is clearly focused, reliable, and prepared to work hard.

- *Knight of Pentacles* indicates someone who works hard in the material world.

- *Queen of Pentacles* indicates someone who deals capably with money, and cares for others.

- *King of Pentacles* indicates someone who has achieved worldly success, and now works hard to create a happy home and family.

Significator Cards

Some tarot readers use a significator card to represent the person who is having the reading. The usual method is to show the court cards to the people you're reading for and ask them to choose the card they feel most closely resembles them.

Traditionally, men chose a king or a knight, and women a queen or a page. Older people chose a king or queen, and younger men and women chose a knight or page. If the person has dark hair, he or she would select a card from the swords suit. Brown-haired people would choose from the wands, people with light-brown hair would choose from the pentacles, and fair-haired people would choose from the suit of cups.

Another method is to use the element that belongs to the client's astrological sign. If the client belongs to a fire sign (Aries, Leo, or Sagittarius), he or she could choose any card from the suit of wands. If the client belongs to an earth sign (Taurus, Virgo, or Capricorn), he or she could choose any card from the suit of pentacles. If the client belongs to an air sign (Gemini, Libra, or Aquarius), he or she could choose any card from the suit of swords. If the client belongs to a water sign (Cancer, Scorpio, or Pisces), he or she could choose any card from the suit of cups.

To save time in practice, I usually select the person's significator card for them by choosing one of the court cards that relates to his or her element.

Mixing the Cards

Most decks of tarot cards are larger than regular playing cards, and this makes them difficult to mix. One way around this problem is to hold the deck of cards vertically, rather than horizontally, and do an overhand shuffle. Shuffle the cards for as long as you wish while thinking about your question. Focus on one question. If you have several questions in your mind, you're likely to receive a confusing answer.

A better method to mix the cards is to spread them facedown onto a table and mix them up until you're absolutely certain you don't know the position of any card. Instead of gathering the cards up again into a pile, take one card at random and hold it in your hand. Take another card from somewhere else on the table and place it on top of the first card. Continue doing this until you're holding all seventy-eight cards in your hand. This method takes time, but you're imbuing each with your energy as you collect them. Consequently, before reassembling the cards, it's a good idea to think about your question and to continue thinking about your need for an answer while you're picking each card up.

Many tarot card readers shuffle their own cards while others are happy for their clients to mix the cards before the reading. If you're doing the mixing, both you and the person you're reading for should think of the question while the cards are being mixed, and the person being read for places his or her hands on the cards before a spread is dealt to impart some of his or her energy into them. I prefer to do the mixing myself and use a different deck when people I read for ask to mix their own cards.

Once the cards have been mixed, the deck is cut. This can be done in any way you wish. Usually, the deck is cut into three piles using the left hand, and then the deck is reassembled by picking the piles up in a different order.

Reversed Cards

After the cards have been mixed, the chances are that some of them will be upside down in relation to the others. These are called *reversed cards*. Some readers interpret these cards negatively and read them as being the reverse of what they would mean if they were upright, rather than reversed.

Other readers, myself included, give the cards the same reading no matter which way up they happen to be. In many decks, especially older ones, the minor arcana cards do not have pictures on them, and some of the cards look the same no matter which way up they happen to be. You might like to experiment and see which method works better for you.

How to Read Tarot

You can read the tarot in many different ways. The simplest method, and a useful way to learn the cards, is to ask a question, mix the cards, and select one at random. You can also do this by randomly selecting a card every morning and carrying it around with you during the day. Look at it from time to time when you have a spare moment. Before you go to bed, see if the card provided an accurate description of your day. I know several people who do this. Most of them use their "card of the day" as a protective amulet, as well as a predictor of the day.

Three- and Five-Card Spreads

Three cards can be dealt to represent the past, present, and future. If they don't provide the necessary information, another three cards can be dealt below the first three to see if they clarify the situation.

I usually prefer to deal five cards in a row, rather than three. The first card is the Past, the second indicates the Present, the third reveals any Mysteries, the fourth provides Suggestions, and the fifth card relates to the Future. The Mystery card reveals anything that is secret, hidden, or possibly overlooked. The Suggestions card provides hints and ideas on where the person can go from here.

Here's a sample reading using the five-card spread:

- The person requesting the reading is a woman in her middle thirties. She is divorced, works in a bank, and lives with her parents. The divorce occurred five years ago. She doesn't particularly enjoy her job, and she is embarrassed that she's still living in the family home. It took her three years after her divorce to start dating again, and she's beginning to think she's destined to be on her own forever. Her question is, "Will I ever meet the right man?"

- She mixes the cards and hands them back. You cut the deck and deal out five cards in a row in front of her. If she's sitting opposite you, you deal the cards from right to left. This means that the first card, indicating the past, is to her left. If you're sitting side by side, you deal the cards from left to right.

- Let's assume that the cards are Strength, Three of Cups, Knight of Cups, Two of Wands, and the Ace of Cups.

- You briefly explain what the five positions represent and then look at the card representing the past. "In the past," you might say, "you showed that you had the necessary fortitude and courage to stand up for yourself. You might even have surprised yourself with your strength of character. You needed this to overcome what must have been a devastating experience, and you grew inwardly as a result. You're not the same person you were then."

- "This card indicates the present," you say. "As you can see, it's a happy card. You're obviously enjoying a good social life, and have good friends and plenty of family support. Although this is all extremely positive, I can tell from your question that you've probably had enough of what might seem like a rather shallow and frivolous lifestyle. You want more, much more, than that."

- "The next card is interesting," you might say, indicating the Knight of Cups. "This is the mystery card, and it shows what you might have forgotten or overlooked. The Knight of Cups indicates a caring and enthusiastic young man. As mysteries can also indicate secrets, it's possible that he's a secret admirer, someone you know, but someone who for some reason is not making his feelings obvious."

- "The fourth card relates to suggestions. As you can see from the card, the Two of Wands shows someone who is thinking deeply before making a decision. That might be you, but it may also indicate your Knight of Cups, who is thinking about the possibility of a relationship with you."

- "Let's see what the future reveals. The Ace of Cups indicates the start of something new. The suit of cups relates very much to love and relationships, and you have three cards from this suit in this spread. That's a very good sign. The Ace of Cups indicates the start of a romantic relationship. Of course, it's up to you how far you want to take it. I'd pay special attention to the Knight of Cups, your mystery man. I think you already know him, but either overlooked him, or thought he wasn't interested."

Most of the time, readings become conversations, and even if this lady didn't say much during the reading, she'll have plenty of questions afterward.

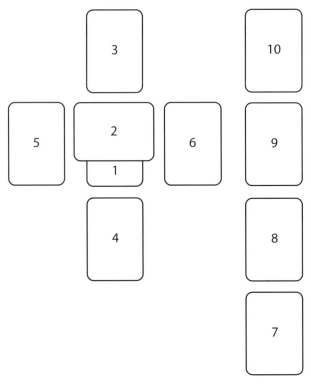

Celtic-cross spread

The Celtic-Cross Spread

The Celtic-cross spread was invented by Arthur Edward Waite and published in his book *The Pictorial Key to the Tarot* in 1911. Many variations of it have been created over the years. I prefer simpler spreads, and use this one only when people request it. However, as it's by far the most popular spread, and because people will sometimes ask you to use it, I'm including Waite's original version here.

1. A significator card is selected and placed faceup on the table.

2. The cards are thoroughly mixed while the person being read for thinks of his or her question.

3. The first card is dealt from the face-down deck and placed face up on top of the significator card, partially obscuring it. As this is done, the reader (you) says, "This covers you." This card provides the first clues as to the nature of the question.

4. The second card (not counting the significator) is dealt and placed face up and crosswise across the first card. The creates the Celtic cross. As this is being done, you say, "This crosses you." This card reveals the type of obstacles that the person being read for is likely to experience.

5. The third card is placed face up above the significator card as you say, "This crowns you." This card provides information about the best possible solution to the client's concern.

6. The fourth card is dealt and placed face up below the significator card. At the same time, you say, "This is beneath you." This card indicates matters from the past that are related to the client's question.

7. The fifth card is placed beside the significator card on the side that the figure on the significator card is looking away from. If there is no person on the card, or if the person is looking straight ahead, the fifth card is placed to the left of the significator card. As this is being done you say, "This is behind you." This card relates to the person's recent past.

8. The sixth card is placed on the opposite side of the significator. This is the direction the significator is looking toward. You say, "This is before you." This card indicates the immediate future.

9. The final four cards are dealt, one at a time, in a vertical line to the right of the cross. The seventh card is the bottom card of this line. As you deal it faceup, say, "This is your Self." This card indicates the person requesting the reading, along with his or her state of mind, thoughts, and feelings.

10. The eighth card is dealt face up above the seventh card as you say, "This is your environment." This reflects the views of other people who are associated with the question.

11. The ninth card is dealt faceup above the eighth card. You say, "This represents your hopes and fears concerning this matter." A positive card in this position denotes the person's hopes, while a negative card reflects the person's fears.

12. The tenth, and final, card is dealt above the ninth one as you say, "This is what will come." This card reveals what is likely to occur.

Naturally, there's a tendency to read the tenth card first as it indicates the outcome. This is not a good idea, though, as all the other cards have a vital part to play, and the final outcome is revealed in all of the cards.

Horoscope Spread

This spread combines the tarot with the twelve houses of astrology to produce a complete reading. The twelve houses are:

1. Personality, physical appearance, childhood, and beginnings

2. Wealth, possessions, money matters, and investments

3. Close relationships, brothers and sisters, communication, and short trips

4. Home, property, family life, and the mother

5. Pleasures, creativity, entertainment, love, and sexuality

6. Health, work, service, and grandparents

7. Partnerships, long term relationships, the husband or wife, and marriage

8. Death, rebirth, losses, and inheritances

9. Philosophy, religion, higher education, travel, and expansion

10. Business, authority, honors, reputation, status, and the father

11. Friends, community service, hopes, and worries

12. Secrets, confinement, loneliness, government, and enemies

The cards are mixed and cut in the normal way and are then dealt, either in a circle, or a straight line. Each card is then interpreted in relation to the particular house it is in. If more information is required about any particular house, an extra card or two can be dealt to help answer the question.

Some readers deal twelve cards faceup and below it deal two more rows of cards face down. The two cards below a particular house are turned over only when more information is required.

Suggested Reading

Donaldson, Terry. *Step-By-Step Tarot*. London: HarperCollins, 1995.

Graham, Sasha, ed. *Tarot Fundamentals*. Torino, Italy: Lo Scarabeo, 2015.

Greer, Mary K. *21 Ways to Read a Tarot Card*. Woodbury, MN: Llewellyn Publications, 2006.

Morrison, Dorothy. *Everyday Tarot Magic*. St. Paul, MN: Llewellyn Publications, 2002.

O'Neill, Robert V. *Tarot Symbolism*. Croydon Hills, Australia: Association for Tarot Studies, 2004.

Pollack, Rachel. *Tarot Wisdom: Spiritual Teachings and Deeper Meanings*. Woodbury, MN: Llewellyn Publications, 2008.

Waite, Arthur Edward. *The Pictorial Key to the Tarot*. New Hyde Park: University Books, Inc., 1959. Originally published in 1911 by William Rider & Son, Limited, London.

Webster, Richard. *Tarot for Everyone*. Torino, Italy: Lo Scarabeo, 2015.

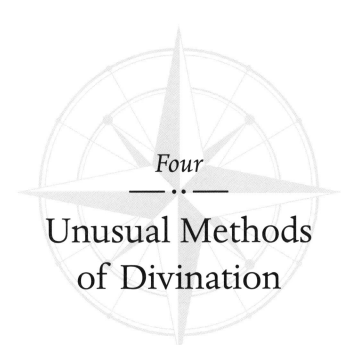

Four

— .. —

Unusual Methods
of Divination

Over the years, I've seen many unusual forms of divination and heard of many more. Here are some interesting methods I've come across.

Banana Reading

I came across this form of divination many years ago at a market in London. I wasn't looking for a psychic reader at the time, but I had to have a reading from the only banana reader I've ever met. He had a line of people waiting for their readings. They started the process by choosing a banana from a large selection laid out on a table. After paying his assistant, the customers were told to peel the banana and eat it while waiting for their turn. I discovered that the lady in front of me was a regular client, and she was happy to tell me how good the banana reader was.

Eventually it was my turn. I handed the man my banana peel and he examined it for about thirty seconds before saying a single word. He spoke for three or four minutes, describing my character before making two or three predictions. He then tossed the peel into a trash can, indicating that the reading was over.

I was impressed at the amount of information he was able to glean from a banana skin, especially as he asked no questions, and didn't seek confirmation of anything he told me.

A year later, I visited London again, and returned to the market to have another reading. Unfortunately, he was no longer there, and no one was able to tell me where he'd gone.

Knee Reading

More than twenty years ago I was reading palms at a psychic fair in Phoenix, Arizona. It wasn't a large fair, and there were about a dozen readers offering their services. There was an empty table next to mine. About an hour after the fair opened, an elderly man put a sign on the table saying "Knee Readings!" I'd never heard of this, and I couldn't wait for him to come back and start reading. He took several trips from his car to the table, to bring in everything he needed. These included several other signs, including one that said, "Ladies Only!"

The fair wasn't busy, yet he had a line of women waiting for him when he finally opened for business. They were almost all repeat clients. I worked steadily, with occasional gaps, but he didn't pause for breath all day.

As we were packing up I asked him about knee reading. He laughed and told me how it started. He and his wife used to read regularly at different fairs. She did tarot readings and he did palmistry. When his wife died, he continued doing the fairs. One day he turned up at a fair and found almost everyone was offering palm readings. He immediately decided he had to do something different, and knee reading was born.

I asked him why he read only for women. "I live on my own," he told me. "I miss female company. Because I'm old, I'm nonthreatening, and women don't mind showing me a knee. Why would I read for men when I'm kept more than busy reading for women?"

Asparagus Reading

Jamima Packington, who lives in Bath, England, is the world's only asparamancer. She discovered her talent at the age of eight after watching her grandmother experimenting with tea leaves. Jamima tosses spears of asparagus into the air and observes the patterns they make when they land on a mat. Jamima usually presents her readings at large events, but doesn't charge for her readings. She uses asparagus to make annual predictions of national and international happenings.

Suggested Reading

Barrie, Josh. "Mystic Veg: Meet the Woman Who Tells the Future from Asparagus." *The Telegraph*. January 18, 2016.

Nephelomancy

Nephelomancy is divination by gazing at the colors, shapes, and patterns made by clouds as they pass across the sky. It's not as easy as it sounds, as the speed and direction the clouds are moving in are also interpreted.

I was introduced to this unusual method of divination by a woman who worked with me in a bookshop in London in the 1960s. She'd grown up in the country and had always looked up to the sky to predict changes in the weather. She was introduced to nephelomancy as a teenager and was instantly captivated, as it gave a new dimension to what she had always done.

She didn't charge for her readings. People would ask her a question, and she'd lie outside in her small back garden and gaze up at the sky. Everything that was immediately above her related to the present. Anything to her right referred to the future, and the past was revealed to her left.

"Wouldn't that all be reversed if you lay down with your head at the other end?" I asked.

"Of course," she explained. "Usually I lie down with my head closest to my back door, but sometimes I lie down with my feet closest. I can even lie down at a 90-degree angle and change the view yet again."

"So what do you do?" I persisted.

"That's easy," she told me. "I don't look up at the sky until I'm lying down. I think I'm guided to lie in the right direction for the particular reading I'm doing."

Sky Stones

I was introduced to sky stones almost fifty years ago while living in Cornwall, England. I happened to see someone I worked with using them to find out what the fishing would be like on the following day. He received a positive response, and the divination proved correct as he caught a large number of fish. I immediately gathered the necessary stones to try it out for myself.

You need three stones: one each of gold, silver, and black. Gold pyrite or tiger's eye is ideal for the gold stone, hematite works well for the silver stone, and obsidian is perfect for the black stone. My stones are approximately an inch in diameter, and I keep them in a small velvet bag.

As this form of divination is thought to be of Celtic origin, it's not surprising that the stones symbolize the three thresholds of dawn (gold), dusk (silver), and midnight (black).

The stones can be used for any question that can be answered by a yes or no.

To use the stones, you hold them loosely in your hand, ask a question, and then gently toss the stones onto a flat surface. If you have an emotional involvement in the answer to the question, you should get someone else to toss the stones while you're thinking about the question.

The stone that is nearer the black stone after they've been tossed provides the answer. If the gold stone is closer, the answer is yes. If the silver stone is closer to the black stone, the answer is no. If the two stones are the same distance away from the black stone, they need to be tossed again.

It's important that you accept the answer the stones provide. Tossing the stones repeatedly in the hope of receiving a different answer implies doubt on the whole procedure, and the stones lose their effectiveness.

If you wish, you can find three stones of about the same size and paint one of them gold, another silver, and the final one black.

Suggested Reading

Webster, Richard. *Omens, Oghams & Oracles*. St. Paul, MN: Llewellyn Publications, 1995.

Dough Reading

Dough reading, sometimes called bread reading, requires a fresh loaf of uncut bread. The crusts are cut off, leaving an oblong piece of dough. A question is asked, and the reader closes her eyes and starts molding the dough into different shapes. She continues doing this for two or three minutes, and, when she feels ready, places it onto a table before opening her eyes. (I've met a few female dough readers, but have yet to encounter a male one.)

The shape that the reader has created is examined from different angles, and the reader interprets the different signs, symbols, and images that the dough has produced.

Some dough readers start the reading while molding the dough, but others wait until after they've studied the shape they've created from the dough.

Gyromancy

Many years ago, when I belonged to a psychic development group, we often finished the evenings with a gyromancy divination. We did it more for fun than anything else, but every now and again useful information came as a result of the exercise.

The process is simple. You'll need twenty-eight sheets of paper. Write the letters of the alphabet, and the words yes and no on them and spread them in a circle around a central object, such as a chair.

Start walking quickly around the chair, and continue doing this until you become giddy. When you reach this stage, you'll start to stagger and lurch. This means you'll make contact with some of the sheets of paper. A second person records all the letters that you touch, until he or she has written down at least ten of them.

Once you've recovered, you can look at the letters you indicated, and see if you can create a message from them.

Ouija Board Reading

Records show that talking boards were used in China in about 1100 CE. In the nineteenth century, Spiritualists used talking boards to communicate with the spirits of the departed. They became extremely popular, and in 1890, a lawyer and inventor called Elijah Bond applied for a patent for a talking board and planchette. In 1901, William Fuld took over the business and began calling the boards Ouija boards. In 1966, the business was sold to Parker Brothers, who in turn sold it to Hasbro in 1991. They still hold the copyrights and patents for the Ouija board today.

Many years ago, corporations would book me to give quick readings at their parties and other entertainments. Most of the time I'd do palmistry and tarot card readings at these, as it's possible to give brief, yet effective, readings using these. Sometimes, if the client requested it, usually on a repeat booking, I'd do other types of readings. If the function was a large one, I'd employ other readers I knew to work with me. One of these used his Ouija board to answer people's questions.

His Ouija board was specially made for him. It was made of plywood, and the top surface containing letters and numbers was beautifully painted. The board was about eight inches square, which is smaller than usual.

He used a guitar pick as a planchette. A planchette is a small heart-shaped piece of wood with three small legs on it. The two back legs contain small castor wheels, and the leg at the pointed part of the heart acts as an indicator as the planchette moves from letter to letter, spelling out a message. Originally, the third leg of a planchette was a pencil, enabling the device to be used for automatic writing. Nowadays, commercially made planchettes usually have small legs, about one inch long, and felt replaces the wheels or castors that used to be used.

Ouija boards are usually used to gain messages from the spirits of people who have died. However, the Ouija board reader told everyone who'd listen that he didn't believe in any of that, and he used the board to answer people's questions. He believed the answers came from people's subconscious minds.

He and his client sat opposite each other. The planchette was placed in the middle of the board, and both of them rested a forefinger on the planchette. The client would state his or her question, and after several seconds the planchette started to move and spelled out an answer.

He's the only person I've met who used a Ouija board this way. Commercially made Ouija boards can be bought at almost any toy store. You might prefer to make your own by writing the letters and numbers in three rows or in a circle on a sheet of poster board. Add the words *yes*, *no*, and *goodbye*. Cover this with a sheet of glass, and use a mouth-down glass as a planchette.

You can use the Ouija board on your own or with as many as six people resting a finger on the planchette. It's a good idea to have someone else write down the letters the planchette indicates, as it can move extremely quickly.

Be patient when you first experiment with the Ouija board. It can take several minutes for the planchette to start moving. Once you become used to it, you'll find the planchette will start moving within thirty seconds.

Shell Reading

Thirty years ago it was rare to find anyone who practiced shell divination. However, it seems to have become much more popular over the last fifteen or twenty years.

Almost every child must have placed a shell against their ear and listened to what appears to be sounds of the sea. In fact, what they're hearing is the sound of blood flowing through the vessels in their ear.

One method of shell reading involves listening carefully to the sounds that come through the shell. Some people close their eyes while doing this to eliminate any potential distractions. After a while, brief conversations can be heard. At first it seems impossible to pick up any words, but with practice, you'll be able to pick up a word here and there. In time you'll be able to hear entire conversations. Most of the time these will have little relevance to what is occurring in your life. Consequently, you need to mentally break into the conversation by asking a question. According to people I've spoken to who practice shell divination, the question is usually followed by a few moments of silence, and then the conversation resumes and, hopefully, but not always, will answer your question.

Another method used by Santeria and diviners in West Africa involves tossing cowrie shells. Most diviners use sixteen shells, but more or less can be used. These land on the divination mat with either the side containing a longitudinal slit, or the rounded side, uppermost. In practice, most shell diviners grind away part of the rounded side to make another opening on the side opposite the longitudinal slit. The number of shells that fall on the divining mat slit or rounded side up are interpreted to create the reading.

Knife Reading

Although this oracle shouldn't be taken too seriously, you'll find plenty of people who'd love to try it. I was first introduced to it as a teenager. I was at a party, and late in the evening one of the other guests told us about it. We quickly gathered the necessary implements, someone wrote the predictions, and we all had a turn.

Required: A large dinner plate, a table knife, and at least twelve predictions.

Method

The predictions are arranged around the plate. The table knife is placed on the dinner plate and everyone has a turn at spinning it. The prediction that the blade is pointing at when it stops moving is the reading for the person who spun the knife. Here are some possible "prophecies" that could be used:

- Good news is coming your way.
- Your project will be successful.
- Success after difficulties.
- Someone admires you.

- This is a good time to make travel plans.

- Think carefully before accepting unsolicited advice.

- Someone needs your help.

- Your finances will improve soon.

- Expect the unexpected.

- Love from afar.

- The good you do will be returned multiplied.

- Look out for a new opportunity.

One version of this is to have everyone write a prediction. This is folded, so no one knows what it is until the knife indicates it. If you try this method, stress that this method of divination is largely for entertainment, and consequently the predictions should all be lighthearted and positive.

Toothpick Reading

Toothpick reading is similar to tea leaf and asparagus reading, as the patterns created by the toothpicks are interpreted. Over the years, I've met several people who read the toothpicks for themselves and others. One man I met kept his toothpicks in a small round metal container that he carried with him, ready for use at any time.

Required: 30 to 40 toothpicks.

Method

Clasp the toothpicks together in your fist, and hold them several inches above a tabletop. Think of a question you'd like to have answered, and open your fist, allowing the toothpicks to drop to the table. Examine the different shapes the toothpicks create on the table, and use your imagination to interpret them.

Five

— .. —

How to Choose the Right Oracle for You

In the previous chapters we've looked at more than forty types of divination. If you're interested in divining for yourself or others, you may have found an oracle that appeals to you. You might even have become interested in the subject by discovering a particular oracle by chance. That's what happened to me when I was nine years old. In fact, if I hadn't discovered my neighbor was a palmist, I might never have become interested in divination at all.

You might already have the necessary tools for a particular type of divination at hand, such as playing cards or dice. This makes it easy to experiment with the system to see if you enjoy using it.

There may be other reasons why you decide on a particular oracle. When I made up my mind in the mid-1970s to become a psychic reader, divination was illegal where I lived. However, astrology seemed to be acceptable. Consequently, I studied astrology for several years, as it was the only way I could practice my skills legally. If it hadn't been for the legal situation, I might never have taken it up.

Some people choose a particular oracle because it's popular. However, others do the opposite and deliberately choose an unusual form of divination, purely because it's different.

If you haven't found the right oracle yet, try all the methods that interest you. You don't have to stick with one modality. You also don't have to rush into any particular method, either. Take your time, evaluate and experiment, and only then make your decision.

Here are a number of factors you should think about before choosing any system of divination.

Passion

The best divination method for you is the one that excites and motivates you. When you experiment, you'll find some oracles that seem interesting and others that have no appeal at all. Look at the ones that seem promising. Does one of them inspire you? Do you feel enthusiastic at the thought of practicing it?

A year or two ago, a young friend of mine took up tea leaf reading. When I asked her why she chose that particular form of divination, she told me, "The tea leaves speak to me." She hadn't experienced that with the other forms of divination she'd tried. She now works every Saturday at a local tea and coffee shop and is as passionate about tea leaf reading now as she was when she took it up.

Time

No matter what system you choose, you'll need to learn how to use it. Some oracles are simple to learn and use, but others, such as astrology, take years to master. With most oracles you can start giving brief readings quickly by telling people you're studying a particular oracle but are still learning how to do it. People will be delighted to have a reading from you, even when you tell them you're a beginner. It's essential to do this, as you need practical, as well as theoretical, experience to help you learn.

Most systems take time to learn, and you need to decide if you're prepared to put in the necessary amount of time and effort to become proficient at it.

Aesthetics

To enjoy working with them, you must like the look of the tools you use. Everyone enjoys handling and looking at attractive objects. This is a simple matter with tarot cards. There are literally hundreds of different decks of tarot cards on the market, and if this is the oracle you prefer, you should select a deck that appeals to you.

There isn't as much choice with other systems. You can find rune stones in a variety of forms, including stones, modeling clay, wood, metal, and even plastic. Oghams are usually made from wood. However, if you're prepared to pay for it, you can buy sets of oghams in which each few is made from the tree that it represents. You can do I Ching readings using any three coins, but it looks so much better, and you'll feel better too, if you use Chinese coins or yarrow sticks.

You can choose from a huge selection of crystals and gemstones. Because I like to handle them and feel their vibrations before buying them, I prefer to buy them at New Age stores and markets. However, if this isn't possible, you can easily find them online.

No matter what oracle you choose, try to use tools that you enjoy handling and looking at.

Interest

You need to have a genuine interest in the divination system you choose. You'll lose interest and get bored if the system is too simple or you can't be bothered learning more about it. Ideally, you want a system that isn't too hard to learn but is involved enough to ensure you can keep learning more and more about it, hopefully for the rest of your life.

Tools

Most systems require tools of one sort or another. If you want to read the tarot, for instance, you'll need a deck of tarot cards. The same thing applies with the runes, dice, dominoes, and playing cards. With some systems, such as palmistry, face reading, and dream interpretation, all you need is someone to read for. Other oracles, such as numerology and geomancy, need nothing more than pen and paper. Even with tea leaf reading, you'll need tea leaves and the necessary equipment to make a cup of tea.

As people get to hear about your reading skills, they'll request your services no matter where you happen to be. Playing cards are small enough to carry, but even if you don't have a deck with you, you'll probably be able to find a deck nearby. At one time you could find tea leaves, a teapot, and a cup and saucer almost everywhere you went. Today, as most people use tea bags, this isn't always the case. However, you might find it hard to get your hands on a crystal ball, or even tarot cards, unless you carry the necessary tools with you. Consequently, portability is another factor to consider.

Care of Your Tools

No matter what system you use, you'll have to treat your reading tools with love and respect. If you're using playing cards, for instance, you should dust them with talcum powder every now and again. You should also replace them at the first signs of wear and tear. This creates a professional image. I cringe every time I see someone reading from a grimy old deck of cards.

If you read the crystal ball, you'll need a square of velvet to rest the crystal ball on when giving a reading, and to wrap it in for protection when it's not being used.

You shouldn't use your reading tools for any other purposes. Don't play games with your set of dominoes or play cards or gamble with the playing cards you use for divination.

Money

Many systems require an investment of time or money to obtain the necessary tools. This could be a factor in deciding what system to use.

A deck of tarot cards is inexpensive and easy to obtain. You could buy a set of rune stones or ogham fews, but you can make a set for almost nothing. It will take time and a small financial outlay to obtain an attractive set of gemstones. If you want to read seashells, you'll probably be able to find suitable shells if you live close to the sea, but it becomes much more difficult and expensive if you live a thousand miles away. Probably the most expensive divination tool is a crystal ball, yet even with this you can practice with a glass of water or an acrylic ball, and if you find it appeals to you, ultimately buy a good crystal ball.

Familiarity

If you want to become a full or part-time reader, you need to use an oracle that people are familiar with. Someone who wants a reading is more likely to choose a tarot reader than someone who reads dominoes or practices augury. In my own work, I've found the most popular systems to be the tarot, palmistry, numerology, and flower reading.

I've found it helpful to be able to offer more than one type of reading. If you've chosen a popular oracle as your "main" system, you can choose something more esoteric for your second oracle.

Hobby or a Business

You can dabble with as many forms of divination as you wish if you're doing it for a hobby and using them to help friends and family. If you're reading purely for people you know, they won't expect you to know the answers to all their questions. However, even as a hobbyist you should learn as much as you can about your areas of interest.

An acquaintance of mine is an authority on the tarot. She's the most knowledgeable person I've ever met on this subject. She's an attorney, and the tarot is her hobby and passion. She does occasional readings for friends and to help raise money for the charities she supports, but she has no interest in making money from it.

People who divine as a hobby vary in their knowledge of the oracle they use. There's nothing wrong with that. However, if you intend making a career out of it at some stage, you need to study the subject and learn as much as you can. Some of your clients will know a great deal about your modality, and you need to know more than they do. Ideally, the learning should be a lifelong process. I've been reading books on divination for well over fifty years, and I am still studying books on my specific interests. I also read books on other forms of divination, and I learn from them, too.

In the end, it doesn't matter if it's a hobby or a business, you should love whatever it is, and learn as much as you can about it.

Six

Preparing for Divination

There are numerous rituals associated with divination. Unfortunately, many of them are superstitions that have little or no relevance to the proposed divination. Some people feel that because a divination has always been done in a certain way, that's the only way in which it can be done. Some rituals are helpful, which is why people have always performed divinations at certain times and dates. Naturally, you can perform a divination whenever you wish, but there are a number of factors that are worth considering if you're performing an important divination.

Timing

Timing has always been considered an important element in divination. Thousands of years ago, the priestesses at the Oracle at Delphi knew this and answered questions on only one day a month, and the priestesses saw no one during the three months of winter.

You can perform a divination at any time you wish. If this wasn't the case, professional diviners would only be able to work at certain times. However, if your divination is extremely important, you can perform it at the best time possible by aligning it with the seasons, movements of the planets, and the days of the week.

Sun Signs

Different energies are created by whatever sign of the zodiac the Sun happens to be in at any given time. These can be harnessed and used to add power to your divinations.

Sun in Aries

This is a good time for divinations involving new ventures, ambition, leadership, assertiveness, enthusiasm, and worthwhile goals.

Sun in Taurus

This is a good time for divinations involving self-improvement, harmony, peace, prosperity, security, dependability, stability, and love.

Sun in Gemini

This is a good time for divinations involving luck, knowledge, communication, social activities, travel, and dealings with others.

Sun in Cancer

This is a good time for divinations involving home, relationships, love, the emotions, and giving of yourself.

Sun in Leo

This is a good time for divinations involving passion, courage, willpower, physical activities, generosity, ambition, and expansion.

Sun in Virgo

This is a good time for divinations involving the home, domesticity, service, organization, health, responsibilities, and caution.

Sun in Libra

This is a good time for divinations involving balance, harmony, commitments, idealism, spirituality, justice, and legal matters.

Sun in Scorpio

This is a good time for divinations involving desire, sexuality, power, leadership, transformation, protection, and self-defense.

Sun in Sagittarius

This is a good time for divinations involving enthusiasm, independence, education, spirituality, philosophy, and eliminating anything you no longer need in your life.

Sun in Capricorn

This is a good time for divinations involving fertility, helping others, ambition, achievement, business activities, responsibility, and steady growth.

Sun in Aquarius

This is a good time for divinations involving helping others rather than yourself. It's also a good time for divinations involving anything that is fresh, new, creative, or different.

Sun in Pisces

This is a good time for divinations involving compassion, healing, dreams, faith, spirituality, psychic ability, and the emotions.

Moon Signs

The Moon has always been used to determine the best times to do a variety of activities, including divination. The best time for any form of divination is said to be when the Moon is in Gemini. (There are a number of sites online that will tell you where the Moon is on any particular date. I like: http://www.lunarium.co.uk/calendar/universal.jsp)

Moon in Aries

This is a good time for any divinations involving business, new projects, investments, personal development, or success. Any divinations involving standing up for yourself are also favored.

Moon in Taurus

This is a good time for any divinations involving home, family, romance, stability, creativity, the arts, prosperity, and getting on well with others.

Moon in Gemini

This is a good time for any divinations involving communication, self-expression, variety, luck, and success. As mentioned earlier, it's a good time for any form of divination.

Moon in Cancer

This is a good time for any divinations involving love, emotions, family members, security, loyalty, acceptance, recognition, and the home. Any type of divination can be performed at this time.

Moon in Leo

This is a good time for any divinations involving sport, theater, passion, leadership, confidence, generosity, and trust.

Moon in Virgo

This is a good time for any divinations involving health, the home, practicality, persistence, the intellect, and employment.

Moon in Libra

This is a good time for any divinations involving relationships, love, marriage, divorce, partnerships, legal concerns, and getting along with others.

Moon in Scorpio

This is a good time for any divinations involving sex, lust, passion, fertility, courage, speaking one's mind, and the cycles of life.

Moon in Sagittarius

This is a good time for any divinations involving adventure, travel, spirituality, higher learning, and all forms of divination.

Moon in Capricorn

This is a good time for any divinations involving business, career, ambition, and success.

Moon in Aquarius

This is a good time for any divinations involving dreams, friendships, mysteries, secrets, and anything that is different or unconventional.

Moon in Pisces

This is a good time for any divinations involving personal growth, dreams, and goals. It's a good time for any form of divination.

Days of the Week

Each day of the week contains different energies that can be useful in divinations.

Sunday (Sun)

Sunday is a good day for divinations involving family, children, friends, authority figures, leadership, career advancement, prosperity, power, and success.

Monday (Moon)

Monday is a good day for divinations involving romance, love, emotions, nurturing, fertility, and all divinations involving women. It's also a good time for divinations concerning water, intuition, and short trips.

Tuesday (Mars)

Tuesday is a good day for divinations involving courage, action, fortitude, power, competitions, money, medicine, gardening, and moving ahead despite obstacles and negativity.

Wednesday (Mercury)

Wednesday is a good day for divinations involving all forms of communication, creativity, thought, self-expression, learning, memory, neighbors, addictions, and the arts.

Thursday (Jupiter)

Thursday is a good day for divinations involving growth, money, finances, prosperity, and all forms of expansion and financial gain. It's also good for divinations involving sport, competition, health, love, and long-distance travel.

Friday (Venus)

Friday is a good day for divinations involving sexuality, love, romance, beauty, fertility, and peace of mind. It's also a good time for divinations relating to healing, social activities, loyalty, and faithfulness.

Saturday (Saturn)

Saturday is a good day for divinations involving gardening, produce, planting, nurturing, protection, and good luck. It's also a good time for divinations relating to endurance, obstacles, and limitations.

Time of Day

Once you've chosen the right day on which to perform your divination, you can fine-tune it by performing it at a particular time of day.

Sunrise

Sunrise is the perfect time of day to perform divinations that relate to self-improvement, conquering addictions and bad habits, and anything relating to work and career.

Midday

The Sun is strongest in the middle of the day. This makes it a powerful time to perform any divinations involving strength, motivation, and major goals.

Sunset

Sunset is the perfect time of day to perform any rituals relating to self-improvement, calmness, stability, and self-control.

Nighttime

After the Sun has fully set is a good time for any divinations involving love, sexuality, and viewing matters in a different light.

Solstices and Equinoxes

The four seasonal cycles provide additional impetus to divinations. Equinoxes have always been considered important, as they occur when day and night are approximately equal in length. Solstices occur when the Sun is at its highest or lowest position relative to the equator.

The period between the spring equinox (March) to the summer solstice (June) is a good time for any divinations involving new beginnings. It's a time of gestation.

The period from the summer solstice (June) to the autumn equinox (September) is a good time for any divinations involving endings, results, conclusions, and reaping your rightful rewards.

The period from the autumn equinox (September) to the winter solstice (December) is a good time for any divinations involving looking ahead, planning, and goal-setting.

The period from the winter solstice (December) to the vernal (spring) equinox (March) is a good time for divinations concerning birth, new life, planning new ventures, and manifestation.

The Esbats

Witches perform lunar rituals at the time of the Full Moon. This is because they believe the Moon possesses more energy at Full Moon than at any other time, and any rituals or divinations performed at this time will make maximum use of the Moon's energy. If your divination involves increase, or helping others, an esbat would be a good time to perform it.

An Open Mind

For divination to work, you must be willing to suspend disbelief and be prepared to act on your feelings and intuition. Many people find this hard to do. This isn't surprising, as we live in a world where most people like to see themselves as logical and rational. Although you need to be open to psychic energies, you should also keep your feet on the ground and use thought and reason as well.

Motivation

You need to be clear about your reasons for performing a particular divination. Do you feel it might give you apparent power over others? Do divinations help you make sense of life? Are you searching for hidden knowledge? Do you want to help others? There are many reasons why people become interested in divination, and you need to ensure that your divinations are intended to help and guide others, rather than be a means of bolstering your self-esteem and ego.

Rituals

A ritual is anything that is repeatedly done in a certain manner. Religious services are rituals. In fact, rituals are often performed to help people gain a closer connection with the divine. Many of the most important aspects of our lives, such as weddings, funerals, birthday celebrations, and other milestones, are rituals. However, rituals are not always about important events. Brushing your teeth might well be a ritual. Even the way you get out of bed in the morning and get ready for work could be considered a ritual.

Many diviners use rituals to help them get into the right state of mind to perform a divination. This may be something simple, such as a short prayer. It might be a full ceremony, involving casting a circle, lighting candles, and asking angels for protection. It could even be something unique to the particular diviner. One diviner I know blows on his tarot cards before using them. His partner, who is also a reader, lights a candle before starting her divinations. Another reader I've met holds her crystals in her cupped hands and says a brief prayer before conducting her divinations. One reader I consulted vigorously rubbed the wooden box she kept her dice in before opening it and allowing the dice to drop to the table. These are all ritualistic practices that enable the diviner to get into the right state of mind before the divination begins.

Rituals of this sort are often performed to help the reader make contact with the divine. However, the goal could be completely different. It might be as simple as enabling the reader to get into the right state of mind before starting the reading.

One reader I know initially performed a short ritual before his readings to give him the necessary confidence to proceed. He started doing this when he first became a reader, and it's now become part of the way he does his readings.

Creating a small ritual for yourself can be helpful when preparing for a reading. It can help you align your conscious and subconscious minds, gain a closer connection with the ultimate source, enter into a quiet meditative state, or even help you gain confidence. Any ritual you do should be personal to you.

An example of a simple ritual might be for the reader and the client to each light a white candle while thinking about what they hope to achieve from the divination. The candles are snuffed out at the end of the divination.

Conclusion

Divination has been popular throughout history, and people today are just as curious about the future as their ancestors were hundreds, and even thousands, of years ago. Amidst all the hustle and bustle of life today, people need all the help they can get to survive and succeed. As long as people have worries and concerns, they'll be interested in gaining insights about the future.

I hope you've tried out some of the different methods of divination covered in this book. With practice, you'll find it a simple matter to get into the calm, peaceful, relaxed, meditative state that will enable you to glimpse into the future. Trust your instincts, feelings, and intuitions. Believe, or at least suspend your disbelief, while performing your divinations. Divination will help you gain a closer connection to the universe, and it will also provide you with guidance and advice that you may not have been able to access in any other way.

As your divination skills increase, so will your intuition—and your popularity. You'll find divination to be a practical tool that will enable you to receive divinely inspired answers to your questions.

I wish you great success in this fascinating field.

Appendix:
Different Types of Divination

Abacomancy: divination by examining the patterns made when dust, sand, or ashes are dropped onto a flat surface.

Acultomancy: divination with needles. Twenty-one needles are placed in a shallow dish. Water is slowly added, causing the needles to move and create patterns that are interpreted.

Aeromancy: divination by signs in the air, such as cloud formations and movements, comets, storms, winds, fog, rainbows, and other events or atmospheric conditions.

Ailuromancy: divination by observing the behavior and actions of cats.

Alectromancy: divination using roosters. Twenty-six pieces of paper, each containing one letter of the alphabet, are placed in a circle, and a kernel of dried corn is placed on each. A rooster is placed in the center of the circle. The letters from which the rooster pecks the grain are formed into a message that divines the future. An alternative method is to recite the letters of the alphabet and record the letters the rooster crows at.

Aleuromancy: divination with flour. A variety of possible outcomes are written on small slips of paper that are rolled into balls of flour dough. Usually they are then baked. The balls are thoroughly mixed, and one is chosen. The message inside predicts the future outcome of the question.

Alomancy: divination with salt. Salt crystals are tossed into the air and observed as they're descending. The patterns the salt creates on the ground are also interpreted.

Alphitomancy: divination to determine the innocence or guilt of someone by having this person eat a cake made from wheat or barley. The person's actions are interpreted. If the person digests the cake easily, he or she is considered innocent.

Alveromancy: divination from sounds. The sound can be anything. Once it's heard, any ensuing sounds from the same source are interpreted. Speaking generally, sounds that get louder indicate danger.

Ambulomancy: divination by walking. This includes the number of steps taken, the speed of walking, and what is observed while taking the walk.

Amniomancy: divination of a child's future by examining the caul that occasionally surrounds a baby's head at birth. Usually the midwife performs the divination.

Anthomancy: divination from flowers. The number of flowers, their colors, and how they're arranged can all be interpreted.

Anthracomancy: divination by gazing at the embers of burning coals.

Anthropomancy: divination by observing the sounds and actions of a human being sacrificed. Another form of this examines the entrails of the dead or dying victims.

Apantomancy: divination from unexpected encounters with animals and birds. The Mexican coat of arms shows a golden eagle sitting on a cactus eating a snake. This was seen as an omen by ancient Aztec diviners, and Mexico City was built on the spot where it occurred. A variation of apantomancy is to divine anything that happens to be present.

Arithmomancy: divination with numbers, usually associated with their alphabetical associations. See also Numerology.

Astragalomancy: divination with knucklebones or dice. The original astragalomancy practitioners used the anklebones of sheep. These were tossed onto the ground and interpreted. Later, letters, words, or symbols were written onto twelve knucklebones that were tossed onto the ground. The positions of the bones and the symbols that were face up were interpreted.

Astragyromancy: divination using special dice that contain letters and numbers.

Astrology: divination from the movements of the stars and planets.

Atramentamancy: a form of scrying using a small amount of ink poured into the palm of the right hand.

Augury: divination from the sounds and movements of birds.

Austromancy: divination by studying the power and direction of winds.

Autonography: divination using a planchette or pen. This is usually called *automatic writing*.

Axinomancy: divination by an axe or hatchet. When the axe is tossed, the direction the handle indicates is interpreted.

Batrachomancy: divination from the sounds, appearance, and actions of toads, frogs, and newts.

Belomancy: divination from arrows. The more common method involves shooting an arrow straight up into the air and observing where it lands. A second method involves shooting the arrow at a rock and interpreting the marks the arrowhead makes against the rock. On occasions answers would be attached to three arrows. The arrow that flew the farthest provided the correct answer.

Bibliomancy: divination from a book. A question is asked and then a book is opened at a random page to determine the answer. Any book can be used, but the Bible and the *Complete Works of Shakespeare* are the most popular for this form of divination. Books can also be used to answer yes or no questions. The question is asked, and the book opened at a random page. With your eyes closed, you run a finger around the page, stopping whenever you wish. Count the number of letters in the sentence you landed on, ignoring any punctuation. If the sentence has an even number of letters, the answer is yes. An odd number means no.

Bletonism: The ability to detect the movements of underground water. It's another name for dowsing and is named after a late eighteenth-century, or early-nineteenth century, French dowser called Bleton.

Botanomancy: divination from the sound of leaves being crushed or tossed into a fire. See also Causimomancy.

Brontomancy: divination from the intensity and duration of thunder. See also Ceraunomancy.

Capnomancy: divination from observing the patterns of smoke rising from a fire.

Cartomancy: divination from playing cards or tarot cards.

Catoptromancy: divination by observing the reflections produced by polished metal plates. This is a form of scrying.

Causimomancy: divination from burning leaves and the branches of trees. The fire and smoke were both interpreted. See also Botanomancy.

Ceneromancy: divination from the ashes remaining after a fire.

Ceraunomancy: divination from lightning and thunder. See also Brontomancy.

Ceromancy: divination by interpreting melted wax.

Ceroscopy: divination from pouring molten wax into cold water.

Cheiromancy: divination from the marks and lines on the palms of a person's hands.

Chirognomy: divination from the shape of someone's hands.

Chronomancy: divination by using time to determine lucky and unlucky days.

Clamancy: divination by interpreting the vocal sounds people make in different situations. This varies from a grunt to a cry of surprise. The volume, pitch, length, and unusualness of the sound are all included in the divination.

Cledonomancy: divination by hearing chance words.

Cleidomancy: divination from a key suspended from a cord or chain.

Cleromancy: divination by lots. Cleromancy frequently refers to divination with dice or dominoes.

Conchomancy: divination with seashells, especially cowrie shells.

Coscinomancy: divination by a sieve. A sieve, balanced by a pair of tongs held by two assistants, moves or turns around when the name of a guilty person is mentioned.

Cromniomancy: divination with onions. Names of different people are placed under each onion plant. Usually, they're names of potential marriage partners. The first onion to sprout answers the question.

Crystallomancy: divination with a crystal ball. This is a form of scrying, and originally the calm surface of water in a pond or lake was used. Nostradamus famously used a bowl of water to make his predictions. The ancient Arabs often used ink in a small container. Other methods involve mirrors, either glass or obsidian. Dr. John Dee, Queen Elizabeth I's astrologer, employed a scryer named Edward Kelley to scry in an obsidian mirror. Highly polished stones are also sometimes used.

Cubomancy: divination with dice. It's similar to astragalomancy, though the dice contain dots, instead of symbols, to indicate the numbers.

Cyclomancy: divination using a turning wheel. Names, or answers to questions, are written around the rim. The wheel contains a marker. The wheel is spun, and when it came to a stop would indicate one of the messages. This would provide the answer.

Cylicomancy: divination using cups of water. A form of scrying.

Dactylomancy: divination with a tripod placed in a bowl that has letters of the alphabet around the rim. People place their fingers on the tripod and it moves to indicate different letters. In some ways, this could be considered the predecessor of the Ouija board. Frequently, a ring would be suspended from the tripod, and it would swing in different directions to spell out the answer.

Daphnomancy: divination by listening to the sounds made by laurel branches being burned in an open fire. The louder the sounds, the more positive the outcome.

Demonomancy: divination by evoking demons and evaluating the answers they provide to your questions. This form of divination is dangerous as it involves black magic.

Empyromancy: divination by examining objects that have been burned in a sacrificial fire.

Extispicy: divination by examining the entrails of a sacrificed animal.

Felidomancy: divination by observing the movements and actions of felines.

Floromancy: divination with flowers.

Gastromancy: divination by interpreting the sounds made by stomach rumbles.

Geloscopy: divination from the sounds of someone's laugh.

Geomancy: divination from the earth. Dots are randomly made in bare earth and are then interpreted. Geomancy also means divination by studying cracks made by the Sun's rays in mud.

Graphology: analyzing character through handwriting.

Gyromancy: divination by walking in a circle containing each letter of the alphabet. When the person becomes dizzy, the letters he or she stumbles on to are recorded and interpreted.

Halomancy: divination from the patterns and shapes made by sprinkling salt onto a flat surface.

Hemomancy: a form of scrying using a drop or two of blood.

Heptatoscopy: divination by examining the liver of a sacrificed animal. References to this can be found in the Bible. It was practiced in most parts of the ancient world, but like extispicy, it died out long ago. People today tend to regard the heart as the seat of the soul. Thousands of years ago, the liver was considered the spiritual home of the soul, which is why hepatoscopy became popular.

Hieroscopy: divination by observing the actions and movements of animals and humans as they're about to be sacrificed.

Hippomancy: divination from horses. The behavior of horses during sacred processions was observed, and predictions were made from their actions.

Hydromancy: divination by water. Water gives life, while the absence of it brings death. It comes from heaven in the form of rain. It possesses cleansing properties that purify people and wash away their sins. In hydromancy the movement the water makes, the direction of its flow, and degree of calmness are all interpreted. Often, a ring, attached to a thread, was dipped into the water and its movements were noted. A yes or no answer could be determined by dropping a pebble into a pool. An odd number of ripples was a good sign. The word *hydromancy* is often used to mean scrying using water.

Ichnomancy: divination using footprints.

Ichthyomancy: divination from the behavior and movements of fish. It's a form of augury. Another form of ichthyomancy involves divination by examining the entrails of a fish.

Iconomancy: divination using religious pictures or icons. The person gazes at the icon and receives information clairvoyantly.

Labiomancy: divination from observing people's lip movements.

Lampadomancy: divination from the observation of flames from a candle or lamp.

Lecanomancy: divination with oil. A small amount of oil is poured into a container of water and the movements and shapes it creates are interpreted. This ancient method of divination is still practiced today.

Libanomancy: divination by smoke. This ancient method of divination was used by the Babylonians. Leaves and small branches from an aromatic plant are cut and dried before being tossed onto red-hot coals. The actions the ensuing smoke made were interpreted to determine future trends.

Lithomancy: divination from polished stones. It's not known how they were used in the past, but it's possible larger stones were used in the same way as a crystal ball. Nowadays, gemstone reading often uses tumbled gemstones.

Lunomancy: divination by examining the shadows created on a person's face by the Moon.

Lychnomancy: divination using the wick of a candle. Visions were sometimes seen in the area of the wick closest to the flame. When this failed to occur, the way the wick burned was analyzed instead.

Macromancy: divination by studying the largest object the diviner can see from where he or she is standing. Size, shape, proximity, and material are all interpreted.

Maculomancy: divination of birthmarks on the body. The size, shape, and placement of each birthmark are interpreted.

Margaritomancy: divination with pearls. A pearl is placed by a fire and covered with a glass. The names of people suspected of committing a crime are spoken. When the name of the guilty party is mentioned, the pearl is said to jump, sometimes even hitting the top of the glass.

Metagnomy: divination by going into a trance state and receiving psychic visions.

Meteoromancy: divination by observing the brightness and direction of meteors, as well as the constellations they appear to come from.

Metoposcopy: divination and character analysis by examining the lines and other markings on someone's forehead.

Micromancy: divination by studying the smallest object the diviner can see. It's the opposite of macromancy.

Moleosophy: divination from moles, birthmarks, and other blemishes on the human body.

Molybdomancy: divination by pouring a small amount of liquid lead into a container of water. The shape the lead created was then interpreted.

Myomancy: divination by observing the movements of rats and mice.

Narcomancy: divination in the form of visions gained while in a drug-induced sleep.

Necromancy: divination by communicating with people who have died.

Nephelomancy: divination by observing the patterns and movements of clouds.

Numerology: divination from the numbers associated with a person's full name at birth as well as the date of birth.

Oculomancy: divination by observing the movements and characteristics of someone's eyes.

Odontomancy: divination from the size, color, uniformity, and spacing of a person's teeth.

Oenomancy: divination from gazing into a glass containing dark-red wine. My family say I do this far too frequently.

Ololygmancy: divination from interpreting the howling of dogs.

Olinomancy: divination from the dregs left behind in a wine glass. Similar to tasseomancy.

Omphalomancy: divination by examining the navel of a mother's first child. This was said to tell her how many more children, or conceptions, she would have.

Oneiromancy: divination by interpreting dreams. As dreams were believed to come from the gods, this was considered a highly powerful method of divination.

Onimancy: divination using olive oil painted onto the fingernails of a young, innocent child's right hand. It's a form of scrying.

Onomancy: divination using the letters of a person's name. This could be described as a shorter and easier version of numerology.

Onychomancy: divination by using polished fingernails as a crystal ball or scrying mirror. People whom I've seen doing this gaze at their own fingernails. However, in medieval times, it was frequently performed by gazing at the fingers of a young, prepubertal boy It is almost always performed outdoors in sunlight. In palmistry, onychomancy means divination from the fingernails.

Oomancy: divination by studying the white of an egg. The raw egg is broken into a glass of water, and the different shapes created by the white of the egg are interpreted. Another version uses the yolk of the egg. The egg is boiled, and the smaller end of the egg is opened. The yolk is then dripped onto a sheet of white paper, and the shapes that are made are interpreted.

Ophiomancy: divination from the actions of snakes and other reptiles.

Ornithomancy: divination from the sight, sounds, and flight of birds.

Osteomancy: divination with bones, usually the shoulder bones of sheep. Astragalomancy also uses bones, but they are used as dice.

Ouranomancy: divination by observing the movements, intensity, and relationships that stars and planets have to each other. Unlike astrology, ouranomancy doesn't map the heavens, but observes the position of the stars at the time of the divination.

Palmistry: divination from the shape, lines, mounts, and other markings on the fingers and palm of the hand.

Pegomancy: divination by observing the patterns made by springs and fountains, especially when stones were tossed into them. A form of hydromancy.

Pessomancy: divination from the patterns made by casting seeds or small stones. Often the seeds and stones are colored or marked to provide further information.

Phrenology: divination from bumps and other features on the head. This system of divination was developed in the late eighteenth century by Franz Joseph Gall, an Austrian physician. It became extremely popular, but it gradually fell out of favor when people who had originally been advocates lost interest.

Phyllomancy: divination from the veins and patterns on leaves. Another version of phyllomancy interprets the sounds made by leaves rustling in a breeze. See also Sycomancy.

Phyllorhodomancy: divination by resting a rose petal in the palm of one hand and slapping with the other. The sound this makes is interpreted. This was a popular form of divination of the ancient Greeks.

Physiognomy: divination by examining facial features, such as the forehead (metoposcopy), face, nose, ears, mouth, eyes, and eyebrows.

Plastromancy: divination with tortoise shells. This was practiced by the Chinese thousands of years ago, and may well be the oldest form of divination. A tortoise shell was heated over a fire, and the cracks in the shell that resulted were interpreted. See also Scapulimancy.

Podomancy: divination from the shape, lines, and markings on the foot.

Psychography: divination by writing under the influence of the spirit world. It's another name for automatic writing. See also Autonography.

Psychomancy: divination with spirits of the dead. Automatic writing and talking boards are examples of this.

Psychometry: divination from the impressions received from a physical object.

Pyromancy: divination by fire. There are a number of variations of this ancient form of divination. One is to gaze into the flames until one enters into a trance state. Often colored powder is tossed into the fire to help the process. Other versions involve studying the flickering movements of the flame on candles and lamps.

Pyroscopy: divination by examining the scorch marks created by flame on a sheet of paper.

Quercusmancy: divination using acorns and oak trees. According to legend, oak trees shed their leaves when an oath was broken. Lovers could each drop an acorn into a container of water. They were destined to marry if the acorns contacted each other. Acorns are often carried as lucky charms, and an old superstition says you'll never grow old as long as you carry one with you.

Retromancy: divination by suddenly looking backward over your shoulder. This enables you to see things from a different point of view, and to also notice things that weren't apparent when you were looking forward.

Rhabdomancy: divination by dowsing using a forked stick or a pendulum.

Rhapsodomancy: divination by opening a book of poetry, and randomly selecting a passage. See also Bibliomancy.

Scapulomancy: divination using bones. More than five thousand years ago the ancient Chinese heated bones and made predictions based on the cracks that were created by the heat. The Romans, Celts, Arabs, and the Labrador tribe of Native Americans all practiced this form of divination.

Scatoscopy: divination from the odor, color, and shape of feces.

Schematomancy: divination from someone's shape and appearance. In some ways, this could be considered a predecessor to body language.

Sciomancy: divination by observing the size and changing shapes of shadows.

Scrying: divination from visions created in clear water, a crystal ball, a mirror, or some other polished surface.

Selenomancy: divination by observing the phases, size, patterns on the surface, and even its appearance through cloud cover, of the Moon.

Sideromancy: divination by tossing an odd number of straws onto a hot iron and observing their movements. Some authorities say that sideromancy was forecasting the future by observing the stars. However, rather than the stars in the sky, this relates to tossing spangles onto the iron and divining the star-like shapes that are formed by them.

Somatomancy: divination from the body. Another name for physiognomy.

Sortilege: divination by the casting of lots, such as dominoes, dice, stones, and other small objects. The I Ching is probably the best-known example of sortilege.

Spodanomancy: divination from ashes. According to Arthur Edward Waite, this method of divination was practiced in Germany in the first half of the nineteenth century. Ashes are spread thickly in the open air in the evening, and a question is written in them using a finger. In the morning, the letters that are still visible are used as oracles.

Stichomancy: an early form of bibliomancy.

Stolisomancy: divination from the clothes someone is wearing.

Sycomancy: divination from leaves. Originally, leaves from a fig tree were preferred, but nowadays leaves from any tree that is closely associated with the person who is doing the divining can be used. Originally, questions were written on the leaves. It was a bad sign if the ink dried quickly, and positive if it took a long time to dry.

Tasseomancy: divination by studying the formations of tea leaves in the bottom of a cup after the tea has been consumed. A variation of this is the interpretation of coffee grounds.

Tephromancy: divination from the ashes of a fire that had consumed a sacrificial victim.

Tiromancy: divination from cheese. Little is known of this ancient form of divination, but it is likely to have been based on its appearance, how the cheese aged, and how much mold it created.

Topomancy: divination by observing the natural forms of nature, such as hills, mountains, streams, rivers, valleys, and plateaus.

Trochomancy: divination by studying the crisscross patterns made by wheel tracks, ideally on a muddy road.

Uromancy: divination from urine.

Xenomancy: divination by interpreting the actions made when encountering strangers.

Xylomancy: divination with wood. A question is asked while walking through a woodland or forest. As soon as the question has been asked, you should stop and look around for any interesting pieces of wood lying on the ground. These are interpreted to answer the question.

Zoomancy: divination from the appearance and actions of animals. A variation of this is the movements of imaginary animals, such as unicorns, sphinxes, and dragons. A form of augury.

Bibliography

Anonymous, *Belle Assemblée or Court and Fashionable Magazine*. London: George B. Whitaker et al., 1828.

Bloomfield, Frena. *The Book of Chinese Beliefs*. London: Arrow Books Limited, 1983.

Brier, Bob. *Ancient Egyptian Magic: Spells, Incarnations, Potions, Stories, and Rituals*. New York: William Morrow and Company, Inc., 1980.

Browning, Robert, and Elizabeth Barrett Barrett. *The Letters of Robert Browning and Elizabeth Barrett Barrett 1845–1846*. London: Smith, Elder & Company, 1900.

Buckland, Raymond. *The Fortune-Telling Book*. Detroit, MI: Visible Ink Press, 2004.

Caulder, Sharon. *Mark of Voodoo: Awakening to My African Spiritual Heritage*. St. Paul, MN: Llewellyn Publications, 2002.

Cunningham, Scott. *Divination for Beginners*. St. Paul, MN: Llewellyn Publications, 1993.

De Givry, Grillot. *A Pictorial Anthology of Witchcraft, Magic, and Alchemy*. London: Spottiswoode, Ballantyne & Co. Ltd., 1931.

Dunne, J. W. *An Experiment with Time*. London: A. & C. Black Limited, 1927.

Fodor, Nandor. *The Unaccountable*. New York: Award Books, 1968.

Forstater, Mark. *The Spiritual Teachings of Marcus Aurelius*. London: Hodder & Stoughton Limited, 2000.

Gibbon, Edward. *The History of the Decline and Fall of the Roman Empire*. London: Joseph Ogle Robinson, 1830.

Glass, Justine. *The Story of Fulfilled Prophecy*. London: Cassell and Company Ltd., 1969.

Gleason, Judith. *A Recitation of Ifa, Oracle of the Yaruba*. New York: Grossman Publishers, 1973.

Harris, Eleanor L. *Ancient Egyptian Divination and Magic*. York Beach, ME: Samuel Weiser, Inc., 1998.

Harris, Martin. "Mormonism—No. 11." *Tiffany's Monthly*, no. 5 (4, 1859): 163–170.

Hawking, Stephen. *Black Holes and Baby Universes*. New York: Bantam Books, 1993.

Hitching, Francis. *Pendulum: The Psi Connection*. London: Fontana Books, 1977.

Hyslop, J. H. *A Case of Veridical Hallucinations*. Proceedings of the American Society for Psychical Research, Volume 3, 1909.

Inglis, Brian, with Ruth West and the Koestler Foundation. *The Unknown Guest: The Mystery of Intuition*. London: Chatto & Windus, Ltd., 1987.

Karcher, Stephen. *The Illustrated Encyclopedia of Divination*. Rockport, MA: Element Books Inc., 1997.

Knuth, Bruce G. *Gems in Myth, Legend and Lore*. Thornton, CO: Jewelers Press, 1999.

Lillie, Arthur. *Modern Mystics and Modern Magic: Containing a Full Biography of Rev. William Stainton Moses*. London: Swan Sonnenschein and Company, 1894.

Loewe, Michael, and Carmen Blacker. *Oracles and Divination*. Boulder, CO: Shambhala Publications, Inc., 1981.

MacLeod, M. and B. Mees. *Runic Amulets and Magic Objects*. Woodbridge, UK: Boydell Press, 2006.

Maven, Max. *Max Maven's Book of Fortunetelling: The Complete Guide to Augury, Soothsaying, and Divination*. New York: Prentice Hall, 1992.

Mehra, Parshotam. *From Conflict to Conciliation: Tibetan Policy Revisited*. Wiesbaden, Germany: Otto Harrassowitz KG, 2004.

Montgomery, Ruth. *The World Before*. New York: Coward, McCann and Geoghegan, Inc., 1976.

Myers, Frederic William Henry. *Human Personality: And its Survival of Bodily Death*. London: Longmans, Green and Company, 1903.

O'Brien, Paul. *Divination: Sacred Tools for Reading the Mind of God*. Portland, OR: Visionary Networks Press, 2007.

Osnos, Evan. *The Next Incarnation. The New Yorker*. October 4, 2010. 63.

Orient, Grand [A. E. Waite], *The Complete Manual of Occult Divination—A Manual of Cartomancy, Volume 1*. London: William Rider, 1912. Reprinted by New Hyde Park: University Books, Inc., 1972.

Peres, Julio Fernando, Alexander Moreira-Almeida, Leonardo Caixeta, Frederico Leao, and Andrew Newberg. "Neuroimaging During Trance State: A Contribution to the Study of Dissociation." *PLoS ONE* 7(11). 2012. http://journals.plos.org/plosone/article?id=10.1371/journal.pone.0049360.

Pickover, Clifford A. *Dreaming the Future: The Fantastic Story of Prediction.* Amherst, MA: Prometheus Books, 2001.

Poinsot, M. C. *The Encyclopedia of Occult Sciences.* New York: Robert M. McBride and Company, 1939.

Raine. J. "Divination in the Fifteenth Century by Aid of a Magical Crystal." *The Archaeological Journal.* London: 1856.

Regardie, Israel. *Practical Guide to Geomantic Divination.* London: Aquarian Press, 1972.

Scot, Reginald. *The Discoverie of Witchcraft.* First published 1584. Many editions available, including New York: Dover Publications, Inc., 1972.

Simoons, Frederick J. *Eat Not This Flesh: Food Avoidances from Prehistory to the Present.* Madison, WI: University of Wisconsin Press, 1961. Revised edition 1994.

Skafte, Dianne. *When Oracles Speak.* London: Thorsons, 1997.

Slate, Dr. Joe H. *Psychic Empowerment.* St. Paul, MN: Llewellyn Publications, 1995.

———. *Psychic Phenomena: New Principles, Techniques and Applications.* Jefferson, NC: McFarland & Company, Inc., 1988.

Struck, Peter T. *Divination and Human Nature: A Cognitive History of Intuition in Classical Antiquity.* Princeton: Princeton University Press, 2016.

Tafel, Dr. J. F. I. *Documents Concerning the Life and Character of Emanuel Swedenborg.* Translated by Rev. I. H. Smithson and George Bush. New York: John Allen, 1847.

Temple, Robert. *Netherworld.* London: Century Hutchinson, 2002.

Ullman, Montague, Stanley Krippner, and Alan Vaughan. *Dream Telepathy: Experiments in Nocturnal ESP.* New York: Macmillan Publishing Company, Inc., 1973.

Waite, Arthur Edward. *The Occult Sciences: A Compendium of Transcendental Doctrine and Experiment.* London: Kegan Paul, Trench, Trubner and Company Limited, 1891.

Webster, Richard. *Color Magic for Beginners.* Woodbury, MN: Llewellyn Publications, 2006.

Weschcke, Carl Llewellyn, and Joe H. Slate. *The Llewellyn Complete Book of Psychic Empowerment.* Woodbury, MN: Llewellyn Publications, 2011.

Williamson, J. N. *The Book of Webster's.* Stamford, CT: Longmeadow Press, 1993.

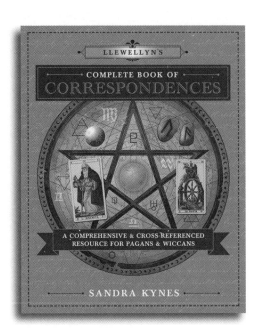

Llewellyn's Complete Book of Correspondences
A Comprehensive & Cross-Referenced Resource for Pagans & Wiccans
SANDRA KYNES

Llewellyn's Complete Book of Correspondences is a clear, straightforward companion for Pagan and Wiccan ritual and spell work. Entries are cross-referenced, indexed, and organized by categories and subcategories, making it easy to find what you need.

This comprehensive reference provides a fascinating look at why correspondences are more than just lists of objects to focus intent on—they are fundamental to how we think. When we use correspondences, we weave together our ideas, beliefs, and energy, creating deeper meaning in our rituals and spell work as we unite our individuality with a larger purpose.

The use of correspondences embodies both physical and symbolic energy and provides the means for uniting the seen and unseen worlds. Packed with content yet easy to use, *Llewellyn's Complete Book of Correspondences* covers traditional correspondences and also provides instruction for forging new ones that hold special meaning for you.

978-0-7387-3253-4, 552 pp., 8 x 10   **$29.99**
